Science and Society

OTHER TITLES IN THE LONGMAN TOPICS READER SERIES

Science and Society

RICHARD W. GRINNELL
Marist College

New York   San Francisco   Boston
London   Toronto   Sydney   Tokyo   Singapore   Madrid
Mexico City   Munich   Paris   Cape Town   Hong Kong   Montreal

Executive Editor: Lynn M. Huddon
Senior Marketing Manager: Sandra McGuire
Production Manager: Bob Ginsberg
Project Coordination, Text Design, and Electronic Page Makeup:
    Carlisle Publishing Services
Cover Design Manager and Cover Designer: Wendy Ann Fredericks
Cover Photo: Jody Dole/Image Bank/Getty Images, Inc.
Senior Manufacturing Buyer: Alfred C. Dorsey
Printer and Binder: RR Donnelley & Sons Company, Harrisonburg
Cover Printer: Phoenix Color Corporation

For permission to use copyrighted material, grateful acknowledgment
is made to the copyright holders on p. 237, which is hereby made part
of this copyright page.

Library of Congress Cataloging-in-Publication Data

Science and society / [edited by] Richard W. Grinnell.
    p. cm. – (A Longman topics reader)
    Includes bibliographical references.
    ISBN 0-321-31811-0
    1. Science—Social aspects.   I. Grinnell, Richard W.

Q175.5.S324 2007
306.4'5—dc22   2006048635

Visit us at www.ablongman.com

ISBN 0-321-31811-0

3 4 5 6 7 8 9 10—DOH—09 08 07

v

Why do some male primates routinely practice violence against females, and some do not? And what do studies of male violence in animals have to tell us about violence against women in human societies? Barbara Smuts' field-work begins to answer these questions.

Using magnetic resonance imaging scanners (the MRI) scientists are now beginning to probe the parts of the brain that we use to make ethical and moral decisions, and are discovering that at least two distinct pathways are being used—one dependent on the evolutionary pressures of the past, the other not.

David Ewing Duncan discovers that having his DNA scanned for possible errors and disease markers opens up a variety of potential ethical and personal anxieties.

Should an otherwise healthy nine-year-old boy be given injections of human growth hormone (hGH) to make him taller? Jenny Everett brings a worried sister's perspective to the process of elective "enheightenment."

Reproductive technology will soon enable us to choose the traits of our offspring. Should we?

Who would be hurt by human cloning? The renowned bio-ethicist Peter Singer argues that the impact upon society of human cloning would be so small that neither the clones nor society would be damaged.

What will the future be like? Look around you. Even Einstein's theories were based upon the insights of the world around him. By considering how science is done now, we can imagine the future.

Science and scientific ways of thinking are so bound up with the way we live our lives that they are, practically, inseparable from our lives themselves. The practical results of scientific inquiry help to fashion the nature of our days, our work, our play, what we think about, and what we fear. Science occupies a particularly influential position in our world because it continually provides us with new tools whose powers are not always evident when we are first offered them, and whose effects are often, initially, beyond our understanding. In some very real ways, science gives us power over ourselves, over others, and over the natural world. But the nature of that power remains undefined, dependent finally upon our understanding of the relationship between science and society. This anthology is designed to enable you to explore that relationship.

Science and Society is a short anthology of readings for college students that focuses on the ways science works with, in, and on our twenty-first century lives. As a whole, the anthology gives you the opportunity to engage with particular and specific types of scientific discovery, as well as the opportunity to join writers and thinkers in contemplation of the impact and importance of those discoveries to the way we live. In its five chapters, the anthology groups essays loosely around the nature of science (in Chapter 1, "What Is Science?"), and the ways science impacts our understanding of ourselves. Essays explore topics related to the way we act and what we do (Chapter 2, "Science and Human Behavior"), the relationship between science and our physical selves (Chapter 3, "Bodies and Genes"), the way science impacts our natural environment (Chapter 4, "Science and the Environment"), and where science is likely to take us in the future (Chapter 5, "Frontiers"). Each essay presents issues for you to engage with and argue about; as a collection, they offer a wide variety of writing models. The apparatus attached to each chapter and to each essay prompts you to think, to discuss, and to write, bringing you closer to understanding the relationship between science and society.

The thirty-one essays in *Science and Society* have been written by working scientists (including scientists whose work has changed the face of our world), science writers (many with science backgrounds, and all with inquisitive and sometimes innovative ways of approaching scientific issues), and cultural critics whose interests focus on science. All are written to be accessible to the general, college-level reader, and have been drawn from books, from popular science magazines (*Discover, Popular Science, Scientific American*), from publications focusing on social and cultural issues (*The New Yorker, Wired, The Atlantic Monthly, The Onion*), from news magazines and newspapers (*Newsweek, Time, The New York Times*), and from the publications of scientific and cultural organizations (*American Scientist, Free Inquiry, Natural History Magazine*). Most of the essays were published in the last five years, as science continually re-imagines and discovers the world around us. But the anthology also includes older pieces by important thinkers and writers of the past to help keep the new ideas in perspective. The resulting collection includes a wide variety of writing styles and narrative voices, and features an array of purposes for writing: to describe, to inform, and to argue. The essays in this collection are designed to engage your attention as readers, as thinkers, and as writers, and to stimulate your response as members of a society in continuous negotiation with science and its products.

ACKNOWLEDGMENTS

I would like to thank Marist College for its interdisciplinary spirit and its support; the reviewers who read an earlier version of *Science and Society* and helped me to effectively fashion this collection (Ken Baake, Texas Tech University; Maggie Griffin, New Mexico Institute of Mining and Technology; Cynthia Haller, York College, The City University of New York; Ted Anton, DePaul University; and Kate Keifer, Colorado State University); my editor at Pearson Longman, Lynn Huddon, whose encouragement, patience, and guidance made this possible; Jon Grinnell, at Gustavus Adolphus College, who provided me with early suggestions and continuous inspiration; Dean Thomas Wermuth, for his ongoing support of my work; Robyn Rosen, my colleague at Marist for advice and inspiration; Robin and Synnøve Grinnell, whose encouragement never failed; and, of course, Leigh Williams, without whom, none of this would have been possible. Finally, I want to thank the scientists and writers who, by helping to describe this amazing world, have made this project an absolute pleasure.

RICHARD W. GRINNELL

Science and Society

What Is Science?

When you pick up this book, you know more or less what it is going to be about. This is a collection of science essays, and you know what science is. You have had to take science classes, after all, and you understand the difference between the study of science and, for example, the study of literature. You also know that, whether you think about it or not, your life is bound up with science. You understand that when you switch on a light, the technology that makes the light possible is the product of the scientific inquiry of people (scientists) who asked questions about the world, developed theories about how electricity might work, and finally turned it into a light and a switch. Though you probably don't think about it, if you did, you would realize that most of the things you live with—your food, your cell phone, your computer, your medication, your running shoes—are all products of science. Similarly, if I tell you that my brother is a scientist (which he is), you immediately have an idea of what kind of person he is, what kind of work he might do. A scientist is something that one can aspire to be, like a fireman or a lawyer. If I tell you that he is a wildlife biologist (which he is), that will probably confound some of your expectations about what he does, but it won't shake your faith in the fact that he is, indeed, a scientist. You know what a scientist is, what science is, and a biologist practices science.

So why begin a book like this with a chapter called "What Is Science?" if you already know the answer? Partly because, though we all subscribe to a general notion of what science is, to talk coherently about the role that science plays in our lives and our society, we need to fine-tune our definitions. We need to understand the issues that haunt the edges of science, and the areas where society and science interact with one another. We all need to have similar answers to the question "What is science?" or our conversations and our debates will do nothing more than confuse us. For example, when we talk about science, do we mean the study of very specific subjects—chemistry, physics, biology—or do we mean a particular way of approaching any subject—the scientific method, for instance? Does a historian practice science when she constructs a hypothesis and then tests it? Or is a historian by definition NOT a scientist? At the end of World War II, when George Orwell asked the question "What is science?", this was his concern, as it was of Lewis Thomas forty years later in his essay "Alchemy." Orwell and Thomas force us to consider science not only as a subject, but as a collection of human practices as well.

This chapter is designed to help you develop a definition of science that tests the edges of how we as a society understand science. It offers you Orwell and Thomas, as well as Stephen Jay Gould ("Sex, Drugs, Disasters, and the Extinction of Dinosaurs"), Carl Sagan ("Why We Need to Understand Science"), Barbara Ehrenreich ("Science, Lies, and the Ultimate Truth"), Lawrence Krauss ("School Districts Want to 'Teach the Controversy.' What Controversy?") and the writers of *The Onion* ("Revolutionary New Insoles Combine Five Forms of Pseudoscience"). These essays, each in a very different way, help to sketch in the boundaries of science by exposing our assumptions, forcing us to draw the line between real and imagined science, and encouraging us to laugh at (and be afraid of) our own scientific ignorance.

In addition, this chapter will stimulate you to do more than simply consider what one does when one "does" science. For science is an inherently social enterprise—it takes place in a particular time and is done by real people with scientific expertise who are subject to the prejudices, the insights, and the limitations of their time. How do these social forces impact what science is or should be? To define science, we will see, is not just to come up with a convenient handful of relevant terms. It is also to draw connections between science as a category and society as a whole. So Peggy Orenstein's "Why Science Must Adapt to Women" and the American Institute of Biological Sciences' "Ethics Statement" join Lawrence Krauss, *The Onion*, Carl Sagan, and George Orwell in suggesting that science has a very cultural, a very human, side. Culture turns out to be an important part of our definition of science. Your job in this chapter is to read, reflect on and respond to these testimonials to the importance and power of science, and then construct your own definition of what science is for us now, at the beginning of the twenty-first century.

What Is Science?

George Orwell

George Orwell (1903–1950) is the pen name of Eric Arthur Blair, a prolific novelist and social critic. He is best known for his novels Animal Farm *(1945) and* 1984 *(1949), which effectively combine story-telling and political and social commentary. In the following essay, first published in the* London Tribune *in 1945, Orwell defines science and uses that definition to challenge his society. As you read this essay, consider whether, sixty years later, Orwell's definition stands up, and whether the concerns he voices continue to be relevant to us today.*

✦

In last week's *Tribune*, there was an interesting letter from Mr. J. Stewart Cook, in which he suggested that the best way of avoiding the danger of a 'scientific hierarchy' would be to see to it that every member of the general public was, as far as possible, scientifically educated. At the same time, scientists should be brought out of their isolation and encouraged to take a greater part in politics and administration.

As a general statement, I think most of us would agree with this, but I notice that, as usual, Mr. Cook does not define science, and merely implies in passing that it means certain exact sciences whose experiments can be made under laboratory conditions. Thus, adult education tends 'to neglect scientific studies in favour of literary, economic and social subjects', economics and sociology not being regarded as branches of science, apparently. This point is of great importance. For the word science is at present used in at least two meanings, and the whole question of scientific education is obscured by the current tendency to dodge from one meaning to the other.

Science is generally taken as meaning either (a) the exact sciences, such as chemistry, physics, etc., or (b) a method of thought which obtains verifiable results by reasoning logically from observed fact.

If you ask any scientist, or indeed almost any educated person, 'What is science?' you are likely to get an answer approximating to (b). In everyday life, however, both in speaking and in writing, when people say 'science' they mean (a). Science means something that happens in a laboratory: the very word calls up a picture of graphs, test-tubes, balances, Bunsen burners, microscopes. A biologist, and astronomer, perhaps a psychologist or a mathematician is described as a 'man of science': no one would think of applying this term to a statesman, a poet, a journalist or even a philosopher. And those who tell us that the young must be scientifically educated mean, almost invariably, that they should be taught more about radioactivity, or the stars, or the physiology of their own bodies, rather than that they should be taught to think more exactly. This confusion of meaning, which is partly deliberate, has in it a great danger. Implied in the demand for more scientific education is the claim that if one has been scientifically trained one's approach to *all* subjects will be more intelligent than if one had had no such training. A scientist's political opinions, it is assumed, his opinions on sociological questions, on morals, on philosophy, perhaps even on the arts, will be more valuable than those of a layman. The world, in other words, would be a better place if the scientists were in control of it. But a 'scientist', as we have just seen, means in practice a specialist in one of the exact sciences. It follows that a chemist or a physicist, as such, is politically more intelligent than a poet or a lawyer, as such. And, in fact, there are already millions of people who do believe this.

But is it really true that a 'scientist', in this narrower sense, is any likelier than other people to approach non-scientific problems in an objective way? There is not much reason for thinking so. Take one simple test—the ability to withstand nationalism. It is often loosely said that 'Science is international', but in practice the scientific workers of all countries line up behind their own governments with fewer scruples than are felt by the writers and the artists. The German scientific community, as a whole, made no resistance to Hitler. Hitler may have ruined the long-term prospects of German science, but there were still plenty of gifted men to do the necessary research on such things as synthetic oil, jet planes, rocket projectiles and the atomic bomb. Without them the German war machine could never have been built up.

On the other hand, what happened to German literature when the Nazis came to power? I believe no exhaustive lists have been published, but I imagine that the number of German scientists— Jews apart—who voluntarily exiled themselves or were persecuted by the règime was much smaller than the number of writers and journalists. More sinister than this, a number of German scientists swallowed the monstrosity of 'racial science'. You can find some of the statements to which they set their names in Professor Brady's *The Spirit and Structure of German Fascism*.

But, in slightly different forms, it is the same picture everywhere. In England, a large proportion of our leading scientists accept the structure of capitalist society, as can be seen from the comparative freedom with which they are given knighthoods, baronetcies and even peerages. Since Tennyson, no English writer worth reading—one might, perhaps, make an exception of Sir Max Beerbohm—has been given a title. And those English scientists who do not simply accept the *status quo* are frequently Communists, which means that, however intellectually scrupulous they may be in their own line of work, they are ready to be uncritical and even dishonest on certain subjects. The fact is that a mere training in one or more of the exact sciences, even combined with very high gifts, is no guarantee of a humane or sceptical outlook. The physicists of half a dozen great nations, all feverishly and secretly working away at the atomic bomb, are a demonstration of this.

But does all this mean that the general public should *not* be more scientifically educated? On the contrary! All it means is that scientific education for the masses will do little good, and probably a lot of harm, if it simply boils down to more physics, more chemistry, more biology, etc., to the detriment of literature and history. Its probable effect on the average human being would be to narrow the range of his thoughts and make him more than ever contemptuous of such knowledge as he did not possess: and his political reactions would probably be somewhat less intelligent than those of an illiterate peasant who retained a few historical memories and a fairly sound aesthetic sense.

Clearly, scientific education ought to mean the implanting of a rational, sceptical, experimental habit of mind. It ought to mean acquiring a *method*—a method that can be used on any problem that one meets—and not simply piling up a lot of facts. Put it in those words, and the apologist of scientific education will usually agree. Press him further, ask him to particularize, and somehow it always turns out that scientific education means more attention to the sciences, in other words—more *facts*. The idea that science means a way of looking at the world, and not simply a body of knowledge, is in practice strongly resisted. I think sheer professional jealousy is part of the reason for this. For if science is simply a method or an attitude, so that anyone whose thought-processes are sufficiently rational can in some sense be described as a scientist—what then becomes of the enormous prestige now enjoyed by the chemist, the physicist, etc. and his claim to be somehow wiser than the rest of us?

A hundred years ago, Charles Kingsley described science as 'making nasty smell in a laboratory'. A year or two ago a young industrial chemist informed me, smugly, that he 'could not see what was the use of poetry'. So the pendulum swings to and fro, but it does not seem to me that one attitude is any better than the other. At the moment, science is on the upgrade, and so we hear, quite rightly, the claim that the masses should be scientifically educated: we do not hear, as we ought, the counter-claim that the scientists themselves would benefit by a little education. Just before writing this, I saw in an American magazine the statement that a number of British and American physicists refused from the start to do research on the atomic bomb, well knowing what use would be made of it. Here you have a group of sane men in the middle of a world of lunatics. And though no names were published, I think it would be a safe guess that all of them were people with some kind of general cultural background, some acquaintance with history or literature or the arts—in short, people whose interests were not, in the current sense of the word, purely scientific.

Topics for Thought and Discussion

1. On one hand, this article is an attempt to *define* science; on another, it is an *argument* for a particular way of understanding science and the consequences of not doing so. Identify the parts of this article that are *definition* and the parts that are *argument*. Do these two essential writing purposes overlap in this article? Do they do so effectively?

2. How does Orwell use Hitler and the events of World War II? What does this writing strategy accomplish for him?

3. For Orwell, what is science and what is its purpose?

4. What does Orwell want out of his readers? Out of you?

5. Orwell agrees both that nonscientists should be better educated in science, and that scientists should be better educated in liberal arts. Which is more important to Orwell? Do you agree? Why or why not? Explain your agreement or disagreement in terms of your own time and concerns.

Suggestions for Writing

1. Update Orwell's argument. Write a letter to a local newspaper (school or community) in which you argue for (or, if you like, against) the need for the balanced education Orwell espouses.

2. How would you answer the question posed in Orwell's title? Write an essay in which you define the term *science* using examples, issues, and concerns from your own time.

Alchemy

LEWIS THOMAS

Lewis Thomas (1913–1993) was a doctor, medical researcher, and hospital administrator whose concern with the growing gap between scientists and the public led him to begin writing. He began with a monthly column in the New England Journal of Medicine, *and ultimately became an award-winning writer, best known for his books* The Lives of a Cell, *which won the National Book Award in 1975, and* The Medusa and the Snail, *which won the American Book Award in 1981. He is the author of many other books, including* The Youngest Science: Notes of a Medicine-Watcher *(1983),* Late Night Thoughts on Listening to Mahler's Ninth Symphony *(1983),* Could I Ask You Something? *(1985), and* The Fragile Species *(1992). In the following essay from* Thoughts on Listening to Mahler's Ninth, *Thomas uses medieval prescientific attempts to understand the world—what is now called* alchemy—*as a way of considering the position of science in human society. As you read, consider Thomas's purpose. Why is he writing this?*

---- ✦ ----

Alchemy began long ago as an expression of the deepest and oldest of human wishes: to discover that the world makes sense. The working assumption—that everything on earth must be made up from a single, primal sort of matter—led to centuries of hard work aimed at isolating the original stuff and rearranging it to the alchemists' liking. If it could be found, nothing would lie beyond human grasp. The transmutation of base metals to gold was only a modest part of the prospect. If you knew about the fundamental substance, you could do much more than make simple money: you could boil up a cure-all for every disease affecting humankind, you could rid the world of evil, and, while doing this, you could make a universal solvent capable of dissolving anything you might want to dissolve. These were heady ideas, and generations of alchemists worked all their lives trying to reduce matter to its ultimate origin.

To be an alchemist was to be a serious professional, requiring long periods of apprenticeship and a great deal of late-night study. From the earliest years of the profession, there was a lot to read. The documents can be traced back to Arabic, Latin, and Greek scholars of the ancient world, and beyond them to Indian Vedic texts as far back as the tenth century B.C. All the old papers contain a formidable array of information, mostly expressed in incantations, which were required learning for every young alchemist and, by design, incomprehensible to everyone else. The word "gibberish" is thought by some to refer back to Jabir ibn Hayyan, an eighth-century alchemist, who lived in fear of being executed for black magic and worded his doctrines so obscurely that almost no one knew what he was talking about.

Indeed, black magic was what most people thought the alchemists were up to in their laboratories, filled with the fumes of arsenic, mercury, and sulphur and the bubbling infusions of all sorts of obscure plants. We tend to look back at them from today's pinnacle of science as figures of fun, eccentric solitary men wearing comical conical hats, engaged in meaningless explorations down one blind alley after another. It was not necessarily so: the work they were doing was hard and frustrating, but it was the start-up of experimental chemistry and physics. The central idea they were obsessed with—that there is a fundamental, elementary particle out of which everything in the universe is made—continues to obsess today's physicists.

They never succeeded in making gold from base metals, nor did they find a universal elixir in their plant extracts; they certainly didn't rid the world of evil. What they did accomplish, however, was no small thing: they got the work going. They fiddled around in their laboratories, talked at one another incessantly, set up one crazy experiment after another, wrote endless reams of notes, which were then translated from Arabic to Greek to Latin and back again, and the work got under way. More workers became interested and then involved in the work, and, as has been happening ever since in science, one thing led to another. As time went on and the work progressed, error after error, new and accurate things began to turn up. Hard facts were learned about the behavior of metals and their alloys, the properties of acids, bases, and salts were recognized, the mathematics of thermodynamics were worked out, and, with just a few jumps through the centuries, the helical molecule of DNA was revealed in all its mystery.

The current anxieties over what science may be doing to human society, including the worries about technology, are no new thing. The third-century Roman emperor Diocletian decreed that all manuscripts dealing with alchemy were to be destroyed, on grounds that such enterprises were against nature. The work went on in secrecy, and, although some of the material was lost, a great deal was translated into other languages, passed around, and preserved.

The association of alchemy with black magic has persisted in the public mind throughout the long history of the endeavor, partly because the objective—the transmutation of one sort of substance into another—seemed magical by definition. Partly also because of the hybrid term: *al* was simply the Arabic article, but *chemy* came from a word meaning "the black land," *Khemia*, the Greek name for Egypt. Another, similar-sounding word, *khumeia*, meant an infusion or elixir, and this was incorporated as a part of the meaning. The Egyptian origin is very old, extending back to Thoth, the god of magic (who later reappeared as Hermes Trismegistus, master of the hermetic seal required by alchemists for the vacuums they believed were needed in their work). The notion of alchemy may be as old as language, and the idea that language and magic are somehow related is also old. "Grammar," after all, was a word used in the Middle Ages to denote high learning, but it also implied a practicing familiarity with alchemy. *Gramarye*, an older term for grammar, signified occult learning and necromancy. "Glamour," of all words, was the Scottish word for grammar, and it meant, precisely, a spell, casting enchantment.

Medicine, from its dark origins in old shamanism millennia ago, became closely linked in the Middle Ages with alchemy. The preoccupation of alchemists with metals and their properties led to experiments—mostly feckless ones, looking back—with the therapeutic use of all sorts of metals. Paracelsus, a prominent physician of the sixteenth century, achieved fame from his enthusiastic use of mercury and arsenic, based on what now seems a wholly mystical commitment to alchemical philosophy as the key to understanding the universe and the human body simultaneously. Under his influence, three centuries of patients with all varieties of illness were treated with strong potions of metals, chiefly mercury, and vigorous purgation became standard medical practice.

Physics and chemistry have grown to scientific maturity, medicine is on its way to growing up, and it is hard to find traces anywhere of the earlier fumblings toward a genuine scientific method. Alchemy exists only as a museum piece, an intellectual fossil, so antique that we no longer need be embarrassed by the memory, but the memory is there. Science began by fumbling. It works because the people involved in it work, and *work together*. They become excited and exasperated, they exchange their bits of information at a full shout, and, the most wonderful thing of all, they keep *at* one another.

Something rather like this may be going on now, without realizing it, in the latest and grandest of all fields of science. People in my field, and some of my colleagues in the real "hard" sciences such as physics and chemistry, have a tendency to take lightly and often disparagingly the efforts of workers in the so-called social sciences. We like to refer to their data as soft. We do not acknowledge as we should the differences between the various disciplines within behavioral research—we speak of analytical psychiatry, sociology, linguistics, economics, and computer intelligence as though these inquiries were all of a piece, with all parties wearing the same old comical conical hats. It is of course not so. The principal feature that the social sciences share these days is the attraction they exert on considerable numbers of students, who see the prospect of exploring human behavior as irresistible and hope fervently that a powerful scientific method for doing the exploring can be worked out. All of the matters on the social-science agenda seem more urgent to these young people than they did at any other time in human memory. It may turn out, years hence, that a solid discipline of human science will have come into existence, hard as quantum physics, filled with deep insights, plagued as physics still is by ambiguities but with new rules and new ways of getting things done. Like, for instance, getting rid of thermonuclear weapons, patriotic rhetoric, and nationalism all at once. If anything like this does turn up we will be looking back at today's social scientists, and their close colleagues the humanists, as having launched the new science in a way not all that different from the accomplishment of the old alchemists, by simply working on the problem—this time, the fundamental, primal universality of the human mind.

Topics for Thought and Discussion

1. According to Thomas, why might an understanding of the history of ancient science and medicine—alchemy—be useful to us today? How does Thomas's conclusion help to reinforce this argument?
2. Thomas writes eloquently, and one of the things he does particularly well is knit his paragraphs together with transitions. Look at the first five paragraphs of this essay and describe as clearly as you can what he does to provide transitions between and among the paragraphs. How does he make his essay so smooth?
3. How does Thomas answer the question "What is science"?
4. Thomas describes the fear and persecution that scientists and alchemists faced at the hands of medieval society. In retrospect, those fears probably seem unfounded to us. But what about the fears currently being voiced about science in our own time? Are our own fears (about stem-cell research, cloning, genetic modification, and so on) like, or unlike, the fears of the past described by Thomas? Should we be afraid of science?

Suggestions for Writing

1. Construct an argument in which you grapple with the question "Should we be afraid of science?" Assume a position and support it with sound reasoning and effective analysis.
2. Write an essay in which you enter into a dialogue with Thomas on an important element of his argument. Identify and summarize his position, and then agree or disagree with it using your own sense of science today.

Why We Need to Understand Science

CARL SAGAN

Carl Sagan (1934–1996) was a renowned astronomer and astrophysicist, but is probably best known as the host of the popular television series, "Cosmos," and as a writer who worked to bring science into the popular culture of the late twentieth century. He is the author of numerous articles and books, among which are The Dragons of Eden *(1977),* Boca's Brain *(1979),* Pale Blue Dot *(1994), and* Billions and Billions: Thoughts on Life and Death at the Brink of the Millennium *(1997), and a novel,* First Contact *(1985), a bestseller later made into a major motion picture. The following essay, first published in 1989 in* Parade Magazine, *posits the question "Why study science?" and argues for the importance of science to the security and prosperity of the United States. As you read this article, consider how Sagan structures his argument. Why does he begin as he begins, and what kinds of evidence does he use? Does the article and its evidence seem dated now, or is Sagan's thesis still relevant?*

---------------- ✦ ----------------

A s I got off the plane, he was waiting for me, holding up a sign with my name on it. I was on my way to a conference of scientists and TV broadcasters, and the organizers had kindly sent a driver.

"Do you mind if I ask you a question?" he said as we waited for my bag. "Isn't it confusing to have the same name as that science guy?"

It took me a moment to understand. Was he pulling my leg? "I *am* that science guy," I said. He smiled. "Sorry. That's my problem. I thought it was yours too." He put out his hand. "My name is William F. Buckley." (Well, his name wasn't *exactly* William F. Buckley, but he did have the name of a contentious TV interviewer, for which he doubtless took a lot of good-natured ribbing.)

As we settled into the car for the long drive, he told me he was glad I was "that science guy"—he had so many questions to ask about science. Would I mind? And so we got to talking. But not about science. He wanted to discuss UFOs, "channeling" (a way to hear what's on the minds of dead people—not much it turns out), crystals, astrology. . . . He introduced each subject with real enthusiasm, and each time I had to disappoint him: "The evidence is crummy," I kept saying. "There's a much simpler explanation." As we drove on through the rain, I could see him getting glummer. I was attacking not just pseudoscience but also a facet of his inner life.

And yet there is so much in real science that's equally exciting, more mysterious, a greater intellectual challenge—as well as being a lot closer to the truth. Did he know about the molecular building blocks of life sitting out there in the cold, tenuous gas between the stars? Had he heard of the footprints of our ancestors found in four-million-year-old volcanic ash? What about the raising of the Himalayas when India went crashing into Asia? Or how viruses subvert cells, or the radio search for extraterrestrial intelligence or the ancient civilization of Ebla? Mr. "Buckley"—well-spoken, intelligent, curious—had heard virtually nothing of modern science. He *wanted* to know about science. It's just that all the science got filtered out before it reached him. What society permitted to trickle through was mainly pretense and confusion. And it had never taught him how to distinguish real science from the cheap imitation.

All over America there are smart, even gifted, people who have a built-in passion for science. But that passion is unrequited. A recent survey suggests that 94 percent of Americans are "scientifically illiterate."

A PRESCRIPTION FOR DISASTER

We live in a society exquisitely dependent on science and technology, in which hardly anyone knows anything about science and technology. This is a clear prescription for disaster. It's dangerous and stupid for us to remain ignorant about global warming, say, or ozone depletion, toxic and radioactive wastes, acid rain. Jobs and wages depend on science and technology. If the United States can't manufacture, at high quality and low price, products people want to buy, then industries will drift out of the United States and transfer a little prosperity to another part of the world. Because of the low birthrate in the sixties and seventies, the National Science Foundation projects a shortage of nearly a million professional scientists and engineers by 2010. Where will they come from? What about fusion, supercomputers, abortion, massive reductions in strategic weapons, addiction, high-resolution television, airline and airport safety, food additives, animal rights, superconductivity, Midgetman vs. rail-garrison MX missiles, going to Mars, finding cures for AIDS and cancer? How can we decide national policy if we don't understand the underlying issues?

I know that science and technology are not just cornucopias pouring good deeds out into the world. Scientists not only conceived nuclear weapons: they also took political leaders by the lapels, arguing that their nation—whichever it happened to be— had to have one first. Then they arranged to manufacture 60,000 of them. Our technology has produced thalidomide, CFCs, Agent Orange, nerve gas, and industries so powerful they can ruin the climate of the planet. There's a *reason* people are nervous about science and technology.

And so the image of the mad scientist haunts our world— from Dr. Faust to Dr. Frankenstein to Dr. Strangelove to the white-coated loonies of Saturday morning children's television. (All of this doesn't inspire budding scientists.) But there's no way back. We can't just conclude that science puts too much power into the hands of morally feeble technologists or corrupt, power-crazed politicians and decide to get rid of it. Advances in medicine and agriculture have saved more lives than have been lost in all the wars in history. Advances in transportation, communication, and entertainment have transformed the world. The sword of science is double-edged. Rather, its awesome power forces on all of us, including politicians, a new responsibility—more attention to the long-term consequences of technology, a global and trans-generational perspective, an incentive to avoid easy appeals to nationalism and chauvinism. Mistakes are becoming too expensive.

Science is much more than a body of knowledge. It is a way of thinking. This is central to its success. Science invites us to let the facts in, even when they don't conform to our preconceptions. It counsels us to carry alternative hypotheses in our heads and see which best match the facts. It urges on us a fine balance between no-holds-barred openness to new ideas, however heretical, and the most rigorous skeptical scrutiny of everything—new ideas *and* established wisdom. We need wide appreciation of this kind of thinking. It works. It's an essential tool for a democracy in an age of change. Our task is not just to train more scientists but also to deepen public understanding of science.

HOW BAD IS IT? VERY BAD

"It's Official," reads one newspaper headline. "We Stink in Science." Less than half of all Americans know that the earth moves around the sun and takes a year to do it—a fact established a few centuries ago. In tests of average 17-year-olds in many world regions, the United States ranked dead last in algebra. On identical tests, the U.S. kids averaged 43 percent and their Japanese counterparts 78 percent. In my book 78 percent is pretty good—it corresponds to a C+, or maybe even a B−; 43 percent is an F. In a chemistry test, students in only two of thirteen nations did worse than the U.S. Compared to us, Britain, Singapore, and Hong Kong were so high they were almost off-scale, and 25 percent of Canadian 18-year-olds knew just as much chemistry as a select 1 percent of American high school seniors (in their second chemistry course, and most of them in "advanced" programs). The best of 20 fifth-grade classrooms in Minneapolis was outpaced by every one of the 20 classrooms in Sendal, Japan, and 19 out of 20 in Taipei, Taiwan. South Korean students were far ahead of American students in all aspects of mathematics and science, and 13-year-olds in British Columbia (in Western Canada) outpaced their U.S. counterparts across the boards (in some areas they did better than the Koreans). Of the U.S. kids, 22 percent say they dislike school; only 8 percent of the Koreans do. Yet two-thirds of the Americans, but only a quarter of the Koreans, say they are "good at mathematics."

WHY WE'RE FLUNKING

How do British Columbia, Japan, Britain, and Korea manage so much better than we do? During the Great Depression, teachers enjoyed job security, good salaries, respectability. Teaching was an admired profession, partly because learning was widely recognized as the road out of poverty. Little of that is true today. And so science (and other) teaching is too often incompetently or uninspiringly done, its practitioners, astonishingly, having little or no training in their subjects—sometimes themselves unable to distinguish science from pseudoscience. Those who do have the training often get higher-paying jobs elsewhere.

We need more money for teachers' training and salaries, and for laboratories—so kids will get hands-on experience rather than just reading what's in the book. But all across America, school-bond issues on the ballot are regularly defeated. U.S. parents are much more satisfied with what their children are learning in science and math than are, say, Japanese and Taiwanese parents—whose children are doing so much better. No one suggests that property taxes be used to provide for the military budget, or for agriculture, or for cleaning up toxic wastes. Why just education? Why not support it from general taxes on the local and state levels? What about a special education tax for those industries with special needs for technically trained workers?

American kids don't do enough schoolwork. The average high school student spends 3.5 hours a week on homework. The total time devoted to studies, in and out of the classroom, is about 20 hours a week. Japanese *fifth*-graders average 33 hours a week.

But most American kids aren't stupid. Part of the reason they don't study hard is that they've received few tangible benefits when they do. Competency (that is, actually knowing the stuff) in verbal skills, mathematics, and science these days doesn't increase earnings for average young men in their first eight years out of high school—many of whom take service rather than industrial jobs.

In the productive sectors of the economy, though, the story is different. There are furniture factories, for example, in danger of going out of business—not because there are no customers, but because few entry-level workers can do simple arithmetic. A major electronics company reports that 80 percent of its job applicants can't pass a *fifth*-grade math test—and that's an American, not a Korean, fifth-grade test. The United States is already losing some $25 billion a year (mainly in lost productivity and the cost of remedial education) because workers, to too great a degree, can't read, write, count, or think. Parents should know that their children's livelihoods may depend on how much math and science they know. Now, while the kids are in school, is the time for them to learn. Parents might encourage their schools to offer—and their kids to take—comprehensible, well-taught advanced science courses. They might also limit the amount of mind-numbing TV their children watch.

WHAT WE CAN DO

Those in America with the most favorable view of science tend to be young, well-to-do, college-educated white males. But three-quarters of new American workers between now and 2001 will be women, nonwhites, and immigrants. Discriminating against them isn't only unjust, it's also self-defeating. It deprives the American economy of desperately needed skilled workers.

Black and Hispanic students are doing better in standardized science tests now than in the late 1960s, but they're the only ones who are. The average math gap between white and black U.S. high school graduates is still huge—two to three grade levels; but the gap between white U.S. high school graduates and those in, say, Japan, Canada, Great Britain, or Finland is more than *twice* as big. If you're poorly motivated and poorly educated, you won't know much—no mystery here. Suburban blacks with college-educated parents do just as well in college as suburban whites with college-educated parents. Enrolling a poor child in a Head Start program doubles his or her chances to be employed later in life; one who completes an Upward Bound program is four times as likely to get a college education. If we're serious, we know what to do.

What about college and university? There are obvious steps similar to what should be done in high schools: salaries for teachers that approach what they could get in industry: more scholarships, fellowships, and laboratory equipment; laboratory science courses required of everyone to graduate: and special attention paid to those traditionally steered away from science. We should also provide the financial and moral encouragement for academic scientists to spend more time on public education—lectures, newspaper and magazine articles, television appearances. This requires scientists to make themselves understandable and fun to listen to. To me, it seems strange that some scientists, who depend on public funding for their research, are reluctant to explain to the public what it is that they do. Fortunately, the number of scientists willing to speak to the public—and capably—has been increasing each year. But there are not yet nearly enough.

Virtually every newspaper in America has a daily astrology column. How many have a daily science column? When I was growing up, my father would bring home a daily paper and consume (often with great gusto) the baseball box scores. There they were, to me dry as dust, with obscure abbreviations (W, SS, SO, W-L, AB, RBI), but they spoke to him. Newspapers everywhere printed them. I figured maybe they weren't too hard for me. Eventually I got caught up in the world of baseball statistics. (I know it helped me in learning decimals, and I still cringe a little when I hear that someone is "batting a thousand." But 1.000 is not 1,000. The lucky player is batting one.)

Or take a look at the financial pages. Any introductory material? Explanatory footnotes? Definitions of abbreviations? Often there's none. It's sink or swim. Look at those acres of statistics! Yet people voluntarily read the stuff. It's not beyond their ability. It's only a matter of motivation. Why can't we do the same with math, science, and technology?

By far the most effective means of raising interest in science is television. There's lots of pseudoscience on television, a fair amount of medicine and technology, but hardly any science—especially on the three big commercial networks, whose executives think science programming means rating declines and lost profits, and nothing else matters. Why in all America is there no TV drama that has as its hero someone devoted to figuring out how the universe works?

Stirring projects in science and technology attract and inspire youngsters. The number of science Ph.D.s peaked around the time of the Apollo program and declined thereafter. This is an important potential side-effect of such projects as sending humans to Mars, the Superconducting Supercollider to explore the fine structure of matter, and the program to map all human genes.

Every now and then, I'm lucky enough to teach a class in kindergarten or the first grade. Many of these children are curious, intellectually vigorous, ask provocative and insightful questions, and exhibit great enthusiasm for science. When I talk to high school students, I find something different. They memorize "facts." But, by and large, the joy of discovery, the life behind those facts, has gone out of them. They're worried about asking "dumb" questions; they're willing to accept inadequate answers; they don't pose follow-up questions; the room is awash with sidelong glances to judge, second by second, the approval of their peers. Something has happened between first and twelfth grade, and it's not just puberty. I'd guess that its partly peer pressure *not* to excel (except in sports); partly that the society teaches short-term gratification; partly the impression that science or math won't buy you a sports car; partly that so little is expected of students; and partly that there are so few role models for intelligent discussion of science and technology or for learning for its own sake.

But there's something else: Many adults are put off when youngsters pose scientific questions. Children ask why the sun is yellow, or what a dream is, or how deep you can dig a hole, or when is the world's birthday, or why we have toes. Too many teachers and parents answer with irritation or ridicule, or quickly move on to something else. Why adults should pretend to omniscience before a five-year-old, I can't for the life of me understand. What's wrong with admitting that you don't know? Children soon recognize that somehow this kind of question annoys many adults. A few more experiences like this, and another child has been lost to science.

There are many better responses. If we have an idea of the answer, we could try to explain. If we don't, we could go to the encyclopedia or library. Or we might say to the child: "I don't know the answer. Maybe no one knows. Maybe when you grow up, you'll be the first to find out."

But mere encouragement isn't enough. We must also give children the tools to winnow the wheat from the chaff. I'm haunted by the vision of a generation of Americans unable to distinguish reality from fantasy, hopefully clutching their crystals for comfort, unequipped even to frame the right questions or to recognize the answers. I want us to rescue Mr. "Buckley" and the millions like him. I also want us to stop turning out leaden, incurious, unimaginative high school seniors. I think America needs, and deserves, a citizenry with minds wide awake and a basic understanding of how the world works.

Public understanding of science is more central to our national security than half a dozen strategic weapons systems. The submediocre performance of American youngsters in science and math, and the widespread adult ignorance and apathy about science and math, should sound an urgent alarm.

Topics for Thought and Discussion

1. Comment on the form of Sagan's essay, from his choice of opening to his use of subtitles. Why does he choose this form?

2. How does Sagan structure his argument? Why does he begin as he begins, and what kinds of evidence does he use?

3. At the beginning of his essay, Sagan writes: "We live in a society exquisitely dependent on science and technology, in which hardly anyone knows anything about science and technology. This is a clear prescription for disaster." What sorts of disasters does he anticipate? From your own perspective, what are the dangers inherent in this kind of society? Does Sagan overstate, or understate them?

4. According to Sagan, why do we "stink at science"? What does Sagan claim is wrong with America's relationship to science? What are some of the things he claims must be done?

5. How do you feel about science? Can you identify some of the forces that influenced you to feel this way? Does Sagan identify them?

Suggestions for Writing

1. Conduct a survey of the popular media with which you are familiar (television programming, films, video games, music, advertising, etc.) and collect raw material on how science is (or is not) presented in popular culture today. Are scientists heroes? Villains? Absent? Present? Use this material in a class discussion: From the research, can the class generalize about the role of science in popular culture? What are your conclusions? Alternatively, write a descriptive or argumentative essay using data you have collected.

2. Write a personal experience essay in which you relate a moment in your own life that influenced your relationship with science. Use this experience to teach your audience something about how a relationship with science is made, or unmade.

3. Brainstorm several ways to popularize science. What are some practical things we can do to make science more popular? Write an essay or a letter to the editor in which you, like Sagan, advise society on ways to increase the popularity of science.

Revolutionary New Insoles Combine Five Forms of Pseudoscience

FROM *THE ONION*

The Onion *is a humor magazine published every week as a current-events newspaper. Begun in 1988 in Madison, Wisconsin (and still based there), it now has a national readership of almost a million people each week.* The Onion's *book* Our Dumb Century *(1999) was a number-one* New York Times *bestseller. Every year,* The Onion *publishes collections of the year's articles, among them* The Onion's Finest News Reporting *(2000),* The Onion Ad Nauseam: Complete News Archives *(2000–2004), and* The Onion Platinum Prestige Encore Gold Premium Collector's Collection *(2003). In the following article from 2000,* The Onion *reports on a new, almost-scientific product. As you read, note the style and form of this piece. How do style and form contribute to the purpose of the article?*

———————— ✦ ————————

MASSILLON, OH—Stressed and sore-footed Americans everywhere are clamoring for the exciting new MagnaSoles shoe inserts, which stimulate and soothe the wearer's feet using no fewer than five forms of pseudoscience.

"What makes MagnaSoles different from other insoles is the way it harnesses the power of magnetism to properly align the bio-magnetic field around your foot," said Dr. Arthur Bluni, the pseu-doscientist who developed the product for Massillon-based Integrated Products. "Its patented Magna-Grid design, which features more than 200 isometrically aligned Contour Points™, actually soothes while it heals, restoring the foot's natural bio-flow."

"MagnaSoles is not just a shoe insert," Bluni continued, "it's a total foot-rejuvenation system."

According to scientific-sounding literature trumpeting the new insoles, the Contour Points™ also take advantage of the semi-plausible medical technique known as reflexology. Practiced in the Occident for over 11 years, reflexology, the literature explains, establishes a correspondence between every point on the human foot and another part of the body, enabling your soles to heal your entire body as you walk.

But while other insoles have used magnets and reflexology as keys to their appearance of usefulness, MagnaSoles go several steps further. According to the product's website, "Only Magna-Soles utilize the healing power of crystals to re-stimulate dead foot cells with vibrational biofeedback . . . a process similar to that by which medicine makes people better."

In addition, MagnaSoles employ a brand-new, cutting-edge form of pseudoscience known as Terranometry, developed specially for Integrated Products by some of the nation's top pseudoscientists.

"The principles of Terranometry state that the Earth resonates on a very precise frequency, which it imparts to the surfaces it touches," said Dr. Wayne Frankel, the California State University biotrician who discovered Terranometry. "If the frequency of one's foot is out of alignment with the Earth, the entire body will suffer. Special resonator nodules implanted at key spots in MagnaSoles convert the wearer's own energy to match the Earth's natural vibrational rate of 32.805 kilofrankels. The resultant harmonic energy field rearranges the foot's naturally occurring atoms, converting the pain-nuclei into pleasing comfortrons."

Released less than a week ago, the $19.95 insoles are already proving popular among consumers, who are hailing them as a welcome alternative to expensive, effective forms of traditional medicine.

"I twisted my ankle something awful a few months ago, and the pain was so bad, I could barely walk a single step," said

Helene Kuhn of Edison, NJ. "But after wearing MagnaSoles for seven weeks, I've noticed a significant decrease in pain and can now walk comfortably. Just try to prove that MagnaSoles didn't heal me!"

Equally impressed was chronic back-pain sufferer Geoff DeAngelis of Tacoma, WA.

"Why should I pay thousands of dollars to have my spine realigned with physical therapy when I can pay $20 for insoles clearly endorsed by an intelligent-looking man in a white lab coat?" DeAngelis asked. "MagnaSoles really seem like they're working."

Topics for Thought and Discussion

1. Look at the form of this essay. Note the short paragraphs and the extensive use of quotations. What would you call this kind of writing? Why is this form appropriate for this essay? How does the form of the essay contribute to its purpose?

2. This essay pokes fun at pseudoscience and our own gullibility when it comes to believing pseudoscientific claims. Read through the essay again and mark or make a list of all of the terms and techniques that *The Onion* uses to emphasize the unreliability of this science. What do the writers do to call attention to the lack of scientific credibility?

3. *Scientific literacy* is our ability to understand scientific language and to differentiate between real science and "pseudoscience." Look at the list of techniques you came up with in question #2, and use those terms and techniques to consider how this essay comments on our general scientific literacy. How does it use our scientific literacy as a source of comedy while criticizing our lack of scientific literacy at the same time?

4. Why might products like MagnaSoles use pseudoscientific jargon to sell their products? What does this tell us about the authority, and the role, of science in our culture?

Suggestions for Writing

1. Using this article as evidence, write an essay in which you define the terms *science* and *pseudoscience*, emphasizing the differences between the two.

2. In the above article, the absurdity of the pseudoscientific claims is funny and borders on the ridiculous. But is there a sense in which pseudoscience (and you'll need to clearly define the term) can be dangerous? Write an essay in which you argue for either the harmfulness, or the harmlessness, of pseudoscience (particularly in the form presented by *The Onion*).

Sex, Drugs, Disasters, and the Extinction of Dinosaurs

STEPHEN JAY GOULD

Stephen Jay Gould (1941–2002) was a paleontologist and evolutionary biologist who spent his professional career at Harvard University. He is responsible for the theory of punctuated equilibrium, which modified Darwin's general theory of evolution to explain rapid periods of evolution. Though an important scientist and theorist, Gould is probably best known as a writer capable of making complex scientific ideas accessible to the general public. For almost thirty years he wrote a regular column for Natural History *magazine, and he published dozens of books aimed at making science interesting and clear to nonscientists. Among his best known books are* The Mismeasure of Man *(1981), which won the National Book Critics' Circle Award;* Wonderful Life *(1989), which won the Science Book Prize;* Full House: The Spread of Excellence from Plato to Darwin *(1996);* Rocks of Ages: Science and Religion in the Fullness of Life *(1999); and* The Hedgehog, the Fox, and the Magister's Pox: Mending the Gap Between Science and the Humanities *(2003). Probably Gould's biggest contribution to the popularizing of science, however, came in his collections of essays from* Natural History *magazine:* Ever Since Darwin: Reflections in Natural History *(1977);* The Panda's Thumb: More Reflections in Natural History *(1980), which won the American Book Award for Science;* Hen's Teeth and Horse's Toes: Further Reflections in Natural History *(1983);* The Flamingo's Smile *(1985);* Bully for Brontosaurus *(1991);* Dinosaur in a Haystack *(1995);* Leonardo's Mountain of Clams and the Diet of Worms *(1998); and* The Lying Stones of Marrakech *(2000) among others. The following essay is from his collection* The Flamingo's Smile. *In it, Gould contrasts good and bad science by looking at the question of what killed the dinosaurs. As you read this essay, notice the way Gould's personality surfaces in his writing. How does his personality contribute to, or detract from, the ideas he presents?*

───────── ✦ ─────────

Science, in its most fundamental definition, is a fruitful mode of inquiry, not a list of enticing conclusions. The conclusions are the consequence, not the essence.

My greatest unhappiness with most popular presentations of science concerns their failure to separate fascinating claims from the methods that scientists use to establish the facts of nature. Journalists, and the public, thrive on controversial and stunning statements. But science is, basically, a way of knowing—in P. B. Medawar's apt words, "the art of the soluble." If the growing corps of popular science writers would focus on *how* scientists develop and defend those fascinating claims, they would make their greatest possible contribution to public understanding.

Consider three ideas, proposed in perfect seriousness to explain that greatest of all titillating puzzles—the extinction of dinosaurs. Since these three notions invoke the primally fascinating themes of our culture—sex, drugs, and violence—they surely reside in the category of fascinating claims. I want to show why two of them rank as silly speculation, while the other represents science at its grandest and most useful.

Science works with testable proposals. If, after much compilation and scrutiny of data, new information continues to affirm a hypothesis, we may accept it provisionally and gain confidence as further evidence mounts. We can never be completely sure that a hypothesis is right, though we may be able to show with confidence that it is wrong. The best scientific hypotheses are also generous and expansive: they suggest extensions and implications that enlighten related, and even far distant, subjects. Simply consider how the idea of evolution has influenced virtually every intellectual field.

Useless speculation, on the other hand, is restrictive. It generates no testable hypothesis, and offers no way to obtain potentially refuting evidence. Please note that I am not speaking of truth or falsity. The speculation may well be true; still, if it provides, in principle, no material for affirmation or rejection, we can make nothing of it. It must simply stand forever as an intriguing idea. Useless speculation turns in on itself and leads nowhere; good science, containing both seeds for its potential refutation and implications for more and different testable knowledge, reaches out. But, enough preaching. Let's move on to dinosaurs, and the three proposals for their extinction.

1. Sex: Testes function only in a narrow range of temperature. (Those of mammals hang externally in a scrotal sac because internal body temperatures are too high for their proper function.) A worldwide rise in temperature at the close of the Cretaceous period caused the testes of dinosaurs to stop functioning and led to their extinction by sterilization of males.

2. Drugs: Angiosperms (flowering plants) first evolved toward the end of the dinosaurs' reign. Many of these plants

contain psychoactive agents, avoided by mammals today as a result of their bitter taste. Dinosaurs had neither means to taste the bitterness nor livers effective enough to detoxify the substances. They died of massive overdoses.

3. Disasters: A large comet or asteroid struck the earth some 65 million years ago, lofting a cloud of dust into the sky and blocking sunlight, thereby suppressing photosynthesis and so drastically lowering world temperatures that dinosaurs and hosts of other creatures became extinct.

Before analyzing these three tantalizing statements, we must establish a basic ground rule often violated in proposals for the dinosaurs' demise. *There is no separate problem of the extinction of dinosaurs.* Too often we divorce specific events from their wider contexts and systems of cause and effect. The fundamental fact of dinosaur extinction is its synchrony with the demise of so many other groups across a wide range of habitats, from terrestrial to marine.

The history of life has been punctuated by brief episodes of mass extinction. A recent analysis by University of Chicago paleontologists Jack Sepkoski and Dave Raup, based on the best and most exhaustive tabulation of data ever assembled, shows clearly that five episodes of mass dying stand well above the "background" extinctions of normal times (when we consider all mass extinctions, large and small, they seem to fall in a regular 26-million-year cycle. . . .). The Cretaceous debacle, occurring 65 million years ago and separating the Mesozoic and Cenozoic eras of our geological time scale, ranks prominently among the five. Nearly all the marine plankton (single-celled floating creatures) died with geological suddenness; among marine invertebrates, nearly 15 percent of all families perished, including many previously dominant groups, especially the ammonites (relatives of squids in coiled shells). On land, the dinosaurs disappeared after more than 100 million years of unchallenged domination.

In this context, speculations limited to dinosaurs alone ignore the larger phenomenon. We need a coordinated explanation for a system of events that includes the extinction of dinosaurs as one component. Thus it makes little sense, though it may fuel our desire to view mammals as inevitable inheritors of the earth, to guess that dinosaurs died because small mammals ate their eggs (a perennial favorite among untestable speculations). It seems most unlikely that some disaster peculiar to dinosaurs befell these massive beasts—and that the debacle happened to strike just when one of history's five great dyings had enveloped the earth for completely different reasons.

The testicular theory, an old favorite from the 1940s, had its root in an interesting and thoroughly respectable study of temperature tolerances in the American alligator, published in the staid *Bulletin of the American Museum of Natural History* in 1946 by three experts on living and fossil reptiles—E. H. Colbert, my own first teacher in paleontology; R. B. Cowles; and C. M. Bogert.

The first sentence of their summary reveals a purpose beyond alligators: "This report describes an attempt to infer the reactions of extinct reptiles, especially the dinosaurs, to high temperatures as based upon reactions observed in the modern alligator." They studied, by rectal thermometry, the body temperatures of alligators under changing conditions of heating and cooling. (Well, let's face it, you wouldn't want to try sticking a thermometer under a 'gator's tongue.) The predictions under test go way back to an old theory first stated by Galileo in the 1630s—the unequal scaling of surfaces and volumes. As an animal, or any object, grows (provided its shape doesn't change), surface areas must increase more slowly than volumes—since surfaces get larger as length squared, while volumes increase much more rapidly, as length cubed. Therefore, small animals have high ratios of surface to volume, while large animals cover themselves with relatively little surface.

Among cold-blooded animals lacking any physiological mechanism for keeping their temperatures constant, small creatures have a hell of a time keeping warm—because they lose so much heat through their relatively large surfaces. On the other hand, large animals, with their relatively small surfaces, may lose heat so slowly that, once warm, they may maintain effectively constant temperatures against ordinary fluctuations of climate. (In fact, the resolution of the "hot-blooded dinosaur" controversy that burned so brightly a few years back may simply be that, while large dinosaurs possessed no physiological mechanism for constant temperature, and were not therefore warm-blooded in the technical sense, their large size and relatively small surface area kept them warm.)

Colbert, Cowles, and Bogert compared the warming rates of small and large alligators. As predicted, the small fellows heated up (and cooled down) more quickly. When exposed to a warm sun, a tiny 50-gram (1.76-ounce) alligator heated up one degree Celsius every minute and a half, while a large alligator, 260 times bigger at 13,000 grams (28.7 pounds), took seven and a half minutes to gain a degree. Extrapolating up to an adult 10-ton dinosaur, they concluded that a one-degree rise in body temperature would take eighty-six hours. If large animals absorb heat so slowly (through their relatively small surfaces), they will also be unable to shed any excess heat gained when temperatures rise above a favorable level. The authors then guessed that large dinosaurs lived at or near their optimum temperatures; Cowles suggested that a rise in global temperatures just before the Cretaceous extinction caused the dinosaurs to heat up beyond their optimal tolerance—and, being so large, they couldn't shed the unwanted heat. (In a most unusual statement within a scientific paper, Colbert and Bogert then explicitly disavowed this speculative extension of their empirical work on alligators.) Cowles conceded that this excess heat probably wasn't enough to kill or even to enervate the great beasts, but since testes often function within a narrow range of temperature, he proposed that this global rise might have sterilized all the males, causing extinction by natural contraception.

The overdose theory has recently been supported by UCLA psychiatrist Ronald K. Siegel. Siegel has gathered, he claims, more than 2,000 records of animals who, when given access, administer various drugs to themselves—from a mere swig of alcohol to massive doses of the big H. Elephants will swill the equivalent of twenty beers at a time, but do not like alcohol in concentrations greater than 7 percent. In a silly bit of anthropocentric speculation, Siegel states that "elephants drink, perhaps, to forget . . . the anxiety produced by shrinking rangeland and the competition for food."

Since fertile imaginations can apply almost any hot idea to the extinction of dinosaurs, Siegel found a way. Flowering plants did not evolve until late in the dinosaurs' reign. These plants also produced an array of aromatic, amino-acid-based alkaloids—the major group of psychoactive agents. Most mammals are "smart" enough to avoid these potential poisons. The alkaloids simply don't taste good (they are bitter); in any case, we mammals have livers happily supplied with the capacity to detoxify them. But, Siegel speculates, perhaps dinosaurs could neither taste the bitterness nor detoxify the substances once ingested. He recently told members of the American Psychological Association: "I'm not suggesting that all dinosaurs OD'd on plant drugs, but it certainly was a factor." He also argued that death by overdose may help explain why so many dinosaur fossils are found in contorted positions. (Do not go gentle into that good night.)

Extraterrestrial catastrophes have long pedigrees in the popular literature of extinction, but the subject exploded again in 1979, after a long lull, when the father-son, physicist-geologist team of Luis and Walter Alvarez proposed that an asteroid, some 10 km in diameter, struck the earth 65 million years ago (comets, rather than asteroids, have since gained favor. . . . Good science is self-corrective).

The force of such a collision would be immense, greater by far than the megatonnage of all the world's nuclear weapons. . . . In trying to reconstruct a scenario that would explain the simultaneous dying of dinosaurs on land and so many creatures in the sea, the Alvarezes proposed that a gigantic dust cloud, generated by particles blown aloft in the impact, would so darken the earth that photosynthesis would cease and temperatures drop precipitously. (Rage, rage against the dying of the light.) The single-celled photosynthetic oceanic plankton, with life cycles measured in weeks, would perish outright, but land plants might survive through the dormancy of their seeds (land plants were not much affected by the Cretaceous extinction, and any adequate theory must account for the curious pattern of differential survival). Dinosaurs would die by starvation and freezing; small, warm-blooded mammals, with more modest requirements for food and better regulation of body temperature, would squeak through. "Let the bastards freeze in the dark," as bumper stickers of our chauvinistic neighbors in sunbelt states proclaimed several years ago during the Northeast's winter oil crisis.

All three theories, testicular malfunction, psychoactive overdosing, and asteroidal zapping, grab our attention mightily. As pure phenomenology, they rank about equally high on the hit parade of primal fascination. Yet one represents expansive science, the others restrictive and untestable speculation. The proper criterion lies in evidence and methodology; we must probe behind the superficial fascination of particular claims.

How could we possibly decide whether the hypothesis of testicular frying is right or wrong? We would have to know things that the fossil record cannot provide. What temperatures were optimal for dinosaurs? Could they avoid the absorption of excess heat by staying in the shade, or in caves? At what temperatures did their testicles cease to function? Were late Cretaceous climates ever warm enough to drive the internal temperatures of dinosaurs close to this ceiling? Testicles simply don't fossilize, and how could we infer their temperature tolerances even if they did? In short, Cowles's hypothesis is only an intriguing speculation leading nowhere. The most damning statement against it appeared right at the conclusion of Colbert, Cowles, and Bogert's paper, when they admitted: "It is difficult to advance any definite arguments against this hypothesis." My statement may seem paradoxical—isn't a hypothesis really good if you can't devise any arguments against it? Quite the contrary. It is untestable and unusable.

Siegel's overdosing has even less going for it. At least Cowles extrapolated his conclusion from some good data on alligators. And he didn't completely violate the primary guideline of citing dinosaur extinction in the context of a general mass dying—for rise in temperature could be the root cause of a general catastrophe, zapping dinosaurs by testicular malfunction and different groups for other reasons. But Siegel's speculation cannot touch the extinction of ammonites or oceanic plankton (diatoms make their own food with good sweet sunlight; they don't OD on the chemicals of terrestrial plants). It is simply a gratuitous, attention-grabbing guess. It cannot be tested, for how can we know what dinosaurs tasted and what their livers could do? Livers don't fossilize any better than testicles.

The hypothesis doesn't even make any sense in its own context. Angiosperms were in full flower ten million years before dinosaurs went the way of all flesh. Why did it take so long? As for the pains of a chemical death recorded in contortions of fossils, I regret to say (or rather I'm pleased to note for the dinosaurs' sake) that Siegel's knowledge of geology must be a bit deficient; muscles contract after death and geological strata rise and fall with motions of the earth's crust after burial—more than enough reason to distort a fossil's pristine appearance.

The impact story, on the other hand, has a sound basis in evidence. It can be tested, extended, refined and, if wrong, disproved. The Alvarezes did not just construct an arresting guess for public consumption. They proposed their hypothesis after laborious geochemical studies with Frank Asaro and Helen Michel had revealed a massive increase of iridium in rocks deposited right at the time of the extinction. Iridium, a rare metal of the platinum group, is virtually absent from indigenous rocks of the earth's crust; most of our iridium arrives on extraterrestrial objects that strike the earth.

The Alvarez hypothesis bore immediate fruit. Based originally on evidence from two European localities, it led geochemists throughout the world to examine other sediments of the same age. They found abnormally high amounts of iridium everywhere—from continental rocks of the western United States to deep sea cores from the South Atlantic.

Cowles proposed his testicular hypothesis in the mid-1940s. Where has it gone since then? Absolutely nowhere, because scientists can do nothing with it. The hypothesis must stand as a curious appendage to a solid study of alligators. Siegel's overdose scenario will also win a few press notices and fade into oblivion. The Alvarezes' asteroid falls into a different category altogether, and much of the popular commentary has missed this essential distinction by focusing on the impact and its attendant results, and forgetting what really matters to a scientist—the iridium. If you talk just about asteroids, dust, and darkness, you tell stories no better and no more entertaining than fried testicles or terminal trips. It is the iridium—the source of testable evidence—that counts and forges the crucial distinction between speculation and science.

The proof, to twist a phrase, lies in the doing. Cowles's hypothesis has generated nothing in thirty-five years. Since its proposal in 1979, the Alvarez hypothesis has spawned hundreds of studies, a major conference, and attendant publications. Geologists are fired up. They are looking for iridium at all other extinction boundaries. Every week exposes a new wrinkle in the scientific press. Further evidence that the Cretaceous iridium represents extraterrestrial impact and not indigenous volcanism continues to accumulate. As I revise this essay in November 1984 (this paragraph will be out of date when the book is published), new data include chemical "signatures" of other isotopes indicating unearthly provenance, glass spherules of a size and sort produced by impact and not by volcanic eruptions, and high-pressure varieties of silica formed (so far as we know) only under the tremendous shock of impact.

My point is simply this: Whatever the eventual outcome (I suspect it will be positive), the Alvarez hypothesis is exciting, fruitful science because it generates tests, provides us with things to do, and expands outward. We are having fun, battling back and forth, moving toward a resolution, and extending the hypothesis beyond its original scope. . . .

As just one example of the unexpected, distant cross-fertilization that good science engenders, the Alvarez hypothesis made a major contribution to a theme that has riveted public attention in the past few months—so-called nuclear winter. . . . In a speech delivered in April 1982, Luis Alvarez calculated the energy that a ten-kilometer asteroid would release on impact. He compared such an explosion with a full nuclear exchange and implied that all-out nuclear war might unleash similar consequences.

This theme of impact leading to massive dust clouds and falling temperatures formed an important input to the decision of Carl Sagan and a group of colleagues to model the climatic consequences of nuclear holocaust. Full nuclear exchange would probably generate the same kind of dust cloud and darkening that may have wiped out the dinosaurs. Temperatures would drop precipitously and agriculture might become impossible. Avoidance of nuclear war is fundamentally an ethical and political imperative, but we must know the factual consequences to make firm judgments. I am heartened by a final link across disciplines and deep concerns—another criterion, by the way, of science at its best: A recognition of the very phenomenon that made our evolution possible by exterminating the previously dominant dinosaurs and clearing a way for the evolution of large mammals, including us, might actually help to save us from joining those magnificent beasts in contorted poses among the strata of the earth.

Topics for Thought and Discussion

1. Gould defines science in his first line. How does the rest of his essay support, modify, or challenge that definition? Summarize from Gould's essay his complete definition of science.
2. What are the primary reasons, according to Gould, that the testicular theory and the drug-overdose theory are not good science? Give specifics from the essay to support your discussion.
3. In what ways does Gould himself come in to this essay? What do his personality and his point of view contribute to the essay and to the argument?
4. Describe some of the less conventional moves Gould makes as a writer. For example, why does he, a scientist, insert lines from Dylan Thomas's poem "Do Not Go Gentle into That Good Night" into his explanation? What else about Gould's argument surprises you?

Suggestions for Writing

1. Write an abstract (a summary of approximately 250 words) of Gould's essay. Remember that your challenge is to capture the essential elements of Gould's essay and condense them to one page. For this assignment, do not directly quote from the essay, and do not refer specifically to Gould.
2. Gould's essay is now more than twenty years old. Research the state of the dinosaur extinction controversy today. In a short essay, evaluate the current state of the issue, and evaluate Gould's prediction that the Alvarez hypothesis will ultimately provide the most convincing science. Was Gould right?

Science, Lies, and the Ultimate Truth

BARBARA EHRENREICH

Barbara Ehrenreich is a writer and social critic whose work has appeared in numerous publications. Initially trained as a scientist, Ehrenreich is best known now as a prolific commentator on American culture. She has written many books, including Complaints and Disorders: The Sexual Politics of Sickness *(1973, with Dierdre English);* For Her Own Good: One Hundred Fifty Years of the Experts' Advice to Women *(1978, also with Dierdre English);* Witches, Midwives and Nurses: A History of Women Healers *(1972);* The Hearts of Men: American Dreams and the Flight from Commitment *(1987);* Fear of Falling: The Inner Life of the Middle Class *(1989);* The Worst Years of Our Lives: Irreverent Notes from a Decade ·of Greed *(1990);* The Snarling Citizen *(1995);* Blood Rites: Origins and History of the Passions of War *(1998);* Nickel and Dimed: On (Not) Getting by in America *(2002); and* Bait and Switch: The (Futile) Pursuit of the American Dream *(2005). The following essay first appeared in* Time *magazine in 1991. What does Ehrenreich claim about the sanctity of science?*

———————— ✦ ————————

If there is any specimen lower than a fornicating preacher, it must be a shady scientist. The dissolute evangelist betrays his one revealed Truth, but the scientist who rushes half-cocked into print or, worse yet, falsifies the data subverts the idea of truth. Cold fusion in a teacup? Or, as biologists (then at Massachusetts Institute of Technology) David Baltimore and Thereza Imanishi-Kari claimed in a controversial 1986 article that the U.S. National Institutes of Health has now judged to be fraudulent, genes from one mouse mysteriously "imitating" those from another? Sure, and parallel lines might as well meet somewhere or apples leap up back onto trees.

Baltimore, the Nobel laureate and since 1990 president of Rockefeller University, has apologized, after a fashion, for his role in the alleged fraud, and many feel that the matter should be left to rest. He didn't, after all, falsify the data himself; he merely signed on as senior scientist to Imanishi-Kari's now discredited findings. But when a young postdoctoral fellow named Margot O'Toole tried to blow the whistle, Baltimore pooh-poohed

O'Toole's evidence and stood by while she lost her job. Then, as the feds closed in, he launched a bold, misguided defense of the sanctity of science. What does one more lie matter anyway? Politicians "misspeak" and are forgiven by their followers. Pop singers have been known to dub in better voices. Literary deconstructionists say there's no truth anyway, just ideologies and points of view. Lies, you might say, are the great lubricant of our way of life. They sell products, flatter the powerful, appease the electorate and save vast sums from the IRS. Imanishi-Kari's lie didn't even hurt anyone: no bridges fell, no patients died.

But science is different, and the difference does define a kind of sanctity. Although we think of it as the most secular of human enterprises, there is a little-known spiritual side to science, with its own stern ethical implications. Through research, we seek to know that ultimate Other, which could be called Nature if the term didn't sound so tame and beaten, or God if the word weren't loaded with so much human hope and superstition. Think of it more neutrally as the nameless Subject of so much that happens, like the It in "It is raining": something "out there" and vastly different from ourselves, but not so alien that we cannot hope to know Its ways.

When I was a graduate student in biology—at Rockefeller, where Baltimore also earned his Ph.D.—I would have winced at all this metaphysics. The ethos of the acolyte was humility and patience. If the experiment didn't succeed, you did it again, and then scratched your head and tried a new approach. There were mistakes, but mistakes could be corrected, which is why you reported exactly how you did things, step by step, so others could prove you right or wrong. There were even, sometimes, corners cut: a little rounding off, an anomalous finding overlooked.

But falsifying data lay outside our moral universe. The least you could do as a scientist was record exactly what you observed (in ink, in notebooks that never left the lab). The most you could do was to arrange the experimental circumstances so as to entrap the elusive It and squeeze out some small confession: This is how the enzyme works, or the protein folds, or the gene makes known its message. But always, and no matter what, you let It do the talking. And when it spoke, which wasn't often, your reward, as one of my professors used to say, was "to wake up screaming in the night"—at the cunning of Its logic and the elegance of Its design.

This was the ideal, anyway. But Big Science costs big bucks and breeds a more mundane and calculating kind of outlook. It takes hundreds of thousands of dollars a year to run a biological laboratory with electron microscopes, ultracentrifuges, amino-acid analyzers, Ph.D.s and technicians. The big bucks tend to go to big shots like Baltimore, whose machines and underlings must grind out "results" in massive volume. In the past two decades, as federal funding for basic research has ebbed, the pressure to produce has risen to dangerous levels. At the same time, the worldly rewards of success have expanded to include fat paychecks (from patents and sidelines in the biotech business) as well as power and celebrity status. And these are the circumstances that invite deception.

Imanishi-Kari succumbed, apparently, to the desire to make a name for herself and hence, no doubt, expand her capacity for honest research. But Baltimore is a more disturbing case. He already had the name, the resources and the power that younger scientists covet. What he forgot is that although humans may respect these things, the truth does not. What he lost sight of, in the smugness of success, is that truth is no respecter of hierarchy or fame. It can come out of the mouths of mere underlings, like the valiant O'Toole.

And if no one was physically hurt, still there was damage done. Scientists worldwide briefly believed the bogus "findings" and altered their views accordingly or wasted time trying to follow the false lead in their labs. Then there is the inevitable damage from the exposure of the lie: millions of people, reading of the scandal, must have felt their deepest cynicism confirmed. If a Nobel laureate in science could sink to the moral level of Milli Vanilli or a White House spin doctor, then maybe the deconstructionists are right and there is no truth anywhere, only self-interest masked as objective fact.

Baltimore should issue a fuller apology, accounting for his alleged cover-up of the initial fraud. Then he should reflect for a week or two and consider stepping down from his position as president of Rockefeller University and de facto science statesman. Give him a modest lab to work in, maybe one in the old Rockefeller buildings where the microbe hunters toiled decades ago. I picture something with a river view, where it is impossible to forget that Manhattan is an island, that the earth is a planet, and that there is something out there much larger, and possibly even cleverer, than ourselves.

Topics for Thought and Discussion

1. According to Ehrenreich, why is a "shady scientist" worse than a "fornicating preacher"? Discuss Ehrenreich's sense of scientific sanctity—her belief in a metaphysical practice of science and an ultimate Truth that is the goal of science. How credible are Ehrenreich's ideas?

2. Examine carefully Ehrenreich's introduction and describe the techniques she uses to hook her reader. How does she maintain reader interest?

3. Examine carefully Ehrenreich's conclusion. Describe its various elements. For what does she call?
4. According to Ehrenreich, what is the relationship between "big bucks," "big science," and deception? How big a problem do you think this is?

Suggestions for Writing

1. A number of recent studies suggest that cheating has become endemic in school and in all areas of the American workplace. How significant is this for science? Should science and scientists be different than the rest of society? Write a response to Ehrenreich in which you use your own sense of right and wrong to revisit (now, fifteen years later) her concerns about the dangers "the lie" poses to science.
2. Conduct a survey of fellow students in which you ask them whether they believe science should be held to different standards of truth and honesty than other human endeavors such as business and politics. Summarize your findings in a one-page statement.
3. Science has suffered some high-profile cases of fraud in recent years. Conduct research into the kinds of scientific malfeasance that have made headlines in the last year. Write an essay in which you describe the particular challenges facing scientific ethics today.

Why Science Must Adapt to Women:
An Elite Survivor Assesses the Hidden Costs of Exclusion
PEGGY ORENSTEIN

Peggy Orenstein is a writer known for her interest in the experience of women in American culture. She is the author of Schoolgirls: Young Women, Self-Esteem, and the Confidence Gap *(1994), and* Flux: Women on Sex, Work, Love, Kids, and Life in a Half-Changed World *(2000). She is also a regular contributor to periodicals, including* Discover Magazine, *in which the following essay appeared in 2002. As you read this essay, pay particular attention to the shape of Orenstein's argument. What is she requesting from you, her reader?*

━━━━━━━━━━ ✦ ━━━━━━━━━━

Elizabeth Blackburn is talking about chromosomes, which isn't surprising: She is the biologist who in 1978 first established that telomeres, caps on the ends of chromosomes, protect critical genetic material from eroding during cell division. Seven years later, she and molecular biologist Carol Greider discovered the enzyme telomerase. Both findings offer tantalizing clues to the mysteries of aging and cancer. In as many as 90 percent of metastatic cancers, for instance, telomerase is wildly over-expressed. Blackburn's work has launched one of the hottest fields in cell biology. Her office in the Blackburn Lab at the University of California at San Francisco is chockablock with awards; it also sports a poster depicting dancing chromosomes tipped with merry, Day-Glo telomeres.

What has Blackburn riled up at the moment, however, has nothing to do with her research. She is focused on the Xs and Ys of chromosomes and why it is that more XX types—women—disappear from academic science. Nearly half of undergraduate science and engineering degrees are earned by women, but that number plummets to a third at the doctoral level, propped up by high numbers in fields such as psychology. Just 22 percent of doctorates in physics and 12 percent in engineering are awarded to women. At the faculty level, women's representation shrinks to 20 percent, concentrated, after controlling for age, in the lower ranks and at less prestigious institutions. In the rarefied air of the National Academy of Sciences, women's membership hovers around 7 percent. Blackburn is one of these elite survivors.

"The argument has been that the pipeline will take care of this," Blackburn says, referring to the idea that if enough women are encouraged to enter science early, the gender gap, over time, will disappear. "But the pipeline has been good for a number of years, and it hasn't taken care of it. In biology it's especially insidious because 50 percent of grad students are female. This has been the case for quite some time. Yet when I was chair of my department, I was the only woman chair in the entire medical school. We are putting a lot of our students off continuing—both men and women, but more women. They vote with their feet."

Make no mistake, Blackburn has flourished in the culture of science. But when she entered in the 1970s, the expectation was that once the pesky problem of overt discrimination was solved, women would adapt to science. Three decades later, she believes that hypothesis was wrong. To create true equality—to ensure that the best minds continue—she feels that science will have to adapt to women.

It is no secret why women scientists flow out of the academic pipeline. Numerous studies have shown that subtle, often unintentional bias combined with a tenure process that overlaps childbearing years has a corrosive effect. A study of 2,000 science and engineering doctoral students sponsored by the National Science Foundation in 1996 found that men were more likely than women to report that they were taken seriously by faculty. They were also more likely to have received help designing research, writing grant proposals, coauthoring publications, and learning management skills.

According to Gerhard Sonnert, a sociologist of science at Harvard University who published a large-scale study on gender and science in 1995, women are often put off by the combative style that's rewarded in scientific research, as well as the emphasis on self-promotion. "There's an accepted language of science that has entered into the folklore and become the field," Blackburn says. "Women don't necessarily speak that exact same language, which is not to say that the language they use is not as good. It is. But all those subtle ways women present things that are different from men, even their tone of voice, play into how what they're presenting is accepted, its authority." What's more, women who do take on an aggressive style are often labeled "difficult."

Women who stick to the academic track may run into further obstacles when they go job hunting. Rhea Steinpreis, a neuroscientist at the University of Wisconsin–Milwaukee, sent more than 230 curricula vitae to randomly selected professors, asking them to evaluate the fitness of the candidate as a job applicant. The CVs were identical in every respect but one: Half were sent by "Karen Miller" and half by "Brian Miller." Fewer than half the professors would hire Karen; Brian was endorsed by two-thirds.

Sometimes women fight back: In 1999 a group of female faculty at the Massachusetts Institute of Technology presented a report to the president of the institution quantifying a culture that marginalized women. In addition to lower pay, they documented discrimination in hiring, promotions, and awards; exclusion from leadership positions; inequities in lab size; and hostility toward family responsibilities. Meanwhile, faculty ratios hadn't budged in two decades. Perhaps the saddest aspect of the report was that because female faculty members had little contact with one another, they tended to see their ill treatment as a unique, isolated event rather than the result of gender bias. When they quit, as many did, they blamed themselves for their inability to thrive.

Elizabeth Blackburn is hard-pressed to recall ever being told that because she was female she couldn't be a scientist. Growing up in Tasmania, Australia, the second of seven children whose parents were both family physicians, she considered science a birthright. She was further insulated from stereotyping by attending an all-girls school and an all-female college.

Blackburn went on to graduate school at Cambridge and a postdoctoral fellowship at Yale, where she recalls her mentor, cell biologist Joe Gall, as particularly supportive. Looking back on her career, however, she believes she was subject to plenty of bias; like many successful women in nontraditional fields, she was just particularly adept at denying it. "I was oblivious for a long time," she recalls, "and that's the way I coped. It was very much a defense. If I had stopped and thought about it, I would've felt so vulnerable to it."

As she talks, Blackburn sits in the living room of the house she shares with her husband, John Sedat, a cell biologist and microscopy expert at UCSF who works on three-dimensional structures of chromosomes in nuclei, and their 15-year-old son, Ben. It's a typically chilly San Francisco summer Sunday. Wisps of fog slide by, rendering the view as undefined as the cost to a woman of blocking out an unfriendly culture. "I spent so much time exhausted and anxious," Blackburn sighs. "It was a different kind of tension than for my male colleagues. And I can't really say what that means. Was I more afraid of being wrong? I don't know."

Not until she was an assistant professor at the University of California at Berkeley and saw a talented female colleague turned down for tenure did Blackburn realize that denial might not protect her. "That was my first wake-up-and-smell-the-coffee feeling," she says. "For a long time, I was stupid enough to think it's only the science that counts. That's a great comfort because you love doing your science. But realistically I knew—I know now—that's not the whole thing."

What propelled Blackburn forward was passion for the work. She is a driven, gifted scientist, and the exciting results of her research reinforced her commitment. If they hadn't, she wonders whether she would have persisted. Like many women, she was tempted to dribble out of the pipeline toward the end of her postdoc. "At one point I thought I was pregnant," she says. "And I thought, 'Oh well, I'll just have a child, and I won't have to think about this pressure.' I don't know if that would've been short term or not. I look back and think how easily one can be deflected because one is at a daunting stage such as having to go out and look for a job."

Blackburn had only one child, at 38, after her appointment to the safe haven of full professorship. When she was placed on bed rest for the last five months of the pregnancy, she offered to take the time as a sabbatical with reduced pay. Her department head, a man, informed her that she was entitled to a leave with full salary. "Here I was, all apologetic," she says. "I was *inviting* discrimination. It was pathetic. Even at the time, I realized that. But I felt like, here I am not keeping up my end of the bargain."

After Ben was born, she moved to UCSF. For years, she says, her life consisted of exactly two things: work and family, which makes her sympathetic to other parents in her lab. "Many women wonder, 'How am I going to do this and have a family?' Because part of the culture of science is that if you're not there until late, you're not really doing it, which is the biggest pile of crap. All these hours and chatting and things like that don't make the science better."

She and Sedat were lucky and affluent enough to find a child-care provider they trusted. *Luck* is a word that Blackburn uses often. She feels lucky to have had encouraging mentors, lucky that her research vindicated her commitment, lucky to have found consistent, loving child care for Ben, lucky to have satisfying work, a happy marriage, and parenthood. Listening to her, though, one wonders: Serendipity plays a role in every life, but is it disproportionately necessary for a woman who wants to pursue academic research? "Someone once asked me how I did it as a woman," Blackburn recalls. "I said something that surprised even me at the time: 'I disguised myself as a man.' I had not really realized until that conversation that that's what I was doing. At the time, I didn't think of it as a sad thing, but it is sad."

She does not perpetuate that strategy. Her lab is half female; a bulletin board is covered with photos of pregnant grad students and postdocs. Some of her students have gone on to mentor others. And 20 years after she and Greider discovered telomerase, the research on the enzyme is largely dominated by women.

Blackburn packs me off to lunch one afternoon with three of the most promising young women scientists in her lab. Jue Lin, 32, is a postdoc in molecular biology with a Ph.D. from Cornell. Melissa Rivera, 30, who did her undergraduate work at MIT, will soon move on to a postdoc at the University of Texas at Austin. Carol Anderson, 29, is a graduate student in molecular biology with a B.S. from Yale. Rivera and Anderson are single. Lin is married with two toddlers.

We stroll down the hill to a Thai place in San Francisco's Sunset District, taking a circuitous route to avoid the steepest streets. While each of these women had once assumed that she would become a principal investigator, they are no longer quite so sure. All three consider their doubts to be personal, yet they sound awfully familiar to me. "It's just, you've got to be this person that I don't want to be in order to be successful as a scientist," Rivera says. "You have to be competitive, and grab things from wherever you can get them, and be protective of what you present."

But surely they're accustomed to competition. "This is different," Lin says. "It's not just about studying and getting good grades. I've always done well at that. This is politics." In addition to, or perhaps because of, her disenchantment, the demands of work seem to conflict with family life. "When I'm in the lab, I think about what's going on in the house," she says. "At home I think, 'I could be working, I could be getting something done.'"

Rivera has put her social life on hold until she finishes her degree. At 30, she is more interested in biology than in her biological clock, but when she projects forward, she's apprehensive. "By the time I'll be established, I'll be 40," she says. "So then I get to maybe date and get married and have children. People can do it, and they do, but meanwhile, you're working 12 hours a day. It's not human."

Anderson, the youngest, frowns. "Maybe it's not necessary to work 16 hours a day to be successful," she says. "I wanted to be in Liz's lab, to have an example of someone who was successful but lives a balanced life." She has joined a support program for women graduate students in the sciences. Does she expect to become an advocate for change? "I would," she says, "but I'm not sure what change needs to happen. The problem isn't clearly defined."

"How do you get rid of those subtle biases?" Rivera asks of no one in particular.

"It takes effort," Anderson says. "Women mentoring other women, supporting each other—which won't happen if women don't go into academic science."

On the way back to the lab, the three enthuse about Blackburn. "Liz is really special," Rivera says. "My next principal investigator is also a woman. She's not typical either. Maybe if I see a lot of P.I.'s like them, it will make a difference. The door is still open. Ask me again in five years. Maybe I'll see that I can do this and still be me."

Blackburn is troubled by the younger women's perception of what it takes to be a successful academic. True, she says, the pressure is more intense for this generation, male or female, at all career stages. But those three could more than meet the challenge. "How many years have these women spent doing incredibly difficult, demanding work? Ten? Thirteen? They ought to get more choices and not feel intimidated after all that. If you have a passion for the work, you should be able to go for it."

Maybe they will. Recently, there have been signs of change. A follow-up to the MIT report, issued in March, showed that while the institution still had a long way to go, it had made progress: More women had been appointed to leadership roles, salaries had increased, collegiality had improved. The university is considering innovative hiring practices and has changed the tenure process to allow time out for childbearing. Other universities have launched their own investigations. Some already offer on-site day care, part-time positions, housing, and mentoring.

For more radical thinkers like Debra Rolison, head of the Advanced Electrochemical Materials Section at the Naval Research Lab in Washington, D.C., waiting for reform isn't acceptable. She believes taxpayers shouldn't support discriminatory institutions. Title IX legislation ought to be applied to hiring practices in academic science, she says. "It's simple. We should yank all federal funds if departments are not hiring women commensurate to how they're training them. You can bet that would solve the problem quickly."

In late June, Blackburn is in Washington, D.C., serving on the President's Bioethics Council on Stem Cell Research. Other scientists had declined to participate, believing the committee would be stacked toward conservatives. Perhaps those years of being a lone female voice make her more willing to stand up for the minority position. "This research is enormously important," she says. "There are intractable diseases out there, and we can't continue with business as usual."

When the council breaks after three days, she is cautiously optimistic. A narrow majority of the members have been swayed to her point of view: Ban reproductive cloning but proceed with cloning for research under strict regulation. Will that position be reflected in the final report? "They could easily present this in a way that would hang up the research, that would effectively make it impossible to proceed," Blackburn warns. (The following month, when the report became public, it did disappoint. It advised a four-year moratorium, an option that had hardly been discussed by the group. Discouraged, Blackburn skipped the next meeting.)

For now she has brought her son, Ben, with her, and they're eager to hit the museums. I ask Ben how he copes with his mother's frequent travels. Even as the question escapes my mouth, I realize it reflects my own unconscious bias: Would I ask the son of a male biologist whether his father's travel schedule upsets him? Am I not implying that Ben *ought* to resent his mother's work?

The truth is that when Ben was younger, Blackburn's absence did make him anxious, which worried her. She cut back on trips and stayed away no more than two nights at a time. She and Sedat never traveled simultaneously. Today Ben seems enviably close to both parents and quietly proud of his mother's accomplishments. "I don't like her going away," he says thoughtfully. "But this council is a worthy cause, and it's important for her to make some good happen. I'm in agreement with her on these issues; we share the same opinion—and she didn't prime me to say that!"

It is difficult to believe there could be any barriers left for Blackburn to break through, but I can't resist asking. She has been nominated for a Nobel Prize, an honor only 10 women scientists have won since it was first awarded in 1901. Will those XX chromosomes undermine telomerase's chance for glory? "If you look at the track record, it would certainly factor against it," she says, then smiles wryly. "But every now and then, you know, someone has to make a gesture to prove the track record is wrong."

Topics for Thought and Discussion

1. Orenstein cares about the issues she writes about and wants you to care about them, too. What techniques does she use to make you care? What elements (examples, evidence, statistics, interviews, anecdotes, dialogue, logic, emotion) does she use to make this essay accessible and to get her point across?
2. What are the advantages and disadvantages of focusing an article like this one on a prominent scientist like Elizabeth Blackburn? Does it make accomplishing Orenstein's purpose easier or harder?
3. What, according to Blackburn, is the "pipeline argument"? Why has the pipeline not worked to bring more women into science?
4. What is the difference between women adapting to science and science adapting to women? How is this difference central to Orenstein's argument?
5. What does Blackburn mean when she says she "disguised" herself as a man to be successful? How is this an indictment of science, and how—according to Orenstein—does science need to change?

Suggestions for Writing

1. Choose a science major at your school (or at a local college or university) and do some research by looking at the school's catalogue or Web site. What is the percentage of faculty who are women? What are their ranks? Who is the

chair of the department? From your research, would you say that the problems described by Blackburn and Orenstein have been resolved at your college/university? Write an analysis that summarizes your findings.

2. Write a personal memoir that describes an experience you have had in the classroom that has taught you something about the relationship between gender and science. What were the consequences of this event, and what have you learned? In your experience, is Orenstein (and Blackburn) right?

3. Evaluate your own experience with science, and list several suggestions that could make undergraduate science a friendlier "place" for women.

School Boards Want to 'Teach the Controversy.' What Controversy?

LAWRENCE KRAUSS

Lawrence Krauss is the Ambrose Swasey Professor of Physics, Professor of Astronomy, chair of the Department of Physics, and the Director of the Center for Education and Research in Cosmology and Astrophysics at Case Western Reserve University. An expert on particle astrophysics, he is also a prolific popularizer of science and cosmology. A frequent guest on radio and television programs, Dr. Krauss is the author of many books, including Fear of Physics: A Guide for the Perplexed *(1993);* The Physics of Star Trek *(1995);* Beyond Star Trek: From Alien Invasion to the End of Time *(1997);* Quintessence: The Mystery of the Missing Mass *(2000);* Atom: A Single Oxygen Atom's Journey from the Big Bang to Life on Earth . . . and Beyond *(2001); and most recently,* Hiding in the Mirror: The Mysterious Allure of Extra Dimensions *(2005). The following article appeared as an opinion piece in the* New York Times *in 2005. As you read, notice the assumptions that Dr. Krauss makes about the roles of science and faith in society.*

---- ✦ ----

The recent so-called debates on the teaching of evolution in Kansas have me thinking about different theological reactions to the teaching of evolution.

The Roman Catholic Church, which stands on common ground with conservative Christians in opposition to abortion, and which is doctrinally committed to notions like the Virgin Birth, apparently has no problem with the notion of evolution as it is currently studied by biologists, including supposedly "controversial" ideas like common ancestry of all life forms.

Popes from Pius XII to John Paul II have reaffirmed that the process of evolution in no way violates the teachings of the church. Pope Benedict XVI, when he was Cardinal Joseph Ratzinger, presided over the church's International Theological Commission, which stated that "since it has been demonstrated that all living organisms on earth are genetically related, it is virtually certain that all living organisms have descended from this first organism."

At the same time, those who wish to include "intelligent design" in the science curriculum insist that if we leave the creator out of discussions of the origin and evolution of life, then such "naturalism" must be incomplete—and that it opens the door to moral relativism and many of the other ills that go along with it.

The ultimate extension of this position may be Representative Tom DeLay's comment that the tragedy at Columbine happened "because our school systems teach our children that they are nothing but glorified apes who have evolutionized out of some primordial mud." Evolutionary biology is not the only science that appears to raise theological issues.

As a cosmologist, I am reminded of a controversy that arose from the development of a consistent mathematical solution of Einstein's equations, devised in 1931 by Georges Lemaître, a Catholic priest and physicist.

The solution required what today we call the Big Bang. By confronting the conventional scientific wisdom that the universe was eternal, and instead demonstrating that it was likely to have had a beginning in the finite past—indeed, one that could certainly be said to be born in light—Lemaître was hailed by many, including 20 years later by Pope Pius XII himself, as having scientifically proved Genesis.

Lemaître, however, became convinced that it was inappropriate to use the Big Bang as a basis for theological pronouncements. He initially inserted, then ultimately removed, a paragraph in the draft of his 1931 paper on the Big Bang remarking on the possible theological consequences of his discovery. In the end, he said, "As far as I can see, such a theory remains entirely outside of any metaphysical or religious question."

While this argument may seem strange, Lemaître was grasping something that is missed in the current public debates about evolution. The Big Bang is not a metaphysical theory, but a scientific one: namely one that derives from equations that have been measured to describe the universe, and that makes predictions that one can test.

It is certainly true that one can reflect on the existence of the Big Bang to validate the notion of creation, and with that the notion of God. But such a metaphysical speculation lies outside of the theory itself.

This is why the Catholic Church can confidently believe that God created humans, and at the same time accept the overwhelming scientific evidence in favor of common evolutionary ancestry of life on earth.

One can choose to view chance selection as obvious evidence that there is no God, as Dr. Richard Dawkins, an evolutionary biologist and uncompromising atheist, might argue, or to conclude instead that God chooses to work through natural means. In the latter case, the overwhelming evidence that natural selection has determined the evolution of life on earth would simply imply that God is "the cause of causes," as Cardinal Ratzinger's document describes it.

The very fact that two such diametrically opposed views can be applied to the same scientific theory demonstrates that the fact of evolution need not dictate theology. In other words, the apparently contentious questions are not scientific ones. It is possible for profoundly atheist evolutionary biologists like Dr. Dawkins and deeply spiritual ones like Dr. Kenneth Miller of Brown University, who writes extensively on evolution, to be in complete agreement about the scientific mechanism governing biological evolution, and the fact that life has evolved via natural selection.

Students are completely free to make up their own minds, in any case. What is at issue is whether they will be taught the science that should allow them to make an informed judgment. But impugning the substance of the science, or requiring the introduction of essentially theological ideas like "intelligent design" into the curriculum, merely muddies the water by imposing theological speculations on a scientific theory. Evolution, like Lemaître's Big Bang, is itself "entirely outside of any metaphysical or religious question."

The Discovery Institute, which promotes "intelligent design," a newer version of creationism, argues that schools should "Teach the Controversy." But there is no scientific controversy.

State school board science standards would do better to include a statement like this: While well-tested theories like evolution and the Big Bang have provided remarkable new insights and predictions about nature, questions of purpose that may underlie these discoveries are outside the scope of science, and scientists themselves have many different views in this regard.

Or one might simply quote Lemaître, who said of the limitations of science and of his own effort to reconcile his scientific discoveries with his parallel religious beliefs: "To search thoroughly for the truth involves a searching of souls as well as of spectra."

Topics for Thought and Discussion

1. Explain what Krauss means when he says that "there is no scientific controversy" about evolution. How does this stand ultimately challenge promoters of "intelligent design"?
2. How does Krauss use the Catholic Church? Consider all of the places that the Church comes into his short essay. Why, in argumentative terms, does he use the Catholic Church?
3. Explain how Krauss attempts to reconcile science and religion. Why, according to Krauss, are they not categorically in opposition to each other?

Suggestions for Writing

1. Write your own meditation on the relationship between science and religion. In your opinion (and, perhaps, your experience), are science and religion in opposition? If so, how do you reconcile the two? If not, how do the two work together?
2. Take a stand on the issue of high school science. Should intelligent design be taught as an alternative scientific approach? Should evolution not be taught? This would make a good research project, as much has been written recently on these issues.
3. The conflict between evolution and intelligent design is a dynamic and fluid one. Survey the headlines from the last six months. What is the state of the issue right now? What are the primary arguments today?

Ethics Statement
AMERICAN INSTITUTE OF BIOLOGICAL SCIENCES

The American Institute of Biological Sciences (AIBS) was established as a national umbrella organization for the biological sciences in 1947 and now represents more than 80 professional societies and organizations with a combined membership exceeding 240,000 scientists and educators. AIBS works to promote biological research and to bridge the gulf between science and society. The following ethics statement, revised in 2002, was designed to give guidance to its members. As you read, notice particularly the elements of the statement that are specific to the practice of science, and which seem to be equally appropriate to all human endeavors. Why is the form of this document appropriate to its content?

————————— ✦ —————————

Preamble: AIBS believes that a code of ethics is basic to the conduct of science and essential to the maintenance of an honorable and respectable profession. Members of AIBS shall conduct their professional lives in accordance with the ethics standards stated below.

Conduct research and teaching in a manner that is consistent with accepted scientific and teaching methods, maintaining the highest standards of honesty and integrity in all professional endeavors.

Comply with all laws and regulations that apply to the treatment of study organisms and other aspects of professional conduct.

Expose scientific fraud and other forms of professional misconduct whenever it is found.

Be civil and respectful in professional interactions, avoiding discrimination based on race, gender, sexual orientation, religion, or age. Treat colleagues, students, and employees fairly.

Be constructive and professional in evaluating the work of colleagues, students, and employees.

Provide recognition of past and present contributions of others to science, and present one's professional opinions only on those topics for which one has training and knowledge.

Promote the free and open exchange of information, not withholding information to substantiate a personal or scientific point of view.

Be candid about potential conflicts of interest in the conduct of professional duties.

Do not speak on behalf of AIBS without written permission from the president of the Institute.

Topics for Thought and Discussion

1. Why do you think that a science organization has an ethics statement? Is it more necessary for science than for other disciplines (like history, or literature, for example)?
2. Choose any one of the preceding precepts and evaluate it. Why is it necessary? What is it designed to control or contain? Is it specific to biology? To science?
3. Describe the form that the AIBS statement takes. Why is this appropriate to the purpose of this text?

Suggestions for Writing

1. Choose a group (professional, campus, social) about which you have some knowledge or in which you are interested. Develop an ethics statement for this group. What kind of ethics are necessary for a sports team? A debate team? A political action club? Identify a group with which you are associated and write a set of ethics statements for it, modeled after the AIBS statement. Be sure to consider form as well as content.

What Is Science?: Exploring Connections

1. Using at least three of the essays from this chapter, construct a comprehensive definition of science.
2. In "What Is Science?" George Orwell claims that science is primarily a way of thinking about the world. How would Carl Sagan ("Why We Need to Understand Science"), Barbara Ehrenreich ("Science, Lies and the Ultimate Truth"), or Stephen Jay Gould ("Sex, Drugs, Disasters, and the Extinction of Dinosaurs") respond? Would they agree? Do you?
3. According to Lewis Thomas ("Alchemy"), George Orwell ("What Is Science?"), Carl Sagan ("Why We Need to Understand Science"), and Lawrence Krauss ("School Boards Want to 'Teach the Controversy.' What Controversy?"), what is the relationship between science and society? What does science owe to society? What does society owe to science? As you come to your own conclusions, differentiate between what you see as the actual relationship between science and society, and what you think *should* be the relationship.
4. Using Orenstein's argument ("Why Science Must Adapt to Women"), and at least two other essays from this chapter, discuss the relationship between science and gender. Do the other essays comment on this question directly, or by what they leave out of their discussions?
5. Ehrenreich's "Science, Lies, and the Ultimate Truth" is also concerned with the ethics of biological research. Apply the ethics from AIBS to the situation described by Ehrenreich. Would this ethics statement fix the problem that Ehrenreich sees?
6. Sagan introduces us to the idea of "pseudoscience" and *The Onion* ("Revolutionary New Insoles Combine Five Forms of Pseudoscience") pushes the idea further. Using these two essays, discuss either the relationship between pseudoscience and science, or what we can learn about the relationship between science and society by looking at pseudoscience.
7. Look at advertising that makes use of scientific claims. How much is real science and how much pseudoscience? What is the role of science in advertising?

Science and Human Behavior

"Know thyself!" This injunction is at least as old as Apollo's oracle at Delphi, and it lies at the foundation of philosophy, history, literature, and most of the rest of the humanities. Why are we the way we are? Why do we behave the way we do? For millennia, philosophers and theologians have struggled to define humanity, often by opposing humanity to the rest of the natural world. Human behavior continues to perplex us, but today what was once primarily a philosophical and religious question is increasingly a scientific one. Evolutionary biologists, evolutionary psychologists, chemists, and physiologists are all adding pieces to the growing picture of how we behave and why. Scientists have discovered that fields as disparate as wildlife biology and chemistry can yield interesting answers to the ancient question "Who am I?"

This chapter provides a range of answers to that seminal question by attempting to answer other, more limited questions.

Why, for example, after September 11th, did we pull together? Why did thousands of people donate blood, money, labor, and materials? How do biologists and psychologists explain altruism? In the course of answering these questions, Natalie Angier ("Of Altruism, Heroism and Nature's Gifts in the Face of Terror") brings us closer to understanding the nature of human society and of the beings that make it up.

Why do I fall in love with the people I do? What makes a relationship last? What makes someone attractive to me and someone else not? Is there such a thing as a love potion? Should there be? In very different ways, both David Buss ("The Strategies of Human Mating") and Gunjan Sinha ("You Dirty Vole") answer this question by investigating what evolutionary psychology and biochemistry can tell us about love and sex, those most perplexing and complex human experiences.

What can male violence against females in baboon and chimpanzee societies teach us about the conditions that foster such violence in human societies? Biopsychologist Barbara Smuts's ("Apes of Wrath") field studies in Africa help her to answer that question, but pose new ones about the direction of human society. Similarly, but drawing upon very different types of technology and science, Carl Zimmer ("Who Would You Save?") looks into how human beings make the ethical decisions they make. What is the biology, what the evolutionary cause, for our ethical choices?

So why do we behave as we do? It is because of chemical reactions in our brains. It is because of evolutionary advantage, and sexual-strategies theory. It is because of group survival and individual reproduction. It is because of physiological adaptation. This chapter will provide you with some questions and some answers, but more than anything, it will provide you with examples of the ways scientists are approaching—and answering—the question of human behavior.

This chapter will also feature a variety of forms by which scientists and writers present their information. From the scientific structure of David Buss's study to Natalie Angier's personal rumination on human altruism, we see the various ways that science is made popular and accessible to the culture and society of which it is a part. So as you read the essays in this chapter, consider not only how we know about ourselves, but how we communicate that knowledge to one another through writing.

Of Altruism, Heroism and Nature's Gifts in the Face of Terror
NATALIE ANGIER

Natalie Angier is one of the premier science writers in the United States today. She is the recipient of the American Association for the Advancement of Science Westinghouse Award for excellence in science journalism, and the Lewis Thomas Award for distinguished writing in the life sciences. She is also a founding staff member of Discover Magazine, *and a winner of the Pulitzer Prize for her science writing while at* The New York Times. *She is a prolific contributor to magazines and the author of many books, including the national bestseller* Woman: An Intimate Geography *(1999),* Natural Obsessions *(1999), and* The Beauty of the Beastly *(1996). She is currently working on* The Canon: What Scientists Wish That Everyone Knew About Science. *She is also the editor of* The Best American Science and Nature Writing 2002. *The following essay was begun the day after the September 11, 2001, terrorist attacks on the United States and published on September 18, 2001 in* The New York Times. *Much has been written about the actions of firefighters, police, and the public during and after the attacks on New York. Note, as you read this essay, the multiple purposes of an article like this one, and the various emotional, practical, and scientific forces Angier brings to bear on her topic.*

✦

September 18, 2001

For the wordless, formless, expectant citizens of tomorrow, here are some postcards of all that matters today:

- Minutes after terrorists slam jet planes into the towers of the World Trade Center, streams of harrowed humanity crowd the emergency stairwells, heading in two directions. While terrified employees scramble down, toward exit doors and survival, hundreds of New York firefighters, each laden with 70 to 100 pounds of lifesaving gear, charge upward, never to be seen again.

- As the last of four hijacked planes advances toward an unknown but surely populated destination, passengers huddle together and plot resistance against their captors, an act that may explain why the plane fails to reach its target, crashing instead into an empty field outside Pittsburgh.

- Hearing of the tragedy whose dimensions cannot be charted or absorbed, tens of thousands of people across the nation storm their local hospitals and blood banks, begging for the chance to give blood, something of themselves to the hearts of the wounded—and the heart of us all—beating against the void.

Altruism and heroism. If not for these twin radiant badges of our humanity, there would be no us, and we know it. And so, when their vile opposite threatened to choke us into submission last Tuesday, we rallied them in quantities so great we surprised even ourselves.

Nothing and nobody can fully explain the source of the emotional genius that has been everywhere on display. Politicians have cast it as evidence of the indomitable spirit of a rock-solid America; pastors have given credit to a more celestial source. And while biologists in no way claim to have discovered the key to human nobility, they do have their own spin on the subject. The altruistic impulse, they say, is a nondenominational gift, the birthright and defining characteristic of the human species.

As they see it, the roots of altruistic behavior far predate *Homo sapiens*, and that is why it seems to flow forth so readily once tapped. Recent studies that model group dynamics suggest that a spirit of cooperation will arise in nature under a wide variety of circumstances.

"There's a general trend in evolutionary biology toward recognizing that very often the best way to compete is to cooperate," said Dr. Barbara Smuts, a professor of anthropology at the University of Michigan, who has published papers on the evolution of altruism. "And that, to me, is a source of some solace and comfort."

Moreover, most biologists concur that the human capacity for language and memory allows altruistic behavior—the desire to give, and to sacrifice for the sake of others—to flourish in measure far beyond the cooperative spirit seen in other species.

With language, they say, people can learn of individuals they have never met and feel compassion for their suffering, and honor and even emulate their heroic deeds. They can also warn one another of any selfish cheaters or malign tricksters lurking in their midst.

"In a large crowd, we know who the good guys are, and we can talk about, and ostracize, the bad ones," said Dr. Craig Packer, a professor of ecology and evolution at the University of Minnesota. "People are very concerned about their reputation, and that, too, can inspire us to be good."

Oh, better than good.

"There's a grandness in the human species that is so striking, and so profoundly different from what we see in other animals," he added. "We are an amalgamation of families working together. This is what civilization is derived from."

At the same time, said biologists, the very conditions that encourage heroics and selflessness can be the source of profound barbarism as well. "Moral behavior is often a within-group phenomenon," said Dr. David Sloan Wilson, a professor of biology at the State University of New York at Binghamton. "Altruism is practiced within your group, and often turned off toward members of other groups."

The desire to understand the nature of altruism has occupied evolutionary thinkers since Charles Darwin, who was fascinated by the apparent existence of altruism among social insects. In ant and bee colonies, sterile female workers labor ceaselessly for their queen, and will even die for her when the nest is threatened. How could such seeming selflessness evolve, when it is exactly those individuals that are behaving altruistically that fail to breed and thereby pass their selfless genes along?

By a similar token, human soldiers who go to war often are at the beginning of their reproductive potential, and many are killed before getting the chance to have children. Why don't the stay-at-homes simply outbreed the do-gooders and thus bury the altruistic impulse along with the casualties of combat?

The question of altruism was at least partly solved when the British evolutionary theorist William Hamilton formulated the idea of inclusive fitness: the notion that individuals can enhance their reproductive success not merely by having young of their own, but by caring for their genetic relatives as well. Among social bees and ants, it turns out, the sister workers are more closely related to one another than parents normally are to their offspring; thus it behooves the workers to care more about current and potential sisters than to fret over their sterile selves.

The concept of inclusive fitness explains many brave acts observed in nature. Dr. Richard Wrangham, a primatologist at Harvard, cites the example of the red colobus monkey. When they are being hunted by chimpanzees, the male monkeys are "amazingly brave," Dr. Wrangham said. "As the biggest and strongest members of their group, they undoubtedly could escape quicker than the others." Instead, the males jump to the front, confronting the chimpanzee hunters while the mothers and offspring jump to safety. Often, the much bigger chimpanzees pull the colobus soldiers off by their tails and slam them to their deaths.

Their courageousness can be explained by the fact that colobus monkeys live in multimale, multifemale groups in which the males are almost always related. So in protecting the young monkeys, the adult males are defending their kin.

Yet, as biologists are learning, there is more to cooperation and generosity than an investment in one's nepotistic patch of DNA. Lately, they have accrued evidence that something like group selection encourages the evolution of traits beneficial to a group, even when members of the group are not related.

In computer simulation studies, Dr. Smuts and her colleagues modeled two types of group-living agents that would behave like herbivores: one that would selfishly consume all the food in a given patch before moving on, and another that would consume resources modestly rather than greedily, thus allowing local plant food to regenerate.

Researchers had assumed that cooperators could collaborate with genetically unrelated cooperators only if they had the cognitive capacity to know goodness when they saw it.

But the data suggested otherwise. "These models showed that under a wide range of simulated environmental conditions you could get selection for prudent, cooperative behavior," Dr. Smuts said, even in the absence of cognition or kinship. "If you happened by chance to get good guys together, they remained together because they created a mutually beneficial environment."

This sort of win-win principle, she said, could explain all sorts of symbiotic arrangements, even among different species—like the tendency of baboons and impalas to associate together because they use each other's warning calls.

Add to this basic mechanistic selection for cooperation the human capacity to recognize and reward behaviors that strengthen the group—the tribe, the state, the church, the platoon—and selflessness thrives and multiplies. So, too, does the need for group identity. Classic so-called minimal group experiments have shown that when people are gathered together and assigned membership in arbitrary groups, called, say, the Greens and the Reds, before long the members begin expressing amity for their fellow Greens or Reds and animosity toward those of the wrong "color."

"Ancestral life frequently consisted of intergroup conflict," Dr. Wilson of SUNY said. "It's part of our mental heritage."

Yet he does not see conflict as inevitable. "It's been shown pretty well that where people place the boundary between us and them is extremely flexible and strategic," he said. "It's possible to widen the moral circle, and I'm optimistic enough to believe it can be done on a worldwide scale."

Ultimately, though, scientists acknowledge that the evolutionary framework for self-sacrificing acts is overlaid by individual choice. And it is there, when individual firefighters or office workers or airplane passengers choose the altruistic path, that science gives way to wonder.

Dr. James J. Moore, a professor of anthropology at the University of California at San Diego, said he had studied many species, including many different primates. "We're the nicest species I know," he said. "To see those guys risking their lives, climbing over rubble on the chance of finding one person alive, well, you wouldn't find baboons doing that." The horrors of last week notwithstanding, he said, "the overall picture to come out about human nature is wonderful."

"For every 50 people making bomb threats now to mosques," he said, "there are 500,000 people around the world behaving just the way we hoped they would, with empathy and expressions of grief. We are amazingly civilized."

True, death-defying acts of heroism may be the province of the few. For the rest of us, simple humanity will do.

Topics for Thought and Discussion

1. Angier's essay is written in very short paragraphs. Why? What does this text structure contribute to her essay and its purpose?
2. How does Angier use emotion to write a scientific essay? What role does emotion play for her, and how does it contribute to her purpose?
3. How do biologists account for the altruistic and heroic actions witnessed on September 11, 2001, and succeeding days?
4. The scientists interviewed by Angier for this article see September 11th, 2001, demonstrating hope for humanity in general. Explain the basis of this hope. Do you agree?

Suggestions for Writing

1. Evaluate your own response to the September 11, 2001 attacks or some other major natural or human event. How can the things you felt, the things you did, and the thoughts and actions of those around you be explained by the evolutionary forces described by Angier?
2. Write an essay in which you comment on altruism in your culture or society. Does it occur in nonemergency situations? Does our culture encourage and reward altruism?

The Strategies of Human Mating
DAVID BUSS

David M. Buss is an evolutionary psychologist at the University of Texas at Austin, and a pioneer in the study of the evolution of human mating. He is widely published; his works include, The Evolution of Desire: Strategies of Human Mating *(1994),* The Dangerous Passion: Why Jealousy Is Necessary in Love and Sex *(2000),*

The Murderer Next Door: Why the Mind Is Designed to Kill *(2005)*, The Handbook of Evolutionary Psychology *(2005), and the award-winning* Evolutionary Psychology: The New Science of the Mind *(2nd edition 2003). He is also the author of numerous articles in popular and scientific journals, and numerous coauthored and edited books. The following essay first appeared in* American Scientist *in 1994. As you read it, note the structure of his argument and how that structure influences the structure of Buss's text. Given your own experience, does Buss seem right?*

———————— ✦ ————————

What do men and women want in a mate? Is there anything consistent about human behavior when it comes to the search for a mate? Would a Gujarati of India be attracted to the same traits in a mate as a Zulu of South Africa or a college student in the midwestern United States?

As a psychologist working in the field of human personality and mating preferences, I have come across many attempts to answer such questions and provide a coherent explanation of human mating patterns. Some theories have suggested that people search for mates who resemble archetypical images of the opposite-sex parent (à la Freud and Jung), or mates with characteristics that are either complementary or similar to one's own qualities, or mates with whom to make an equitable exchange of valuable resources.

These theories have played important roles in our understanding of human mating patterns, but few of them have provided specific predictions that can be tested. Fewer still consider the origins and functions of an individual's mating preferences. What possible function is there to mating with an individual who is an archetypical image of one's opposite-sex parent? Most theories also tend to assume that the processes that guide the mating preferences of men and women are identical, and no sex-differentiated predictions can be derived. The context of the mating behavior is also frequently ignored; the same mating tendencies are posited regardless of circumstances.

Despite the complexity of human mating behavior, it is possible to address these issues in a single, coherent theory. David Schmitt of the University of Michigan and I have recently proposed a framework for understanding the logic of human mating patterns from the standpoint of evolutionary theory. Our theory makes several predictions about the behavior of men and women in the context of their respective sexual strategies. In particular, we discuss the changes that occur when men and women shift their goals from short-term mating (casual sex) to long-term mating (a committed relationship).

Some of the studies we discuss are based on surveys of male and female college students in the United States. In these instances, the sexual attitudes of the sample population may not be reflective of the behavior of people in other cultures. In other instances, however, the results represent a much broader spectrum of the human population. In collaboration with 50 other scientists, we surveyed the mating preferences of more than 10,000 men and women in 37 countries over a six-year period spanning 1984 through 1989. Although no survey, short of canvassing the entire human population, can be considered exhaustive, our study crosses a tremendous diversity of geographic, cultural, political, ethnic, religious, racial, and economic groups. It is the largest survey ever on mate preferences.

What we found is contrary to much current thinking among social scientists, which holds that the process of choosing a mate is highly culture-bound. Instead, our results are consistent with the notion that human beings, like other animals, exhibit species-typical desires when it comes to the selection of a mate. These patterns can be accounted for by our theory of human sexual strategies.

COMPETITION AND CHOICE

Sexual-strategies theory holds that patterns in mating behavior exist because they are evolutionarily advantageous. We are obviously the descendants of people who were able to mate successfully. Our theory assumes that the sexual strategies of our ancestors evolved because they permitted them to survive and produce offspring. Those people who failed to mate successfully because they did not express these strategies are not our ancestors. One simple example is the urge to mate, which is a universal desire among people of all cultures and which is undeniably evolutionary in origin.

Although the types of behavior we consider are more complicated than simply the urge to mate, a brief overview of the relevant background should be adequate to understand the evolutionary logic of human mating strategies. As with many issues in evolutionary biology, this background begins with the work of Charles Darwin.

Darwin was the first to show that mate preferences could affect human evolution. In his seminal 1871 treatise, *The Descent of*

Man and Selection in Relation to Sex, Darwin puzzled over characteristics that seemed to be perplexing when judged merely on the basis of their relative advantage for the animal's survival. How could the brilliant plumage of a male peacock evolve when it obviously increases the bird's risk of predation? Darwin's answer was sexual selection, the evolution of characteristics that confer a reproductive advantage to an organism (rather than a survival advantage). Darwin further divided sexual selection into two processes: intrasexual competition and preferential mate choice.

Intrasexual competition is the less controversial of the two processes. It involves competition between members of the same sex to gain preferential access to mating partners. Characteristics that lead to success in these same-sex competitions—such as greater strength, size, agility, confidence, or cunning—can evolve simply because of the reproductive advantage gained by the victors. Darwin assumed that this is primarily a competitive interaction between males, but recent studies suggest that human females are also very competitive for access to mates.

Preferential mate choice, on the other hand, involves the desire for mating with partners that possess certain characteristics. A consensual desire affects the evolution of characteristics because it gives those possessing the desired characteristics an advantage in obtaining mates over those who do not possess the desired characteristics. Darwin assumed that preferential mate choice operates primarily through females who prefer particular males. (Indeed, he even called this component of sexual selection *female choice.*)

Darwin's theory of mate-choice selection was controversial in part because Darwin simply assumed that females desire males with certain characteristics. Darwin failed to document how such desires might have arisen and how they might be maintained in a population.

The solution to the problem was not forthcoming until 1972, when Robert Trivers, then at Harvard University, proposed that the relative parental investment of the sexes influences the two processes of sexual selection. Specifically, the sex that invests more in offspring is selected to be more discriminating in choosing a mate, whereas the sex that invests less in offspring is more competitive with members of the same sex for sexual access to the high-investing sex. Parental-investment theory accounts, in part, for both the origin and the evolutionary retention of different sexual strategies in males and females.

Consider the necessary *minimum* parental investment by a woman. After internal fertilization, the gestation period lasts about nine months and is usually followed by lactation, which in tribal societies typically can last several years. In contrast, a man's minimum parental investment can be reduced to the contribution of sperm, an effort requiring as little time as a few minutes. This disparity in parental investment means that the replacement of a child who dies (or is deserted) typically costs more (in time and energy) for women than men. Parental-investment theory predicts that women will be more choosy and selective about their mating partners. Where men can provide resources, women should desire those who are able and willing to commit those resources to her and her children.

SEXUAL STRATEGIES

Our evolutionary framework is based on three key ingredients. First, human mating is inherently strategic. These strategies exist because they solved specific problems in human evolutionary history. It is important to recognize that the manifestation of these strategies need not be through conscious psychological mechanisms. Indeed, for the most part we are completely unaware of *why* we find certain qualities attractive in a mate. A second component of our theory is that mating strategies are context-dependent. People behave differently depending on whether the situation presents itself as a short-term or long-term mating prospect. Third, men and women have faced different mating problems over the course of human evolution and, as a consequence, have evolved different strategies.

As outlined here, sexual strategies theory consists of nine hypotheses. We can test these hypotheses by making several predictions about the behavior of men and women faced with a particular mating situation. Even though we make only a few predictions for each hypothesis, it should be clear that many more predictions can be derived to test each hypothesis. We invite the reader to devise his or her own tests of these hypotheses.

Hypothesis 1: Short-term mating is more important for men than women. This hypothesis follows from the fact that men can reduce their parental investment to the absolute minimum and still produce offspring. Consequently, short-term mating should be a key component of the sexual strategies of men, and much less so for women. We tested three predictions based on this hypothesis in a sample of 148 college students (75 men and 73 women) in the midwestern United States.

First, we predict that men will express a greater interest in seeking a short-term mate than will women. We asked the students to rate the degree to which they were currently seeking a short-term mate (defined as a one-night stand or a brief affair) and the degree to which they were currently seeking a long-term mate (defined as a marriage partner). They rated their interests on a 7-point scale, where a rating of 1 corresponds to a complete lack of interest and a 7 corresponds to a high level of interest.

We found that although the sexes do not differ in their stated proclivities for seeking a long-term mate (an average rating of about 3.4 for both sexes), men reported a significantly greater interest (an average rating of about 5) in seeking a short-term sexual partner than did women (about 3). The results also showed that at any given time men are more interested in seeking a short-term rather than a long-term mate, whereas women are more interested in seeking a long-term mate than a short-term mate.

Second, we predict that men will desire a greater number of mates than is desired by women. We asked the same group of college students how many sexual partners they would ideally like to have during a given time interval and during their lifetimes. In this instance men consistently reported that they desired a greater number of sex partners than reported by the women for every interval of time. For example, the average man desired about eight sex partners during the next two years, whereas the average woman desired to have one sex partner. In the course of a lifetime, the average man reported the desire to have about 18 sex partners, whereas the average woman desired no more than 4 or 5 sex partners.

A third prediction that follows from this hypothesis is that men will be more willing to engage in sexual intercourse a shorter period of time after first meeting a potential sex partner. We asked the sample of 148 college students the following question: "If the conditions were right, would you consider having sexual intercourse with someone you viewed as desirable if you had known that person for *(a time period ranging from one hour to five years)*?" For each of 10 time intervals the students were asked to provide a response ranging from −3 (definitely not) to 3 (definitely yes).

After a period of 5 years, the men and women were equally likely to consent to sexual relations, each giving a score of about

2 (probably yes). For all shorter time intervals, men were consistently more likely to consider sexual intercourse. For example, after knowing a potential sex partner for only one week, the average man was still positive about the possibility of having sex, whereas women said that they were highly unlikely to have sex with someone after knowing him for only one week.

This issue was addressed in a novel way by Russell Clark and Elaine Hatfield of the University of Hawaii. They designed a study in which college students were approached by an attractive member of the opposite sex who posed one of three questions after a brief introduction: "Would you go out on a date with me tonight?" "Would you go back to my apartment with me tonight?" or "Would you have sex with me tonight?"

Of the women who were approached, 50 percent agreed to the date, 6 percent agreed to go to the apartment and none agreed to have sex. Many women found the sexual request from a virtual stranger to be odd or insulting. Of the men approached, 50 percent agreed to the date, 69 percent agreed to go back to the woman's apartment and 75 percent agreed to have sex. In contrast to women, many men found the sexual request flattering. Those few men who declined were apologetic about it, citing a fiancée or an unavoidable obligation that particular evening. Apparently, men are willing to solve the problem of partner number by agreeing to have sex with virtual strangers.

Hypothesis 2: Men seeking a short-term mate will solve the problem of identifying women who are sexually accessible. We can make at least two predictions based on this hypothesis. First, men will value qualities that signal immediate sexual accessibility in a short-term mate highly, and less so in a long-term mate. When we asked men in a college sample of 44 men and 42 women to rate the desirability of promiscuity and sexual experience in a mate, both were significantly more valued in a short-term mate. Although men find promiscuity mildly desirable in a short-term mate, it is clearly undesirable in a long-term mate. It is noteworthy that women find promiscuity extremely undesirable in either context.

We also predict that qualities that signal sexual inaccessibility will be disliked by men seeking short-term mates. We asked men to rate the desirability of mates who have a low sex drive, who are prudish or who lack sexual experience. In each instance men expressed a particular dislike for short-term mates with these qualities. A low sex drive and prudishness are also disliked by men in long-term mates, but less so. In contrast, a lack of sexual experience is slightly valued by men in a long-term mate.

Hypothesis 3: Men seeking a short-term mate will minimize commitment and investment. Here we predict that men will find undesirable any cues that signal that a short-term mate wants to extract a commitment. We asked the same group of 44 men to rate the variable *wants a commitment* for short-term and long-term mates. Of all the qualities we addressed, this one showed the most striking dependence on context. The attribute of wanting a commitment was strongly desirable in a long-term mate but strongly undesirable in a short-term mate. This distinction was not nearly so strong for women. Although women strongly wanted commitment from a long-term mate, it was only mildly undesirable in a short-term mate.

Hypotheses 4 and 5: Men seeking a short-term mate will solve the problem of identifying fertile women, whereas men seeking a long-term mate will solve the problem of identifying reproductively valuable women. Because these hypotheses are closely linked it is useful to discuss them together. Fertility and reproductive value are related yet distinct concepts. Fertility refers to the probability that a woman is *currently* able to conceive a child. Reproductive value, on the other hand, is defined actuarially in units of expected future reproduction. In other words, it is the extent to which persons of a given age and sex will contribute, on average, to the ancestry of future generations. For example, a 14-year-old woman has a higher reproductive value than a 24-year-old woman, because her *future* contribution to the gene pool is higher on average. In contrast, the 24-year-old woman is more fertile than the 14-year-old because her *current* probability of reproducing is greater.

Since these qualities cannot be observed directly, men would be expected to be sensitive to cues that might be indicative of a woman's fertility and reproductive value. One might expect that men would prefer younger women as short-term and long-term mates. Again, since age is not something that can be observed directly, men should be sensitive to physical cues that are reliably linked with age. For example, with increasing age, skin tends to wrinkle, hair turns gray and falls out, lips become thinner, ears become larger, facial features become less regular, and muscles lose their tone. Men could solve the problem of identifying reproductively valuable women if they attended to physical features linked with age and health, *and* if their standards of attractiveness evolved to correspond to these features.

As an aside, it is worth noting that cultures do differ in their standards of physical beauty, but less so than anthropologists initially assumed. Cultural differences of physical beauty tend to center on whether relative plumpness or thinness is valued. In cultures where food is relatively scarce, plumpness is valued, whereas cultures with greater abundance value thinness. With the exception of plumpness and thinness, however, the physical cues to youth and health are seen as sexually attractive in all known cultures that have been studied. In no culture do people perceive wrinkled skin, open sores and lesions, thin lips, jaundiced eyes, poor muscle tone, and irregular facial features to be attractive.

A woman's reproductive success, however, is not similarly dependent on solving the problem of fertility in mates. Because a man's reproductive capacity is less closely linked with age and cannot be assessed as accurately from appearance, youth and physical attractiveness in a mate should be less important to women than it is to men.

Among our sample of American college students we asked men and women to evaluate the relative significance (on a scale from 0, unimportant, to 3, important) of the characteristics *good looking* and *physically attractive* in a short-term and a long-term mate. We found that men's preference for physical attractiveness in short-term mates approached the upper limit of the rating scale (about 2.71). Interestingly, this preference was stronger in men seeking short-term mates than in men seeking long-term mates (about 2.31). The results are a little surprising to us because we did not predict that men would place a greater significance on the physical attractiveness of a short-term mate compared to a long-term mate.

Women also favored physical attractiveness in a short-term mate (2.43) and a long-term mate (2.10). Here again, physical attractiveness was more important in short-term mating than in long-term mating. In both contexts, however, physical attractiveness was significantly less important to women than it is to men.

We also tested these predictions in our international survey of 37 cultures. My colleagues in each country asked men and women to evaluate the relative importance of the characteristics *good looking* and *physically attractive* in a mate. As in our American college population, men throughout the world placed a high value on physical attractiveness in a partner.

In each of the 37 cultures men valued physical attractiveness and good looks in a mate more than did their female counterparts. These sex differences are not limited to cultures that are saturated with visual media, Westernized cultures or racial, ethnic, religious or political groups. Worldwide, men place a premium on physical appearance.

A further clue to the significance of reproductive value comes in an international study of divorce. Laura Betzig of the University of Michigan studied the causes of marital dissolution in 89 cultures from around the world. She found that one of the strongest sex-linked causes of divorce was a woman's old age (hence low reproductive value) and the inability to produce children. A woman's old age was significantly more likely to result in divorce than a man's old age.

Hypothesis 6: Men seeking a long-term mate will solve the problem of paternity confidence. Men face an adaptive problem that is not faced by women—the problem of certainty in parenthood. A woman can always be certain that a child is hers, but a man cannot be so sure that his mate's child is his own. Historically, men have sequestered women in various ways through the use of chastity belts, eunuch-guarded harems, surgical procedures and veiling to reduce their sexual attractiveness to other men. Some of these practices continue to this day and have been observed by social scientists in many parts of the world.

Most of these studies have considered three possibilities: (1) the desire for chastity in a mate (cues to *prior* lack of sexual contact with others), (2) the desire for fidelity in mates (cues to no *future* sexual contact with others), and (3) the jealous guarding of mates to prevent sexual contact with other men. We have looked at these issues ourselves in various studies.

In our international study, we examined men's and women's desire for chastity in a potential marriage partner. It proved to be a highly variable trait across cultures. For example, Chinese men and women both feel that it is indispensable in a mate. In the Netherlands and Scandinavia, on the other hand, both sexes see chastity as irrelevant in a mate. Overall, however, in about two-thirds of the international samples, men desire chastity more than women do. Sex differences are especially large among Indonesians, Iranians and Palestinian Arabs. In the remaining one-third of the cultures, no sex differences were found. In no cultures do women desire virginity in a mate more than men. In other words, where there is a difference between the sexes, it is always the case that men place a greater value on chastity.

Although we have yet to examine the desire for mate fidelity in our international sample, in her cross-cultural study Betzig found that the most prevalent cause of divorce was sexual infidelity, a cause that was highly sex-linked. A wife's infidelity was considerably more likely to result in a divorce than a husband's infidelity. Compromising a man's certainty in paternity is apparently seen worldwide as a breach so great that it often causes the irrevocable termination of the long-term marital bond.

We have examined the issue of fidelity among American college students. Indeed, Schmitt and I found that fidelity is the characteristic most valued by men in a long-term mate. It is also highly valued by women, but it ranks only third or fourth in importance, behind such qualities as honesty. It seems that American men are concerned more about the future fidelity of a mate than with her prior abstinence.

Our studies of jealousy reveal an interesting qualitative distinction between men and women. Randy Larsen, Jennifer Semmelroth, Drew Westen and I conducted a series of interviews in which we asked American college students to imagine two scenarios: (1) their partner having sexual intercourse with someone else, or (2) their partner falling in love and forming a deep emotional attachment to someone else. The majority of the men reported that they would be more upset if their mate had sexual intercourse with another man. In contrast, the majority of the women reported that they would be more upset if their mate formed an emotional attachment to another woman.

We also posed the same two scenarios to another group of 60 men and women, but this time we recorded their physiological responses. We placed electrodes on the corrugator muscle in the brow (which contracts during frowning), on two fingers of the right hand to measure skin conductance (or sweating), and the thumb to measure heart rate.

The results provided a striking confirmation of the verbal responses of our earlier study. Men became more physiologically distressed at the thought of their mate's sexual infidelity than their mate's emotional infidelity. In response to the thought of sexual infidelity their skin conductances increased by an average of about 1.5 microSiemens, the frowning muscle showed 7.75 microvolt units of contraction, and their hearts increased by about five beats per minute. In response to the thought of emotional infidelity, the men's skin conductance showed little change from baseline, their frowning increased by only 1.16 units, and their heart rates did not increase. Women, on the other hand, tended to show the opposite pattern. For example, in response to the thought of emotional infidelity, their frowning increased by 8.12 units, whereas the thought of sexual infidelity elicited a response of only 3.03 units.

Hypothesis 7: Women seeking a short-term mate will prefer men willing to impart immediate resources. Women confront a different set of mating problems than those faced by men. They need not consider the problem of partner number, since mating with 100 men in one year would produce no more offspring than mating with just one. Nor do they have to be concerned about the certainty of genetic parenthood. Women also do not need to identify men with the highest fertility since men in their 50s, 60s and 70s can and do sire children.

In species where males invest parentally in offspring, where resources can be accrued and defended, and where males vary in their ability and willingness to channel these resources, females gain a selective advantage by choosing mates who are willing and able to invest resources. Females so choosing afford their offspring better protection, more food and other material advantages that increase their ability to survive and reproduce. Do human females exhibit this behavior pattern? If so, we should be able to make a few predictions.

In short-term contexts, women especially value signs that a man will immediately expend resources on them. We asked 50 female subjects to evaluate the desirability of a few characteristics in a short-term and a long-term mate: *spends a lot of money early on, gives gifts early on,* and *has an extravagant lifestyle.* We found that women place greater importance on these qualities in a short-term mate than in a long-term mate, despite the fact that women are generally less exacting in short-term mating contexts.

We would also predict that women will find undesirable any traits that suggest that a man is reluctant to expend resources on her immediately. When we tested this prediction with the same sample population, we found that women especially dislike men who are stingy early on. Although this attribute is undesirable in a long-term mate as well, it is significantly more so in a short-term mate.

Hypothesis 8: Women will be more selective than men in choosing a short-term mate. This hypothesis follows from the fact that women (more than men) use short-term matings to evaluate prospective long-term mates. We can make several predictions based on this hypothesis.

First, women (more than men) will dislike short-term mates who are already in a relationship. We examined the relative undesirability of a prospective mate who was already in a relationship to 42 men and 44 women, using a scale from −3 (extremely undesirable) to 3 (extremely desirable). Although men were only slightly bothered (averaging a score of about −1.04) by this scenario, women were significantly more reluctant to engage in a relationship with such a mate (average score about −1.70).

We would also predict that women (more than men) will dislike short-term mates who are promiscuous. To a woman, promiscuity indicates that a man is seeking short-term relationships and is less likely to commit to a long-term mating. We tested this prediction in the same sample of 42 men and 44 women using the same rating scale as before. Although men found promiscuity to be of neutral value in a short-term mate, women rated the trait as moderately undesirable (an average of about −2.00).

Finally, because one of the hypothesized functions for female short-term mating is protection from aggressive men, women should value attributes such as physical size and strength in short-term mates more than in long-term mates. When we asked men and women to evaluate the notion of a mate being *physically strong*, we found that women preferred physically strong mates in all contexts more than men did, and that women placed a premium on physical strength in a short-term mate. This was true despite the higher standards women generally hold for a long-term mate.

Hypothesis 9: Women seeking a long-term mate will prefer men who can provide resources for her offspring. In a long-term mating context, we would predict that women (more than men) will desire traits such as a potential mate's ambition, earning capacity, professional degrees and wealth.

In one study we asked a group of 58 men and 50 women to rate the desirability (to the average man and woman) of certain characteristics that are indicators of future resource-acquisition potential. These included such qualities as *is likely to succeed in profession, is likely to earn a lot of money,* and *has a reliable future career.* We found that in each case women desired the attribute more in a long-term mate than in a short-term mate. Moreover, women valued each of these characteristics in a long-term mate more than men did.

In our international study, we also examined men's and women's preferences for long-term mates who can acquire resources. In this case we looked at such attributes as *good financial prospects, social status,* and *ambition-industriousness*—attributes that typically lead to the acquisition of resources. We found that sex differences in the attitudes of men and women were strikingly consistent around the world. In 36 of the 37 cultures, women placed significantly greater value on financial prospects than did men. Although the sex differences were less profound for the other two qualities, in the overwhelming majority of cultures, women desire *social status* and *ambition-industriousness* in a long-term mate more than their male counterparts do.

Finally, in her international study of divorce, Betzig found that a man's failure to provide proper economic support for his wife and children was a significant sex-linked cause of divorce.

CONCLUSION

The results of our work and that of others provide strong evidence that the traditional assumptions about mate preferences—that they are arbitrary and culture-bound—are simply wrong. Darwin's initial insights into sexual selection have turned out to be scientifically profound for people, even though he understood neither their functional-adaptive nature nor the importance of relative parental investment for driving the two components of sexual selection.

Men and women have evolved powerful desires for particular characteristics in a mate. These desires are not arbitrary but are highly patterned and universal. The patterns correspond closely to the specific adaptive problems that men and women have faced during the course of human evolutionary history. These are the problems of paternity certainty, partner number and reproductive capacity for men, and the problems of willingness and ability to invest resources for women.

It turns out that a woman's physical appearance is the most powerful predictor of the occupational status of the man she marries. A woman's appearance is more significant than her intelligence, her level of education or even her original socioeconomic status in determining the mate she will marry. Women who possess the qualities men prefer are most able to translate their preferences into actual mating decisions. Similarly, men possessing what women want—the ability to provide resources—are best able to mate according to their preferences.

Some adaptive problems are faced by men and women equally: identifying mates who show a proclivity to cooperate and mates who show evidence of having good parenting skills. Men do not look at women simply as sex objects, nor do women look at men simply as success objects. One of our most robust observations was that both sexes place tremendous importance on mutual love and kindness when seeking a long-term mate.

The similarities among cultures and between sexes implies a degree of psychological unity or species typicality that transcends geographical, racial, political, ethnic and sexual diversity. Future research could fruitfully examine the ecological and historical sources of diversity while searching for the adaptive functions of the sexual desires that are shared by all members of our species.

Bibliography

Buss, D. 1994. *The Evolution of Desire: Strategies of Human Mating.* New York: Basic Books.

Buss, D. M., et al. 1990. International preferences in selecting mates: A study of 37 cultures. *Journal of Cross-Cultural Psychology* 21:5–47.

Buss, D. M., R. Larsen, D. Westen, and J. Semmelmoth, 1992. Sex differences in jealousy: Evolution, physiology, psychology. *Psychological Science* 3:251–255.

Buss, D. M., and D. P. Schmitt, 1993. Sexual Strategies Theory: An evolutionary perspective on human mating. *Psychological Review* 100:204–232.

Topics for Thought and Discussion

1. Describe the structure of Buss's article. What would you say are the main parts of this essay, and what does he do in each? In what ways does this structure serve Buss's argument?
2. Describe the general principles of "sexual-strategies theory."
3. In your own experience, and in general terms, do Buss's conclusions and hypotheses seem right? Is there something he is leaving out? What do you think of Buss's conclusions?

Suggestions for Writing

1. Choose one of the nine hypotheses Buss provides and design an experiment or a technique by which the hypothesis might be tested. (Do not actually conduct this experiment.)

2. Write an essay in which you investigate some of the ways an individual society's values might modify the evolutionary pressures that Buss describes.
3. Write an essay in which you use your own observations to either support or argue against Buss's conclusions about the strategies of human mating.

You Dirty Vole
GUNJAN SINHA

Gunjan Sinha trained as a molecular geneticist, but early in her career abandoned the lab for writing, and has become an award-winning freelance science and medical journalist. For five years the life sciences editor for Popular Science *magazine, she has written extensively on science and technology for a range of publications. She has also appeared as a science commentator on* Dateline NBC, *and* CNN. *The following article first appeared in* Popular Science *in 2002. As you read, consider how Sinha uses storytelling to transition into more conventional science writing.*

---- ✦ ----

George is a typical midwestern American male in the prime of his life, with an attractive spouse named Martha. George is a devoted husband, Martha an attentive wife. The couple has four young children, a typical home in a lovely valley full of corn and bean fields, and their future looks bright. But George is occasionally unfaithful. So, occasionally, is Martha. No big deal: That's just the way life is in this part of America.

This is a true story, though the names have been changed, and so, for that matter, has the species. George and Martha are prairie voles. They don't marry, of course, or think about being faithful. And a bright future for a vole is typically no more than 60 days of mating and pup-rearing that ends in a fatal encounter with a snake or some other prairie predator.

But if you want to understand more about the conflict in human relationships between faithfulness and philandering, have a peek inside the brain of this wee rodent. Researchers have been studying voles for more than 25 years, and they've learned that the mating behavior of these gregarious creatures uncannily resembles our own—including a familiar pattern of monogamous attachment: Male and female share a home and child care, the occasional dalliance notwithstanding. More important, researchers have discovered what drives the animals' monogamy: brain chemistry. And when it comes to the chemical soup that governs behavior associated with what we call love, prairie vole brains are a lot like ours.

Scientists are careful to refer to what voles engage in as "social monogamy," meaning that although voles prefer to nest and mate with a particular partner, when another vole comes courting, some will stray. And as many as 50 percent of male voles never find a permanent partner. Of course, there is no moral or religious significance to the vole's behavior—monogamous or not. Voles will be voles, because that's their nature.

Still, the parallels to humans are intriguing. "We're not an animal that finds it in our best interest to screw around," says Pepper Schwartz, a sociologist at the University of Washington, yet studies have shown that at least one-third of married people cheat. In many cases, married couples struggle with the simple fact that love and lust aren't always in sync, often tearing us in opposite directions. Vole physiology and behavior reinforce the idea that love and lust are biochemically separate systems, and that the emotional tug of war many of us feel between the two emotions is perfectly natural—a two-headed biological drive that's been hard-wired into our brains through millions of years of evolution.

No one knew that voles were monogamous until Lowell Getz, a now-retired professor of ecology, ethology, and evolution at the University of Illinois, began studying them in 1972. At the time, Getz wanted to figure out why the vole population would boom during certain years and then slowly go bust. He set traps in the grassy plains of Illinois and checked them a few times a day, tagging the voles he caught. What surprised him was how often he'd find the same male and female sitting in a trap together.

Voles build soft nests about 8 inches below ground. A female comes of age when she is about 30 days old: Her need to mate is then switched on as soon as she encounters an unpartnered male and sniffs his urine. About 24 hours later, she's ready to breed—with the male she just met or another unattached one if he's gone. Then, hooked, the pair will stick together through thick and thin, mating and raising young.

Getz found vole mating behavior so curious that he wanted to bring the animals into the lab to study them more carefully. But he was a field biologist, not a lab scientist, so he called Sue Carter, a colleague and neuroendocrinologist. Carter had been studying how sex hormones influence behavior, and investigating monogamy in voles dovetailed nicely with her own research. The animals were small: They made the perfect lab rats.

The scientific literature was already rich with studies on a hormone called oxytocin that is made in mammalian brains and that in some species promotes bonding between males and females and between mothers and offspring. Might oxytocin, swirling around in tiny vole brains, be the catalyst for turning them into the lifelong partners that they are?

Sure enough, when Carter injected female voles with oxytocin, they were less finicky in choosing mates and practically glued themselves to their partners once they had paired. The oxytocin-dosed animals tended to lick and cuddle more than untreated animals, and they avoided strangers. What's more, when Carter injected females with oxytocin-blocking chemicals, the animals deserted their partners.

In people, not only is the hormone secreted by lactating women but studies have shown that oxytocin levels also increase during sexual arousal—and skyrocket during orgasm. In fact, the higher the level of oxytocin circulating in the blood during intercourse, the more intense the orgasm.

But there's more to vole mating than love; there's war too. Male voles are territorial. Once they bond with a female, they spend lots of time guarding her from other suitors, often sitting near the entrance of their burrow and aggressively baring their beaver-like teeth. Carter reasoned that other biochemicals must kick in after mating, chemicals that turn a once laid-back male into a territorial terror. Oxytocin, it turns out, is only part of the story. A related chemical, vasopressin, also occurs in both sexes. Males, however, have much more of it. When Carter dosed male voles with a vasopressin-blocking chemical after mating, their feistiness disappeared. An extra jolt of vasopressin, on the other hand, boosted their territorial behavior and made them more protective of their mates.

Vasopressin is also present in humans. While scientists don't yet know the hormone's exact function in men, they speculate that it works similarly: It is secreted during sexual arousal and promotes bonding. It may even transform some men into jealous boyfriends and husbands. "The biochemistry (of attachment) is probably going to be similar in humans and in (monogamous) animals because it's quite a basic function," says Carter. Because oxytocin and vasopressin are secreted during sexual arousal and orgasm, she says, they are probably the key biochemical players that bond lovers to one another.

But monogamous animals aren't the only ones that have vasopressin and oxytocin in their brains. Philandering animals do too. So what separates faithful creatures from unfaithful ones?

Conveniently for scientists, the generally monogamous prairie vole has a wandering counterpart: the montane vole. When Thomas Insel, a neuroscientist at Emory University, studied the two species' vasopressin receptors (appendages on a cell that catch specific biochemicals) he found them in different places. Prairie voles have receptors for the hormone in their brains' pleasure centers; montane voles have the receptors in other brain areas. In other words, male prairie voles stick with the same partner after mating because it feels good. For montane voles, mating is a listless but necessary affair, rather like scratching an itch.

A BRIEF INQUIRY INTO THE BIOLOGICAL EXPRESSIONS OF HUMAN LOVE

Of course, human love is much more complicated. The biochemistry of attachment isn't yet fully understood, and there's clearly much more to it than oxytocin and vasopressin. Humans experience different kinds of love. There's "compassionate love," associated with feelings of calm, security, social comfort, and emotional union. This kind of love, say scientists, is probably similar to what voles feel toward their partners and involves oxytocin and vasopressin. Romantic love—that crazy obsessive euphoria that people feel when they are "in love"—is very different, as human studies are showing.

Scientists at University College London led by Andreas Bartels recently peered inside the heads of love-obsessed college students. They took 17 young people who claimed to be in love, stuck each of them in an MRI machine, and showed them pictures of their lovers. Blood flow increased to very specific areas of the brain's pleasure center—including some of the same areas that are stimulated when people engage in addictive behaviors. Some of these same areas are also active during sexual arousal, though romantic love and sexual arousal are clearly different: Sex has more to do with hormones like testosterone, which, when given to both men and women, increases sex drive and sexual fantasies. Testosterone, however, doesn't necessarily make people fall in love with, or become attached to, the object of their attraction.

Researchers weren't particularly surprised by the parts of the lovers' brains that were active. What astonished them was that two other brain areas were suppressed—the amygdala and the right prefrontal cortex. The amygdala is associated with negative emotions like fear and anger. The right prefrontal cortex appears to be overly active in people suffering from depression. The positive emotion of love, it seems, suppresses negative emotions. Might that be the scientific basis for why people who are madly in love fail to see the negative traits of their beloved? "Maybe," says Bartels cautiously. "But we haven't proven that yet."

The idea that romantic love activates parts of the brain associated with addiction got Donatella Marazziti at Pisa University in Tuscany wondering if it might be related to obsessive compulsive disorder (OCD). Anyone who has ever been in love knows how consuming the feeling can be. You can think of nothing but your lover every waking moment. Some people with OCD have low levels of the brain chemical serotonin. Might love-obsessed people also have low serotonin levels? Sure enough, when Marazziti and her colleagues tested the blood of 20 students who were madly in love and 20 people with OCD, she found that both groups had low levels of a protein that shuttles serotonin between brain cells.

And what happens when the euphoria of "mad love" wears off? Marazziti tested the blood of a few of the lovers 12 to 18 months later and found that their serotonin levels had returned to normal. That doesn't doom a couple, of course, but it suggests a biological explanation for the evolution of relationships. In many cases, romantic love turns into compassionate love, thanks to oxytocin and vasopressin swirling inside the lovers' brains. This attachment is what keeps many couples together. But because attachment and romantic love involve different biochemical processes, attachment to one person does not suppress lust for another. "The problem is, they are not always well linked," says anthropologist Helen Fisher, who has written several books on love, sex, and marriage.

TYING IT ALL TOGETHER: THE TRAVELING SALESMAN AND THE MARRIAGE VOW

In the wild, about half of male voles wander the fields, never settling down with one partner. These "traveling salesmen," as Lowell Getz calls them, are always "trying to get with other females." Most females prefer to mate with their partners. But if they get the chance, some will mate with other males too. And, according to Jerry Wolff, a biologist at the University of Memphis, female voles sometimes "divorce" their partners. In the lab, he restricts three males at a time in separate but connected chambers and gives a female free range. The female has already paired with one of the males and is pregnant with his pups. Wolff says about a third of the females pick up their nesting materials and move in with a different fellow. Another third actually solicit and successfully mate with one or both of the other males, and the last third remain faithful.

Why are some voles fickle, others faithful? Vole brains differ from one creature to the next. Larry Young, a neuroscientist at Emory University, has found that some animals have more receptors for oxytocin and vasopressin than others. In a recent experiment, he injected a gene into male prairie voles that permanently upped the number of vasopressin receptors in their brains. The animals paired with females even though the two hadn't mated. "Normally they have to mate for at least 24 hours to establish a bond," he says. So the number of receptors can mean the difference between sticking around and skipping out after sex. Might these differences in brain wiring influence human faithfulness? "It's too soon to tell," Young says. But it's "definitely got us very curious."

How does evolution account for the often-conflicting experiences of love and lust, which have caused no small amount of destruction in human history? Fisher speculates that the neural systems of romantic love and attachment evolved for different reasons. Romantic love, she says, evolved to allow people to distinguish between potential mating partners and "to pursue these partners until insemination has occurred." Attachment, she says, "evolved to make you tolerate this individual long enough to raise a child." Pepper Schwartz agrees: "We're biologically wired to be socially monogamous, but it's not a good evolutionary tactic to be sexually monogamous. There need to be ways to keep reproduction going if your mate dies."

Many of our marriage customs, say sociologists, derive from the need to reconcile this tension. "As much as people love passion and romantic love," Schwartz adds, "most people also want to have the bonding sense of loyalty and friendship love as well." Marriage vows are a declaration about romantic love and binding attachment, but also about the role of rational thought and the primacy of mind and mores over impulses.

Scientists hope to do more than simply decode the biochemistry of the emotions associated with love and attachment. Some, like Insel, are searching for treatments for attachment disorders such as autism, as well as pathological behaviors like stalking and violent jealousy. It is not inconceivable that someday there might be sold an attachment drug, a monogamy pill; the mind reels at the marketing possibilities.

Lowell Getz, the grandfather of all this research, couldn't be more thrilled. "I spent almost $1 million of taxpayer money trying to figure out stuff like why sisters don't make it with their brothers," he says. "I don't want to go to my grave feeling like it was a waste."

Topics for Thought and Discussion

1. How appropriate is it for scientists to draw conclusions about human beings from animals like voles? Is it fair and reasonable to reduce something as mysterious and powerful as love to chemical reactions? Explain.
2. What might be the advantages and disadvantages of, as Sinha suggests, "an attachment drug, a monogamy pill"? Would chemically inducing love violate what it means to be "in love"? Explain.
3. What are the purposes of understanding the chemical basis of love? Why pursue this question?
4. What does this science have to tell us about human behavior?

Suggestions for Writing

1. Write an essay in which you define love. See if you can combine cultural conventions about love and romance with the scientific basis of love described by Sinha. Can they be reconciled?
2. Imagine a world in which love can be chemically induced. Is this world a utopia or a dystopia? Describe this world.

Apes of Wrath
BARBARA SMUTS

Barbara Smuts is a professor of psychology and anthropology at the University of Michigan at Ann Arbor, and is an expert on the social behavior of nonhuman animals (particularly primates, wolves, and domestic dogs). She is the author of numerous scholarly and popular scientific articles, as well as the book, Sex and Friendship in Baboons *(first published in 1985 and reprinted in 1999 by Harvard University Press). She has conducted field studies on chimpanzees (with Jane Goodall in Tanzania), baboons (in Kenya and Tanzania), and bottlenose dolphins (off Western Australia). The following article, first published in* Discover *Magazine in 1995, draws upon her experience in the field. As you read, note how Dr. Smuts makes connections between her animal observations and human social relations.*

✦

Nearly 20 years ago I spent a morning dashing up and down the hills of Gombe National Park in Tanzania, trying to keep up with an energetic young female chimpanzee, the focus of my observations for the day. On her rear end she sported the small, bright pink swelling characteristic of the early stages of estrus, the period when female mammals are fertile and sexually receptive. For some hours our run through the park was conducted in quiet, but then, suddenly, a chorus of male chimpanzee pant hoots shattered the tranquility of the forest. My female rushed forward to join the males. She greeted each of them, bowing and then turning to present her swelling for inspection. The males examined her perfunctorily and resumed grooming one another, showing no further interest.

At first I was surprised by their indifference to a potential mate. Then I realized that it would be many days before the female's swelling blossomed into the large, shiny sphere that signals ovulation. In a week or two, I thought, these same males will be vying intensely for a chance to mate with her.

The attack came without warning. One of the males charged toward us, hair on end, looking twice as large as my small female and enraged. As he rushed by he picked her up, hurled her to the ground, and pummeled her. She cringed and screamed. He ran off, rejoining the other males seconds later as if nothing had happened. It was not so easy for the female to return to normal. She whimpered and darted nervous glances at her attacker, as if worried that he might renew his assault.

In the years that followed I witnessed many similar attacks by males against females, among a variety of Old World primates, and eventually I found this sort of aggression against females so puzzling that I began to study it systematically—something that has rarely been done. My long-term research on olive baboons in Kenya showed that, on average, each pregnant or lactating female was attacked by an adult male about once a week and seriously injured about once a year. Estrous females were the target of even more aggression. The obvious question was, Why?

In the late 1970s, while I was in Africa among the baboons, feminists back in the United States were turning their attention to male violence against women. Their concern stimulated a wave of research documenting disturbingly high levels of battering, rape, sexual harassment, and murder. But although scientists investigated this kind of behavior from many perspectives, they mostly ignored the existence of similar behavior in other animals. My observations over the years have convinced me that a deeper understanding of male aggression against females in other species can help us understand its counterpart in our own.

Researchers have observed various male animals—including insects, birds, and mammals—chasing, threatening, and attacking females. Unfortunately, because scientists have rarely studied such aggression in detail, we do not know exactly how common it is. But the males of many of these species are most aggressive toward potential mates, which suggests that they sometimes use violence to gain sexual access.

Jane Goodall provides us with a compelling example of how males use violence to get sex. In her 1986 book, *The Chimpanzees of Gombe*, Goodall describes the chimpanzee dating game. In one of several scenarios, males gather around attractive estrous females and try to lure them away from other males for a one-on-one sexual expedition that may last for days or weeks. But females find some suitors more appealing than others and often resist the advances of less desirable males. Males often rely on aggression to counter female resistance. For example, Goodall describes how Evered, in "persuading" a reluctant Winkle to accompany him into the forest, attacked her six times over the course of five hours, twice severely.

Sometimes, as I saw in Gombe, a male chimpanzee even attacks an estrous female days before he tries to mate with her. Goodall thinks that a male uses such aggression to train a female to fear him so that she will be more likely to surrender to his subsequent sexual advances. Similarly, male hamadryas baboons, who form small harems by kidnapping child brides, maintain a tight rein over their females through threats and intimidation. If, when another male is nearby, a hamadryas female strays even a few feet from her mate, he shoots her a threatening stare and raises his brows. She usually responds by rushing to his side; if not, he bites the back of her neck. The neck bite is ritualized—the male does not actually sink his razor-sharp canines into her flesh—but the threat of injury is clear. By repeating this behavior hundreds of times, the male lays claim to particular females months or even years before mating with them. When a female comes into estrus, she solicits sex only from her harem master, and other males rarely challenge his sexual rights to her.

These chimpanzee and hamadryas males are practicing sexual coercion: male use of force to increase the chances that a female victim will mate with him, or to decrease the chances that she will mate with someone else. But sexual coercion is much more common in some primate species than in others. Orangutans and chimpanzees are the only nonhuman primates whose males in the wild force females to copulate, while males of several other species, such as vervet monkeys and bonobos (pygmy chimpanzees), rarely if ever try to coerce females sexually. Between the two extremes lie many species, like hamadryas baboons, in which males do not force copulation but nonetheless use threats and intimidation to get sex.

These dramatic differences between species provide an opportunity to investigate which factors promote or inhibit sexual coercion. For example, we might expect to find more of it in species in which males are much larger than females—and we do. However, size differences between the sexes are far from the whole story. Chimpanzee and bonobo males both have only a slight size advantage, yet while male chimps frequently resort to force, male bonobos treat the fair sex with more respect. Clearly, then, although size matters, so do other factors. In particular, the social relationships females form with other females and with males appear to be as important.

In some species, females remain in their birth communities their whole lives, joining forces with related females to defend vital food resources against other females. In such "female-bonded" species, females also form alliances against aggressive males. Vervet monkeys are one such species, and among these small and exceptionally feisty African monkeys, related females gang up against males. High-ranking females use their dense network of female alliances to rule the troop; although smaller than males, they slap persistent suitors away like annoying flies. Researchers have observed similar alliances in many other female-bonded species, including other Old World monkeys such as macaques, olive baboons, patas and rhesus monkeys, and gray langurs; New World monkeys such as the capuchin; and prosimians such as the ring-tailed lemur.

Females in other species leave their birth communities at adolescence and spend the rest of their lives cut off from their female kin. In most such species, females do not form strong bonds with other females and rarely support one another against males. Both chimpanzees and hamadryas baboons exhibit this pattern, and, as we saw earlier, in both species females submit to sexual control by males.

This contrast between female-bonded species, in which related females gang together to thwart males, and non-female-bonded species, in which they don't, breaks down when we come to the bonobo. Female bonobos, like their close relatives the chimpanzees, leave their kin and live as adults with unrelated females. Recent field studies show that these unrelated females hang out together and engage in frequent homoerotic behavior, in which they embrace face-to-face and rapidly rub their genitals together; sex seems to cement their bonds. Examining these studies in the context of my own research has convinced me that one way females use these bonds is to form alliances against males, and that, as a consequence, male bonobos do not dominate females or attempt to coerce them sexually. How and why female bonobos, but not chimpanzees, came up with this solution to male violence remains a mystery.

Female primates also use relationships with males to help protect themselves against sexual coercion. Among olive baboons, each adult female typically forms long-lasting "friendships" with a few of the many males in her troop. When a male baboon assaults a female, another male often comes to her rescue; in my troop, nine times out of ten the protector was a friend of the female's. In return for his protection, the defender may enjoy her sexual favors the next time she comes into estrus. There is a dark side to this picture, however. Male baboons frequently threaten or attack their female friends—when, for example, one tries to form a friendship with a new male. Other males apparently recognize friendships and rarely intervene. The female, then, becomes less vulnerable to aggression from males in general, but more vulnerable to aggression from her male friends.

As a final example, consider orangutans. Because their food grows so sparsely, adult females rarely travel with anyone but their dependent offspring. But orangutan females routinely fall victim to forced copulation. Female orangutans, it seems, pay a high price for their solitude.

Some of the factors that influence female vulnerability to male sexual coercion in different species may also help explain such variation among different groups in the same species. For example, in a group of chimpanzees in the Tai Forest in the Ivory Coast, females form closer bonds with one another than do females at Gombe. Tai females may consequently have more egalitarian relationships with males than their Gombe counterparts do.

Such differences between groups especially characterize humans. Among the South American Yanomamo, for instance, men frequently abduct and rape women from neighboring villages and severely beat their wives for suspected adultery. However, among the Aka people of the Central African Republic, male aggression against women has never been observed. Most human societies, of course, fall between these two extremes.

How are we to account for such variation? The same social factors that help explain how sexual coercion differs among nonhuman primates may deepen our understanding of how it varies across different groups of people. In most traditional human societies, a woman leaves her birth community when she marries and goes to live with her husband and his relatives. Without strong bonds to close female kin, she will probably be in danger of sexual coercion. The presence of close female kin, though, may protect her. For example, in a community in Belize, women live near their female relatives. A man will sometimes beat his wife if he becomes jealous or suspects her of infidelity, but when this happens, onlookers run to tell her female kin. Their arrival on the scene, combined with the presence of other glaring women, usually shames the man enough to stop his aggression.

Even in societies in which women live away from their families, kin may provide protection against abusive husbands, though how much protection varies dramatically from one society to the next. In some societies a woman's kin, including her father and brothers, consistently support her against an abusive husband, while in others they rarely help her. Why?

The key may lie in patterns of male-male relationships. Alliances between males are much more highly developed in humans than in other primates, and men frequently rely on such alliances to compete successfully against other men. They often gain more by supporting their male allies than they do by supporting female kin. In addition, men often use their alliances to defeat rivals and abduct or rape their women, as painfully illustrated by recent events in Bosnia. When women live far from close kin, among men who value their alliances with other men more than their bonds with women, they may be even more vulnerable to sexual coercion than many nonhuman primate females.

Like nonhuman primate females, many women form bonds with unrelated males who may protect them from other males. However, reliance on men exacts a cost—women and other primate females often must submit to control by their protectors. Such control is more elaborate in humans because allied men agree to honor one another's proprietary rights over women. In most of the world's cultures, marriage involves not only the exclusion of other men from sexual access to a man's wife—which protects the woman against rape by other men—but also entails the husband's right to complete control over his wife's sexual life, including the right to punish her for real or suspected adultery, to have sex with her whenever he wants, and even to restrict her contact with other people, especially men.

In modern industrial society, many men—perhaps most—maintain such traditional notions of marriage. At the same time, many of the traditional sources of support for women, including censure of abusive husbands by the woman's kinfolk or other community members, are eroding as more and more people end up without nearby kin or long-term neighbors. The increased vulnerability of women isolated from their birth communities, however, is not just a by-product of modern living. Historically, in highly patriarchal societies like those found in China and northern India, married women lived in households ruled by their husband's mother and male kin, and their ties with their own kin were virtually severed. In these societies, today as in the past, the husband's female kin often view the wife as a competitor for resources. Not only do they fail to support her against male coercive control, but they sometimes actively encourage it. This scenario illustrates an important point: women do not invariably support other women against men, in part because women may perceive their interests as best served through alliances with men, not with other women. When men have most of the power and control most of the resources, this looks like a realistic assessment.

Decreasing women's vulnerability to sexual coercion, then, may require fundamental changes in social alliances. Women gave voice to this essential truth with the slogan SISTERHOOD IS POWERFUL —a reference to the importance of women's ability to cooperate with unrelated women as if they were indeed sisters. However, among humans, the male-dominant social system derives support from political, economic, legal, and ideological institutions that other primates can't even dream of. Freedom from male control— including male sexual coercion—therefore requires women to form alliances with one another (and with like-minded men) on a scale beyond that shown by nonhuman primates and humans in the past. Although knowledge of other primates can provide inspiration for this task, its achievement depends on the uniquely human ability to envision a future different from anything that has gone before.

Topics for Thought and Discussion

1. What are the implications of Smuts's title? Tease out all of the possible meanings you can. How does it seem related to the subject?
2. What writing strategies (word choice, analogies, metaphor, description) does Smuts use to anthropomorphize (that is, to make human-like) her nonhuman primates?
3. In her observation of animal groups, what does Smuts conclude about the purpose of male violence against females?
4. Discuss the bridge that Smuts makes between her studies of apes and the behavior of humans. What is the primary lesson that she has learned from animals about preventing violence against women?

Suggestions for Writing

1. Smuts argues at the end of her essay that "among humans, the male-dominant social system derives support from political, economic, legal, and ideological

institutions that other primates can't even dream of." Describe some of these institutions as you see them and in the spirit of Smuts's argument, describe how they will need to change in order to minimize the incidence of violence against women in our society.

2. Look around your own campus and describe in general terms the relationship between women and men. Is this relationship characterized by violence (physical, emotional, verbal)? Bring Smuts into your paper either as a way to understand these relationships, or as a way to argue that your college campus does not suffer from the violence Smuts describes.

Whose Life Would You Save?
CARL ZIMMER

Carl Zimmer is a science writer, lecturer, and radio commentator. He is a contributing editor at Discover Magazine *and has written for* Discover, National Geographic, Newsweek, Natural History, Smithsonian, *and* The New York Times. *He is the author of five books dealing with science and its relationship to society and history, including* At the Water's Edge *(1999),* Parasite Rex *(2000),* Evolution: The Triumph of an Idea *(2001),* Soul Made Flesh *(2004), and most recently,* The Smithsonian Intimate Guide to Human Origins *(2005). The following essay first appeared in* Discover Magazine *in 2004. As you read this essay, note the way that science and technology are being used to attempt to answer questions once thought to be the province of philosophers and humanists.*

---- ✦ ----

Dinner with a philosopher is never just dinner, even when it's at an obscure Indian restaurant on a quiet side street in Princeton with a 30-year-old postdoctoral researcher. Joshua Greene is a man who spends his days thinking about right and wrong and how we separate the two. He has a particular fondness for moral paradoxes, which he collects the way some people collect snow globes.

"Let's say you're walking by a pond and there's a drowning baby," Greene says, over chicken tikka masala. "If you said, 'I've just paid $200 for these shoes and the water would ruin them, so I won't save the baby,' you'd be an awful, horrible person. But there are millions of children around the world in the same situation, where just a little money for medicine or food could save their lives. And yet we don't consider ourselves monsters for having this dinner rather than giving the money to Oxfam. Why is that?" Philosophers pose this sort of puzzle over dinner every day. What's unusual here is what Greene does next to sort out the conundrum. He leaves the restaurant, walks down Nassau Street to the building that houses Princeton University's psychology department, and says hello to graduate student volunteer Nishant Patel. (Greene's volunteers take part in his study anonymously; Patel is not his real name.) They walk downstairs to the basement, where Patel dumps his keys and wallet and shoes in a basket. Greene waves an airport metal-detector paddle up and down Patel's legs, then guides him into an adjoining room dominated by a magnetic resonance imaging scanner. The student lies down on a slab, and Greene closes a cagelike device over his head. Pressing a button, Greene maneuvers Patel's head into a massive doughnut-shaped magnet.

Greene goes back to the control room to calibrate the MRI, then begins to send Patel messages. They are beamed into the scanner by a video projector and bounce off a mirror just above Patel's nose. Among the messages that Greene sends is the following dilemma, cribbed from the final episode of the TV series *M*A*S*H*: A group of villagers is hiding in a basement while enemy soldiers search the rooms above. Suddenly, a baby among them starts to cry. The villagers know that if the soldiers hear it they will come in and kill everyone. "Is it appropriate," the message reads, "for you to smother your child in order to save yourself and the other villagers?"

As Patel ponders this question—and others like it—the MRI scans his brain, revealing crackling clusters of neurons. Over the past four years, Greene has scanned dozens of people making these kinds of moral judgments. What he has found can be unsettling. Most of us would like to believe that when we say something is right or wrong, we are using our powers of reason alone. But Greene argues that our emotions also play a powerful role in our moral judgments, triggering instinctive responses that are the product of millions of years of evolution. "A lot of our deeply felt moral convictions may be quirks of our evolutionary history," he says.

Greene's research has put him at the leading edge of a field so young it still lacks an official name. Moral neuroscience? Neuroethics? Whatever you call it, the promise is profound. "Some people in these experiments think we're putting their soul under the microscope," Greene says, "and in a sense, that is what we're doing."

The puzzle of moral judgments grabbed Greene's attention when he was a philosophy major at Harvard University. Most modern theories of moral reasoning, he learned, were powerfully shaped by one of two great philosophers: Immanuel Kant and John Stuart Mill. Kant believed that pure reason alone could lead us to moral truths. Based on his own pure reasoning, for instance, he declared that it was wrong to use someone for your own ends and that it was right to act only according to principles that everyone could follow.

John Stuart Mill, by contrast, argued that the rules of right and wrong should above all else achieve the greatest good for the greatest number of people, even though particular individuals might be worse off as a result. (This approach became known as utilitarianism, based on the "utility" of a moral rule.) "Kant puts what's right before what's good," says Greene. "Mill puts what's good before what's right."

By the time Greene came to Princeton for graduate school in 1997, however, he had become dissatisfied with utilitarians and Kantians alike. None of them could explain how moral judgments work in the real world. Consider, for example, this thought experiment concocted by the philosophers Judith Jarvis Thompson and Philippa Foot: Imagine you're at the wheel of a trolley and the brakes have failed. You're approaching a fork in the track at top speed. On the left side, five rail workers are fixing the track. On the right side, there is a single worker. If you do nothing, the trolley will bear left and kill the five workers. The only way to save five lives is to take the responsibility for changing the trolley's path by hitting a switch. Then you will kill one worker. What would you do?

Now imagine that you are watching the runaway trolley from a footbridge. This time there is no fork in the track. Instead, five workers are on it, facing certain death. But you happen to be standing next to a big man. If you sneak up on him and push him off the footbridge, he will fall to his death. Because he is so big, he will stop the trolley. Do you willfully kill one man, or do you allow five people to die?

Logically, the questions have similar answers. Yet if you poll your friends, you'll probably find that many more are willing to throw a switch than push someone off a bridge. It is hard to explain why what seems right in one case can seem wrong in another. Sometimes we act more like Kant and sometimes more like Mill. "The trolley problem seemed to boil that conflict down to its essence," Greene says. "If I could figure out how to make sense of that particular problem, I could make sense of the whole Kant-versus-Mill problem in ethics."

The crux of the matter, Greene decided, lay not in the logic of moral judgments but in the role our emotions play in forming them. He began to explore the psychological studies of the 18th-century Scottish philosopher David Hume. Hume argued that people call an act good not because they rationally determine it to be so but because it makes them feel good. They call an act bad because it fills them with disgust. Moral knowledge, Hume wrote, comes partly from an "immediate feeling and finer internal sense."

Moral instincts have deep roots, primatologists have found. Last September, for instance, Sarah Brosnan and Frans de Waal of Emory University reported that monkeys have a sense of fairness. Brosnan and De Waal trained capuchin monkeys to take a pebble from them; if the monkeys gave the pebble back, they got a cucumber. Then they ran the same experiment with two monkeys sitting in adjacent cages so that each could see the other. One monkey still got a cucumber, but the other one got a grape—a tastier reward. More than half the monkeys who got cucumbers balked at the exchange. Sometimes they threw the cucumber at the researchers; sometimes they refused to give the pebble back. Apparently, De Waal says, they realized that they weren't being treated fairly.

In an earlier study, De Waal observed a colony of chimpanzees that got fed by their zookeeper only after they had all gathered in an enclosure. One day, a few young chimps dallied outside for hours, leaving the rest to go hungry. The next day, the other chimps attacked the stragglers, apparently to punish them for their self-ishness. The primates seemed capable of moral judgment without benefit of human reasoning. "Chimps may be smart," Greene says. "But they don't read Kant."

The evolutionary origins of morality are easy to imagine in a so-cial species. A sense of fairness would have helped early primates cooperate. A sense of disgust and anger at cheaters would have helped them avoid falling into squabbling. As our ancestors became more self-aware and acquired language, they would transform those feelings into moral codes that they then taught their children.

This idea made a lot of sense to Greene. For one thing, it showed how moral judgments can feel so real. "We make moral judgments so automatically that we don't really understand how they're formed," he says. It also offered a potential solution to the trolley problem: Although the two scenarios have similar out-comes, they trigger different circuits in the brain. Killing someone with your bare hands would most likely have been recognized as immoral millions of years ago. It summons ancient and over-whelmingly negative emotions—despite any good that may come of the killing. It simply *feels* wrong.

Throwing a switch for a trolley, on the other hand, is not the sort of thing our ancestors confronted. Cause and effect, in this case, are separated by a chain of machines and electrons, so they do not trigger a snap moral judgment. Instead, we rely more on abstract reasoning—weighing costs and benefits, for example—to choose between right and wrong. Or so Greene hypothesized. When he arrived at Princeton, he had no way to look inside people's brains. Then in 1999, Greene learned that the university was building a brain-imaging center.

The heart of the Center for the Study of Brain, Mind, and Behavior is an MRI scanner in the basement of Green Hall. The scanner creates images of the brain by generating an intense magnetic field. Some of the molecules in the brain line up with the field, and the scanner wiggles the field back and forth a few degrees. As the molecules wiggle, they release radio waves. By detecting the waves, the scanner can reconstruct the brain as well as detect where neurons are consuming oxygen—a sign of mental activity. In two seconds, the center's scanner can pinpoint such activity down to a cubic millimeter—about the size of a peppercorn.

When neuroscientists first started scanning brains in the early 1990s, they studied the basic building blocks of thought, such as language, vision, and attention. But in recent years, they've also tried to understand how the brain works when people interact. Humans turn out to have special neural networks that give them what many cognitive neuroscientists call social intelligence. Some regions can respond to smiles, frowns, and other expressions in a tenth of a second. Others help us get inside a person's head and figure out intentions. When neuroscientist Jonathan Cohen came to Princeton to head the center, he hoped he could dedicate some time with the scanner to study the interaction between cognition and emotion. Greene's morality study was a perfect fit.

Working with Cohen and other scientists at the center, Greene decided to compare how the brain responds to different questions. He took the trolley problem as his starting point, then invented questions designed to place volunteers on a spectrum of moral judgment. Some questions involved personal moral choices; some were impersonal but no less moral. Others were utterly innocuous, such as deciding whether to take a train or a bus to work. Greene could then peel away the brain's general decision-making circuits and focus in on the neural patterns that differentiate personal from impersonal thought.

Some scenarios were awful, but Greene suspected people would make quick decisions about them. Should you kill a friend's sick father so he can collect on the insurance policy? Of course not. But other questions—like the one about the smothered baby—were as agonizing as they were gruesome. Greene calls these doozies. "If they weren't creepy, we wouldn't be doing our job," he says.

As Greene's subjects mulled over his questions, the scanner measured the activity in their brains. When all the questions had flashed before the volunteers, Greene was left with gigabytes of data, which then had to be mapped onto a picture of the brain. "It's not hard, like philosophy hard, but there are so many details to keep track of," he says. When he was done, he experienced a "pitter-patter heartbeat moment." Just as he had predicted, personal moral decisions tended to stimulate certain parts of the brain more than impersonal moral decisions.

The more people Greene scanned, the clearer the pattern became: Impersonal moral decisions (like whether to throw a switch on a trolley) triggered many of the same parts of the brain as nonmoral questions do (such as whether you should take the train or the bus to work). Among the regions that became active was a patch on the surface of the brain near the temples. This region, known as the dorsolateral prefrontal cortex, is vital for logical thinking. Neuroscientists believe it helps keep track of several pieces of information at once so that they can be compared. "We're using our brains to make decisions about things that evolution hasn't wired us up for," Greene says.

Personal moral questions lit up other areas. One, located in the cleft of the brain behind the center of the forehead, plays a crucial role in understanding what other people are thinking or feeling. A second, known as the superior temporal sulcus, is located just above the ear; it gathers information about people from the way they move their lips, eyes, and hands. A third, made up of parts of two adjacent regions known as the posterior cingulate and the precuneus, becomes active when people feel strong emotions.

Greene suspects these regions are part of a neural network that produces the emotional instincts behind many of our moral judgments. The superior temporal sulcus may help make us aware of others who would be harmed. Mind reading lets us appreciate their suffering. The precuneus may help trigger a negative feeling—an inarticulate sense, for example, that killing someone is plain wrong.

When Greene and his coworkers first began their study, not a single scan of the brain's moral decision-making process had been published. Now a number of other scientists are investigating the neural basis of morality, and their results are converging on some of the same ideas. "The neuroanatomy seems to be coming together," Greene says.

Another team of neuroscientists at Princeton, for instance, has pinpointed neural circuits that govern the sense of fairness. Economists have known for a long time that humans, like capuchin monkeys, get annoyed to an irrational degree when they feel they're getting shortchanged. A classic example of this phenomenon crops up during the "ultimatum game," in which two players are given a chance to split some money. One player proposes the split, and the other can accept or reject it—but if he rejects it, neither player gets anything.

If both players act in a purely rational way, as most economists assume people act, the game should have a predictable result. The first player will offer the second the worst possible split, and the second will be obliged to accept it. A little money, after all, is better than none. But in experiment after experiment, players tend to offer something close to a 50-50 split. Even more remarkably, when they offer significantly less than half, they're often rejected.

The Princeton team (led by Alan Sanfey, now at the University of Arizona) sought to explain that rejection by having people play the ultimatum game while in the MRI scanner. Their subjects always played the part of the responder. In some cases the proposer was another person; in others it was a computer. Sanfey found that unfair offers from human players—more than those from the computer—triggered pronounced reactions in a strip of the brain called the anterior insula. Previous studies had shown that this area produces feelings of anger and disgust. The stronger the response, Sanfey and his colleagues found, the more likely the subject would reject the offer.

Another way to study moral intuition is to look at brains that lack it. James Blair at the National Institute of Mental Health has spent years performing psychological tests on criminal psychopaths. He has found that they have some puzzling gaps in perception. They can put themselves inside the heads of other people, for example, acknowledging that others feel fear or sadness. But they have a hard time *recognizing* fear or sadness, either on people's faces or in their voices.

Blair says that the roots of criminal psychopathy can first be seen in childhood. An abnormal level of neurotransmitters might make children less empathetic. When most children see others get sad or angry, it disturbs them and makes them want to avoid acting in ways that provoke such reactions. But budding psychopaths don't perceive other people's pain, so they don't learn to rein in their violent outbreaks.

As Greene's database grows, he can see more clearly how the brain's intuitive and reasoning networks are activated. In most cases, one dominates the other. Sometimes, though, they produce opposite responses of equal strength, and the brain has difficulty choosing between them. Part of the evidence for this lies in the time it takes for Greene's volunteers to answer his questions.

Impersonal moral ones and nonmoral ones tend to take about the same time to answer. But when people decide that personally hurting or killing someone is appropriate, it takes them a long time to say yes—twice as long as saying no to these particular kinds of questions. The brain's emotional network says no, Greene's brain scans show, and its reasoning network says yes.

When two areas of the brain come into conflict, researchers have found, an area known as the anterior cingulate cortex, or ACC, switches on to mediate between them. Psychologists can trigger the ACC with a simple game called the Stroop test, in which people have to name the color of a word. If subjects are shown the word blue in red letters, for instance, their responses slow down and the ACC lights up. "It's the area of the brain that says, 'Hey, we've got a problem here,'" Greene says.

Greene's questions, it turns out, pose a sort of moral Stroop test. In cases where people take a long time to answer agonizing personal moral questions, the ACC becomes active. "We predicted that we'd see this, and that's what we got," he says. Greene, in other words, may be exposing the biology of moral anguish.

Of course, not all people feel the same sort of moral anguish. Nor do they all answer Greene's questions the same way. Some aren't willing to push a man over a bridge, but others are. Greene nicknames these two types the Kantians and the utilitarians. As he takes more scans, he hopes to find patterns of brain activity that are unique to each group. "This is what I've wanted to get at from the beginning," Greene says, "to understand what makes some people do some things and other people do other things."

Greene knows that his results can be disturbing: "People sometimes say to me, 'If everyone believed what you say, the whole world would fall apart.'" If right and wrong are nothing more than the instinctive firing of neurons, why bother being good? But Greene insists the evidence coming from neuroimaging can't be ignored. "Once you understand someone's behavior on a sufficiently mechanical level, it's very hard to look at them as evil," he says. "You can look at them as dangerous; you can pity them. But evil doesn't exist on a neuronal level."

By the time Patel emerges from the scanner, rubbing his eyes, it's past 11 P.M. "I can try to print a copy of your brain now or e-mail it to you later," Greene says. Patel looks at the image on the computer screen and decides to pass. "This doesn't feel like you?" Greene says with a sly smile. "You're not going to send this to your mom?"

Soon Greene and Patel, who is Indian, are talking about whether Indians and Americans might answer some moral questions differently. All human societies share certain moral universals, such as fairness and sympathy. But Greene argues that different cultures produce different kinds of moral intuition and different kinds of brains. Indian morality, for instance, focuses more on matters of purity, whereas American morality focuses on individual autonomy. Researchers such as Jonathan Haidt, a psychologist at the University of Virginia, suggest that such differences shape a child's brain at a relatively early age. By the time we become adults, we're wired with emotional responses that guide our judgments for the rest of our lives.

Many of the world's great conflicts may be rooted in such neuronal differences, Greene says, which may explain why the conflicts seem so intractable. "We have people who are talking past each other, thinking the other people are either incredibly dumb or willfully blind to what's right in front of them," Greene says. "It's not just that people disagree; it's that they have a hard time imagining how anyone could disagree on this point that seems so obvious." Some people wonder how anyone could possibly tolerate abortion. Others wonder how women could possibly go out in public without covering their faces. The answer may be that their brains simply don't work the same: Genes, culture, and personal experience have wired their moral circuitry in different patterns.

Greene hopes that research on the brain's moral circuitry may ultimately help resolve some of these seemingly irresolvable disputes. "When you have this understanding, you have a bit of distance between yourself and your gut reaction," he says. "You may not abandon your core values, but it makes you a more reasonable person. Instead of saying, 'I am right, and you are just nuts,' you say, 'This is what I care about, and we have a conflict of interest we have to work around.'"

Greene could go on—that's what philosophers do—but he needs to switch back to being a neuroscientist. It's already late, and Patel's brain will take hours to decode.

Topics for Thought and Discussion

1. Using the stories that Greene uses to test his subjects, and Zimmer's discussion of them, would you say you are a Kantian or a utilitarian? For example, how did you answer the trolley problem?
2. According to Greene, what evolutionary forces contribute to the Kantian and the utilitarian ways of looking at the moral world?
3. What seems to be Greene's purpose with this research? What does he hope the result will be? (See particularly the last page of Zimmer's essay.)

4. Describe the various parts (the structure) of Zimmer's essay. For example, Zimmer frames the essay with narrative events: meeting with Greene for dinner at an Indian restaurant at the beginning, and Greene heading back to the lab to analyze Patel's brain-scan at the end. What other parts of this essay stand out? Why? Is the structure effective?

Suggestions for Writing

1. Write an essay in which you speculate about the consequences of research like Greene's. What are the potential benefits of knowing the location in the brain of different types of moral reasoning? What are the potential costs?
2. Greene argues that our moral decision making is a consequence of evolutionary pressures. Using Zimmer's essay as your source, evaluate the role of evolution in Greene's work. What parts of morality seem to be a consequence of evolution (instead of a consequence of culture, for example)? Fashion your conclusions into a short essay.
3. Conduct research into the ways that MRI scanning is being used to map the human brain, and write a status report. What have scientists discovered about the brain in the last year? What seem to be some of the practical uses for this knowledge?

Science and Human Behavior: Exploring Connections

1. Compare and contrast the scientific basis for David Buss's conclusions in "The Strategies of Human Mating" with the scientific basis of Gunjan Sinha's "You Dirty Vole." How are conclusions drawn? What counts as evidence in both? Are both equally scientific?
2. Can Barbara Smuts's conclusions in "Apes of Wrath" be reconciled with David Buss's conclusions in "The Strategies of Human Mating"? How might the violence Smuts describes be integrated into Buss's conclusions about the evolution of sexual strategies?
3. Using at least three of the essays in this chapter as evidence, what can you conclude about human behavior in general? What forces have created it? How much is biological, how much is physiological, and how much is cultural? What kind of creatures are we?
4. This chapter, in addition to demonstrating a number of important ways that science addresses issues of behavior, has also provided a variety of ways to structure scientific arguments. Using David Buss's article and any two other essays, compare and contrast the structure, strategies, and techniques used by these writers to present scientific material. Do all seem equally effective, or are some essays more effective than others?

Bodies and Genes

As human beings, we have a long track record of engineering ourselves to improve our lives. We do so in simple, unintrusive ways—by applying lipstick, by getting our hair permed, by wearing hiking boots, by tanning, by wearing contact lenses—and in more invasive ways—by getting botox injections, by having our stomachs stapled, and by undergoing cosmetic surgery. We also submit ourselves to myriad medical interventions in order to remain healthy or to improve our health. We are experts at maximizing ourselves and fitting ourselves to the work and the play that we do. If we want to explore the great barrier reef, we get certified in SCUBA and take tanks and a mask to breathe under water. If we want to be more effective as basketball players, we buy specially designed shoes and wear lightweight shorts and shirts. (We also train and practice, but that's another issue altogether.) If we want to see things that are far away, we invest in binoculars or a telescope; if we need to see in the dark, we invest in night-goggles. If we want to be in touch with friends and family, we purchase cell phones (with good calling plans). If we break a leg, we get crutches or a wheelchair. Medical procedures, elective surgery, cosmetics, clothing, tattoos, piercings—all are in our arsenal of body modifications that establish our position in the world. We use a wide variety of assistive technologies (to borrow a term from John Hockenberry's "The New Brainiacs" in Chapter 5), from wheelchairs to pacemakers, from sunglasses to hearing aids, from BlackBerries to cell phones, from insulin pumps to personal computers. These help us regulate our metabolism, extend our sight, extend our ability to communicate, improve our reach, increase our intellect, and enable us to organize our lives. Technology, medicine, and clothing all work for us to make us stronger, faster, more striking, more effective. We accept these ways of modifying ourselves with little reflection and with almost no internal or social anxiety or conflict. After all, we humans used to define ourselves and differentiate ourselves from other animals by the simple fact that we are tool users (we now know that many other animals use tools as well, but tools are still often considered very human adaptations). We use tools, and we modify ourselves, to accomplish what we feel we need to accomplish, and to be the person we feel we need or want to be. And we do it almost without thinking about it.

Science, however, has now given us additional tools—additional ways of modifying ourselves—and these techniques are far more controversial than anything we have used in the past. This chapter focuses on ways that science enables us to go farther. These new strategies are more dramatic, more challenging, and more controversial than buying a winter coat to keep warm, or even having a tummy tuck. What science can do now—or soon will be able to do— is to reengineer us from our DNA up. This, unlike most other modification techniques—laser surgery, the scuba tanks—*is* controversial and is likely to redefine both what it means to be human and the role of science in our society.

This chapter will ask you to consider what we can now know about, and do to, ourselves and others. David Ewing Duncan gets a gene scan and introduces us to what we and others can know about our genes and where that might take society in "DNA as Destiny"; Jenny Everett discusses hGH treatments to make short people taller in "My Little Brother on Drugs"; and Sharon Begley, in "Designer Babies," considers a very near future in which parents can preselect the characteristics of their children. The famous bioethicist, Peter Singer, considers human cloning from a rational ethical perspective in "The Year of the Clones;" and Jennifer Kahn ends the chapter with "Stripped for Parts," a description of the harvesting of human organs for transplant, asking us to consider both the utility, and perhaps the coming obsolescence, of organ transplants themselves. These essays provide us with a picture of the new ways we have to engineer ourselves for the lives we live, and they suggest the extent to which the twenty-first century will be dominated by the biological revolution happening at the level of our DNA.

Science is moving quickly to give us extraordinary power over ourselves and over *homo sapiens* as a species. It will be up to all of us, but particularly up to you, to help us decide what society does with this power. This chapter will ask you to consider what can be done, and what should be done, to our bodies and our genes as we make our way through the twenty-first century.

DNA as Destiny
DAVID EWING DUNCAN

David Ewing Duncan is a successful writer and television and radio producer. He has written numerous books, including the best-selling Calendar: Humanity's Epic Struggle to Determine a True and Accurate Year *(1998), as well as* Residents: The Perils and Promise of Educating Young Doctors *(1996),* Hernando de Soto: A Savage Quest in the Americas *(1996),* Cape to Cairo *(1989),* Pedaling the Ends of the Earth *(1985), and most recently,* The Geneticist Who Played Hoops with My DNA *(2006). He is a frequent contributor to magazines, is a commentator and guest producer on NPR's* Morning Edition, *and a special producer for ABC's* Nightline *and* 20/20, *and for Discovery Television. He is also a contributing editor to* Wired, *where this essay first appeared in November 2002. As you read this essay, notice how Duncan uses his own experience to encourage us to think about the larger issues of genetic testing.*

——————— ✦ ———————

I feel naked. Exposed. As if my skin, bone, muscle tissue, cells have all been peeled back, down to a tidy swirl of DNA. It's the basic stuff of life, the billions of nucleotides that keep me breathing, walking, craving, and just being. Eight hours ago, I gave a few cells, swabbed from inside my cheek, to a team of geneticists. They've spent the day extracting DNA and checking it for dozens of hidden diseases. Eventually, I will be tested for hundreds more. They include, as I will discover, a nucleic time bomb ticking inside my chromosomes that might one day kill me.

For now I remain blissfully ignorant, awaiting the results in an office at Sequenom, one of scores of biotech startups incubating in the canyons north of San Diego. I'm waiting to find out if I have a genetic proclivity for cancer, cardiac disease, deafness, Alzheimer's, or schizophrenia.

This, I'm told, is the first time a healthy human has ever been screened for the full gamut of genetic-disease markers. Everyone has errors in his or her DNA, glitches that may trigger a heart spasm or cause a brain tumor. I'm here to learn mine.

Waiting, I wonder if I carry some sort of Pandora gene, a hereditary predisposition to peek into places I shouldn't. Morbid curiosity is an occupational hazard for a writer, I suppose, but I've never been bothered by it before. Yet now I find myself growing nervous and slightly flushed. I can feel my pulse rising, a cardiovascular response that I will soon discover has, for me, dire implications.

In the coming days, I'll seek a second opinion, of sorts. Curious about where my genes come from, I'll travel to Oxford and visit an "ancestral geneticist" who has agreed to examine my DNA for links back to progenitors whose mutations have been passed on to me. He will reveal the seeds of my individuality and the roots of the diseases that may kill me—and my children.

For now, I wait in an office at Sequenom, a sneak preview of a trip to the DNA doctor, circa 2008. The personalized medicine being pioneered here and elsewhere prefigures a day when everyone's genome will be deposited on a chip or stored on a gene card tucked into a wallet. Physicians will forecast illnesses and prescribe preventive drugs custom-fitted to a patient's DNA, rather than the one-size-fits-all pharmaceuticals that people take today. Gene cards might also be used to find that best-suited career, or a DNA-compatible mate, or, more darkly, to deny someone jobs, dates, and meds because their nucleotides don't measure up.

It's a scenario Andrew Niccol imagined in his 1997 film, *Gattaca*, where embryos in a not-too-distant future are bioengineered for perfection, and where genism—discrimination based on one's DNA—condemns the lesser-gened to scrubbing toilets.

The *Gattaca*-like engineering of defect-free embryos is at least 20 or 30 years away, but Sequenom and others plan to take DNA testing to the masses in just a year or two. The prize: a projected $5 billion market for personalized medicine by 2006, and billions, possibly hundreds of billions, more for those companies that can translate the errors in my genome and yours into custom pharmaceuticals.

Sitting across from me is the man responsible for my gene scan: Andi Braun, chief medical officer at Sequenom. Tall and sinewy, with a long neck, glasses, and short gray hair, Braun, 46, is both jovial and German. Genetic tests are already publicly available for Huntington's disease and cystic fibrosis, but Braun points out that these illnesses are relatively rare. "We are targeting diseases that impact millions," he says in a deep Bavarian accent, envisioning a day when genetic kits that can assay the whole range of human misery will be available at Wal-Mart, as easy to use as a home pregnancy test.

But a kit won't tell me if I'll definitely get a disease, just if I have a bum gene. What Sequenom and others are working toward is pinning down the probability that, for example, a colon cancer gene will actually trigger a tumor. To know this, Braun must analyze the DNA of thousands of people and tally how many have the colon cancer gene, how many actually get the disease, and how many don't. Once this data is gathered and crunched, Braun will be able to tell you, for instance, that if you have the defective DNA, you have a 40 percent chance, or maybe a 75 percent chance, by age 50, or 90. Environmental factors such as eating right—or wrong—and smoking also weigh in. "It's a little like predicting the weather," says Charles Cantor, the company's cofounder and chief scientific officer.

Braun tells me that, for now, his tests offer only a rough sketch of my genetic future. "We can't yet test for everything, and some of the information is only partially understood," he says. It's more of a peek through a rudimentary eyeglass than a Hubble Space Telescope. Yet I will be able to glimpse some of the internal programming bequeathed to me by evolution, and that I, in turn, have bequeathed to my children—Sander, Danielle, and Alex, ages 15, 13, and 7. They are a part of this story, too. Here's where I squirm, because as a father I pass on not only the ingredients of life to my children but the secret codes of their demise—just as I have passed on my blue eyes and a flip in my left brow that my grandmother called "a little lick from God." DNA is not only the book of life, it is also the book of death, says Braun: "We're all going to die, ja?"

Strictly speaking, Braun is not looking for entire genes, the long strings of nucleotides that instruct the body to grow a tooth or create white blood cells to attack an incoming virus. He's after single nucleotide polymorphisms, or SNPs (pronounced "snips"), the tiny genetic variations that account for nearly all differences in humans.

Imagine DNA as a ladder made of rungs—3 billion in all—spiraling upward in a double helix. Each step is a base pair, designated by two letters from the nucleotide alphabet of G, T, A, and C. More than 99 percent of these base pairs are identical in all humans, with only about one in a thousand SNPs diverging to make us distinct. For instance, you might have a CG that makes you susceptible to diabetes, and I might have a CC, which makes it far less likely I will get this disease.

This is all fairly well-known: Genetics 101. What's new is how startups like Sequenom have industrialized the SNP identification process. Andi Braun and Charles Cantor are finding thousands of new SNPs a day, at a cost of about a penny each.

Braun tells me that there are possibly a million SNPs in each person, though only a small fraction are tightly linked with common ailments. These disease-causing SNPs are fueling a biotech bonanza; the hope is that after finding them, the discoverers can design wonder drugs. In the crowded SNP field, Sequenom vies with Iceland-based deCode Genetics, American companies such as Millennium Pharmaceuticals, Orchid BioSciences, and Celera Genomics, as well as multinationals like Eli Lilly and Roche Diagnostics. "It's the Oklahoma Land Grab right now," says Toni Schuh, Sequenom's CEO.

The sun sets outside Braun's office as my results arrive, splayed across his computer screen like tarot cards. I'm trying to maintain a steely, reportorial facade, but my heart continues to race.

Names of SNPs pop up on the screen: connexin 26, implicated in hearing loss; factor V leiden, which causes blood clots; and alpha-1 antitrypsin deficiency, linked to lung and liver disease. Beside each SNP are codes that mean nothing to me: 13q11-q12, 1q23, 14q32.1. Braun explains that these are addresses on the human genome, the PO box numbers of life. For instance, 1q23 is the address for a mutant gene that causes vessels to shrink and impede the flow of blood—it's on chromosome 1. Thankfully, my result is negative. "So, David, you will not get the varicose veins. That's good, ja?" says Braun. One gene down, dozens to go.

Next up is the hemochromatosis gene. This causes one's blood to retain too much iron, which can damage the liver. As Braun explains it, somewhere in the past, an isolated human community lived in an area where the food was poor in iron. Those who developed a mutation that stores high levels of iron survived, and those who didn't became anemic and died, failing to reproduce. However, in these iron-rich times, hemochromatosis is a liability. Today's treatment? Regular bleeding. "You tested negative for this mutation," says Braun. "You do not have to be bled."

I'm also clean for cystic fibrosis and for a SNP connected to lung cancer.

Then comes the bad news. A line of results on Braun's monitor shows up red and is marked "MT," for mutant type. My body's programming code is faulty. There's a glitch in my system. Named ACE (for angiotensin-I converting enzyme), this SNP means my body makes an enzyme that keeps my blood pressure spiked. In plain English, I'm a heart attack risk.

My face drains of color as the news sinks in. I'm not only defective, but down the road, every time I get anxious about my condition, I'll know that I have a much higher chance of dropping dead. I shouldn't be surprised, since I'm told everyone has some sort of disease-causing mutation. Yet I realize that my decision to take a comprehensive DNA test has been based on the rather ridiculous assumption that I would come out of this with a clean genetic bill of health. I almost never get sick, and, at age 44, I seldom think about my physical limitations, or death. This attitude is buttressed by a family largely untouched by disease. The women routinely thrive into their late eighties and nineties. One great-aunt lived to age 101; she used to bake me cupcakes in her retirement home when I was a boy. And some of the Duncan menfolk are pushing 90-plus. My parents, now entering their seventies, are healthy. In a flash of red MTs, I'm glimpsing my own future; my own mortality. I'm slated to keel over, both hands clutching at my heart.

"Do you have any history in your family of high blood pressure or heart disease?" asks Matthew McGinniss, a Sequenom geneticist standing at Braun's side.

"No," I answer, trying to will the color back into my face. Then a second MT pops up on the screen—another high blood pressure mutation. My other cardiac indicators are OK, which is relatively good news, though I'm hardly listening now. I'm already planning a full-scale assault to learn everything I can about fighting heart disease—until McGinniss delivers an unexpected pronouncement. "These mutations are probably irrelevant," he says. Braun agrees: "It's likely that you carry a gene that keeps these faulty ones from causing you trouble—DNA that we have not yet discovered."

The SNPs keep rolling past, revealing more mutations, including a type-2 diabetes susceptibility, which tells me I may want to steer clear of junk food. More bad news: I don't have a SNP called CCR5 that prevents me from acquiring HIV, nor one that seems to shield smokers from lung cancer. "Ja, that's my favorite," says Braun, himself a smoker. "I wonder what Philip Morris would pay for that."

By the time I get home, I realize that all I've really learned is I might get heart disease, and I could get diabetes. And I should avoid smoking and unsafe sex—as if I didn't already know this. Obviously, I'll now watch my blood pressure, exercise more, and lay off the Cap'n Crunch. But beyond this, I have no idea what to make of the message Andi Braun has divined from a trace of my spit.

Looking for guidance, I visit Ann Walker, director of the Graduate Program for Genetic Counseling at the University of

California at Irvine. Walker explains the whats and hows, and the pros and cons, of DNA testing to patients facing hereditary disease, pregnant couples concerned with prenatal disorders, and anyone else contemplating genetic evaluation. It's a tricky job because, as I've learned, genetic data is seldom clear-cut.

Take breast cancer, Walker says. A woman testing positive for BRCA1, the main breast cancer gene, has an 85 percent chance of actually getting the cancer by age 70, a wrenching situation, since the most effective method of prevention is a double mastectomy. What if a woman has the operation and it turns out she's among those 15 percent who carry the mutation but will never get the cancer? Not surprisingly, one study, conducted in Holland, found that half of healthy women whose mothers developed breast cancer opt not to be tested for the gene, preferring ignorance and closer monitoring. Another example is the test for APoE, the Alzheimer's gene. Since the affliction has no cure, most people don't want to know their status. But some do. A positive result, says Walker, allows them to put their affairs in order and prepare for their own dotage. Still, the news can be devastating. One biotech executive told me that a cousin of his committed suicide when he tested positive for Huntington's, having seen the disease slowly destroy his father.

Walker pulls out a chart and asks about my family's medical details, starting with my grandparents and their brothers and sisters: what they suffered and died from, and when. My Texas grandmother died at 92 after a series of strokes. My 91-year-old Missouri grandmom was headed to a vacation in Mexico with her 88-year-old second husband when she got her death sentence—ovarian cancer. The men died younger: my grandfathers in their late sixties, though they both have brothers still alive and healthy in their nineties. To the mix, Walker adds my parents and their siblings, all of whom are alive and healthy in their sixties and seventies; then my generation; and finally our children. She looks up and smiles: "This is a pretty healthy group."

Normally, Walker says, she would send me home. Yet I'm sitting across from her not because my parents carry some perilous SNP, but as a healthy man who is after a forecast of future maladies. "We have no real training yet for this," she says, and tells me the two general rules of genetic counseling: No one should be screened unless there is an effective treatment or readily available counseling; and the information should not bewilder people or present them with unnecessary trauma.

Many worry that these prime directives may be ignored by Sequenom and other startups that need to launch products to survive. FDA testing for new drugs can take up to 10 years, and many biotech firms feel pressure to sell something in the interim. "Most of these companies need revenue," says the University of Pennsylvania's Arthur Caplan, a top bioethicist. "And the products they've got now are diagnostic. Whether they are good ones, useful ones, necessary ones, accurate ones, seems less of a concern than that they be sold." Caplan also notes that the FDA does not regulate these tests. "If it was a birth control test, the FDA would be all over it."

I ask Caplan about the *Gattaca* scenario of genetic discrimination. Will a woman dump me if she finds out about my ACE? Will my insurance company hike my rate? "People are denied insurance and jobs right now," he says, citing sickle-cell anemia, whose sufferers and carriers, mostly black, have faced job loss and discrimination. No federal laws exist to protect us from genism, or from insurers and employers finding out our genetic secrets. "Right now you're likely going to be more disadvantaged than empowered by genetic testing," says Caplan.

After probing my genetic future, I jet to England to investigate my DNA past. Who are these people who have bequeathed me this tainted bloodline? From my grandfather Duncan, an avid genealogist, I already know that my paternal ancestors came from Perth in south-central Scotland. We can trace the name back to an Anglican priest murdered in Glasgow in 1680 by a mob of Puritans. His six sons escaped and settled in Shippensburg, Pennsylvania, where their descendants lived until my great-great-grandfather moved west to Kansas City in the 1860s.

In an Oxford restaurant, over a lean steak and a heart-healthy merlot, I talk with geneticist Bryan Sykes, a linebacker-sized 55-year-old with a baby face and an impish smile. He's a molecular biologist at the university's Institute of Molecular Medicine and the author of the best-selling *Seven Daughters of Eve*. Sykes first made headlines in 1994 when he used DNA to directly link a 5,000-year-old body discovered frozen and intact in an Austrian glacier to a 20th-century Dorset woman named Marie Mosley. This stunning genetic connection between housewife and hunter-gatherer launched Sykes's career as a globe-trotting genetic gumshoe. In 1995, he confirmed that bones dug up near Ekaterinburg, Russia, were the remains of Czar Nicholas II and his family, by comparing the body's DNA with that of the czar's living relatives, including Britain's Prince Philip. Sykes debunked explorer Thor Heyerdahl's *Kon-Tiki* theory by tracing Polynesian genes to Asia and not the Americas, and similarly put the lie to the *Clan of the Cave Bear* hypothesis, which held that the Neanderthal interbred with our ancestors, the Cro-Magnon, when the two subspecies coexisted in Europe 15,000 years ago.

Sykes explains to me that a bit of DNA called mtDNA is key to his investigations. A circular band of genes residing separately from the 23 chromosomes of the double helix, mtDNA is passed down solely through the maternal line. Sykes used mtDNA to discover something astounding: Nearly every European can be traced back to just seven women living 10,000 to 45,000 years ago. In his book, Sykes gives these seven ancestors hokey names and tells us where they most likely lived: Ursula, in Greece (circa 43,000 B.C.), and Velda, in northern Spain (circa 15,000 B.C.), to name two of the "seven daughters of Eve." (Eve was the ur-mother who lived 150,000 years ago in Africa.)

Sykes has taken swab samples from the cheeks of more than 10,000 people, charging $220 to individually determine a person's mtDNA type. "It's not serious genetics," Sykes admits, "but people like to know their roots. It makes genetics less scary and shows us that, through our genes, we are all very closely related." He recently expanded his tests to include non-Europeans. The Asian daughters of Eve are named Emiko, Nene, and Yumio, and their African sisters are Lamia, Latifa, and Ulla, among others.

Before heading to England, I had mailed Sykes a swab of my cheek cells. Over our desserts in Oxford he finally offers up the results. "You are descended from Helena," he pronounces. "She's the most common daughter of Eve, accounting for some 40 percent of Europeans." He hands me a colorful certificate, signed by him, that heralds my many-times-great-grandma and tells me that she lived 20,000 years ago in the Dordogne Valley of France. More interesting is the string of genetic letters from my mtDNA readout that indicates I'm mostly Celtic, which makes sense. But other bits of code reveal traces of Southeast Asian DNA, and even a smidgen of Native American and African.

This doesn't quite have the impact of discovering that I'm likely to die of a heart attack. Nor am I surprised about the African and Indian DNA, since my mother's family has lived in the American South since the 17th century. But Southeast Asian? Sykes laughs. "We are all mutts," he says. "There is no ethnic purity. Somewhere over the years, one of the thousands of ancestors who contributed to your DNA had a child with someone from Southeast Asia." He tells me a story about a blond, blue-eyed surfer from Southern California who went to Hawaii to apply for monies awarded only to those who could prove native Hawaiian descent. The grant-givers laughed—until his DNA turned up traces of Hawaiian.

The next day, in Sykes's lab, we have one more test: running another ancestry marker in my Y chromosome through a database of 10,000 other Ys to see which profile is closest to mine. If my father was in the database, his Y chromosome would be identical, or possibly one small mutation off. A cousin might deviate by one tick. Someone descended from my native county of Perth might be two or three mutations removed, indicating that we share a common ancestor hundreds of years ago. Sykes tells me these comparisons are used routinely in paternity cases. He has another application. He is building up Y-chromosome profiles of surnames: men with the same last name whose DNA confirms that they are related to common ancestors.

After entering my mtDNA code into his laptop, Sykes looks intrigued, then surprised, and suddenly moves to the edge of his seat. Excited, he reports that the closest match is, incredibly, him—Bryan Sykes! "This has never happened," he says, telling me that I am a mere one mutation removed from him, and two from the average profile of a Sykes. He has not collected DNA from many other Duncans, he says, though it appears as if sometime in the past 400 years a Sykes must have ventured into Perth, and then had a child with a Duncan. "That makes us not-so-distant cousins," he says. We check a map of Britain on his wall, and sure enough, the Sykes family's homeland of Yorkshire is less than 200 miles south of Perth.

The fact that Sykes and I are members of the same extended family is just a bizarre coincidence, but it points to applications beyond simple genealogy. "I've been approached by the police to use my surnames data to match up with DNA from an unknown suspect found at a crime scene," says Sykes. Distinctive genetic markers can be found at the roots of many family trees. "This is possible, to narrow down a pool of suspects to a few likely surnames. But it's not nearly ready yet."

Back home in California, I'm sweating on a StairMaster at the gym, wondering about my heart. I wrap my hands around the grips and check my pulse: 129. Normal. I pump harder and top out at 158. Also normal. I think about my visit a few days earlier—prompted by my gene scan—to Robert Superko, a cardiologist. After performing another battery of tests, he gave me the all clear—except for one thing. Apparently, I have yet another lame-heart gene, the atherosclerosis susceptibility gene ATHS, a SNP that causes plaque in my cardiac bloodstream to build up if I don't exercise far more than average—which I do, these days, as a slightly obsessed biker and runner. "As long as you exercise, you'll be fine," Superko advised, a bizarre kind of life sentence that means that I must pedal and jog like a madman or face—what? A triple bypass?

Pumping on the StairMaster, I nudge the setting up a notch, wishing, in a way, that I either knew for sure I was going to die on, say, February 17, 2021, or that I hadn't been tested at all. As it is, the knowledge that I have an ACE and ATHS deep inside me will be nagging me every time I get short of breath.

The last results from my DNA workup have also come in. Andi Braun has tested me for 77 SNPs linked to lifespan in order to assess when and how I might get sick and die. He has given me a score of .49 on his scale. It indicates a lifespan at least 20 percent longer than that of the average American male who, statistically speaking, dies in his 74th year. I will likely live, then, to the age of 88. That's 44 years of StairMaster to go.

Braun warns that this figure does not take into account the many thousands of other SNPs that affect my life, not to mention the possibility that a piano could fall on my head.

That night, I put my 7-year-old, Alex, to bed. His eyes droop under his bright-white head of hair as I finish reading *Captain Underpants* aloud. Feeling his little heart beating as he lies next to me on his bed, I wonder what shockers await him inside his nucleotides, half of which I gave him. As I close the book and then sing him to sleep, I wonder if he has my culprit genes. I don't know, because he hasn't been scanned. For now, he and the rest of humanity are living in nearly the same blissful ignorance as Helena did in long-ago Dordogne. But I do know one thing: Alex has my eyebrow, the "lick of God." I touch his flip in the dark, and touch mine. He stirs, but it's not enough to wake him.

Topics for Thought and Discussion

1. Duncan writes this essay as a narrative—a story that has a beginning and an end, characters, movement, and events. Identify some of the storytelling techniques that he uses. How do they contribute to his purpose in this essay?
2. Duncan seems, at times, to regret having had his DNA scanned. Is it better, do you think, to live (as he puts it) "in blissful ignorance"? What are the pros and cons of this kind of DNA scan?
3. Discuss the potential consequences of genism. Can you imagine a situation in which genism might be allowed?
4. Describe how Duncan's conclusion impacts his essay. How and why is the vignette with his son an appropriate way for him to conclude his essay?

Suggestions for Writing

1. Write your own essay of discovery, using Duncan's story-telling techniques. Your story does not need to be about DNA testing, but can focus on any learning experience that you can present as a journey.
2. Would you want to know? Write an essay in which you describe the circumstances under which you would want to know what your genes foretell, and the circumstances under which you would not.
3. Write a short story in which you grapple with an issue, or issues, drawn from Duncan's essay. It can be set now or in the future.

My Little Brother on Drugs
JENNY EVERETT

Jenny Everett is an assistant editor of Popular Science *magazine and a writer about science and technology whose essays have appeared nationally in* Popular Science *and other science periodicals. The following essay, which first appeared in* Popular Science *in 2004, is both a personal experience essay and an investigation into current attempts to engineer the human body. As you read this, consider what Everett's experience teaches her about these attempts.*

———————————— ◆ ————————————

I swipe an alcohol-soaked gauze pad over my younger brother's left thigh, an inch below the hem of his SpongeBob boxers. As I screw the needle into the injection pen, Alex feeds me instructions. It's my first time, but already it's his 37th.

"Here are the rules: Insert the needle quickly and gently, but only when I say so," he says, taking the pen to pantomime the motion. He removes the first of two protective caps and turns a knob on the pen—one, two, three, four, five clicks—and watches intensely as his dose is released into the barrel.

"Make sure the skin dimples. That means the needle is all the way in," he continues. "Press the button until it clicks, then hold it there for 5 seconds. Keep the skin dimpled, otherwise all the medicine won't go in me. When you take out the needle, do it straight up and fast. And, Jenny, please don't hit a vein. That *huwts* me." Suddenly, dropping his r, Alex sounds much more like his 9-year-old self.

I pinch a clump of skin between my thumb and index finger and wait. "OK," he whispers. But I can't do it. "OK," he repeats.

I pierce the fatty tissue and wince—and take it as a compliment that he doesn't. "Keep dimpling!" he yells.

Here's the thing: My brother isn't sick. He's short. Shorter than every boy and girl in Ms. Lemcke's fourth-grade class, shorter than 97 percent of boys his age. What I've just shot into his 3-foot-11-and-three-quarters-inch, 50-pound body is Humatrope, a lab-brewed human growth hormone (hGH) nearly identical to the hGH secreted by the pituitary gland, the critical metabolic hormone that regulates not only height, as its name suggests, but also cardiac function, fat metabolism and muscle growth.

Alex's quest for "enheightenment," as I've come to call it, began last summer just as the Food and Drug Administration expanded its approved uses of Humatrope, Eli Lilly & Co.'s recombinant hGH, to include children of idiopathic short stature (ISS)—kids who are extremely short for reasons that are not entirely understood. Kids who, like Alex, are teased or ignored by classmates who may trump their height by a foot—but whose "condition" may be caused by nothing more than genetics. This groundbreaking and controversial FDA ruling made Humatrope available to 400,000 American children expected to grow no taller than 5 feet 3 in the case of boys and 4 feet 11 in the case of girls, putting them in the bottom 1.2 percentile. For Alex, the nightly hGH shots will probably continue for six to eight years—all to make this otherwise healthy boy grow taller.

Human growth is an invisible but intense process, an intricate and little understood web of genes, hormones and other variables. Genetics aside, growth hormone may be the single biggest player. Between 10 and 30 times a day, your hypothalamus sends a growth hormone-releasing hormone to the garbanzo-bean-size pituitary gland at the base of your brain. Each time the pituitary gland receives a signal, it spits out a small amount of growth hormone. Although scientists think a small percentage of hGH travels to your bones, a majority of the hormone latches onto binding proteins, which carry it to receptors in your liver cells. This triggers the secretion of insulin-like growth factor-1 (IGF-1), a protein that promotes bone growth in children and teenagers until their growth plates, areas at the ends of the bones, fuse, at around age 17 for boys or 15 for girls. After that, growth hormone continues to regulate the metabolic system, burning fat and building muscle, but we produce exponentially less hGH each decade after puberty. Thus, the teenager who can routinely "supersize it" without consequence ages into the 30-year-old whose beer and burgers go straight to his gut.

In 1971, Berkeley chemist Choh Hao Li synthesized the growth hormone molecule, an enormous biotech breakthrough, and in 1985 synthetic growth hormone was approved by the FDA to treat growth hormone deficiency. Prior to the drug's development, medicinal growth hormone was scarce. What did exist had to be extracted from the pituitary glands of human corpses—most of the time legally, but occasionally by pathologists being paid by suppliers to remove the hormone without permission from the deceased's family. As a result of the shortage, hGH treatment was conservative, reserved for kids who made very little if any growth hormone themselves. Between 1963 and 1985, 7,700 patients in the U.S. took the hormone. Ultimately, 26 of these patients died of Creutzfeldt-Jakob disease (CJD); the fatal brain disease that's similar to mad cow is thought to have contaminated a batch of the pituitary hormone doled out in the '60s and '70s. The FDA banned growth hormone when the first two cases of CJD were reported in early 1985—just in time for the agency's approval, later that year, of the synthetic version.

Suddenly, the growth hormone supply was unlimited, safer and less expensive, opening the door for looser diagnoses, along with higher and more frequent doses. By 1988 what had once been a niche drug prescribed to treat dwarfism was shattering all market expectations, chalking up more than a half billion dollars in annual sales.

At the time, I was 11 years old, and a ripe candidate for growth hormone supplementation. I had been born in the fifth percentile for height, but at age 5 my "growth velocity" started slipping, and by 11, I was hovering below the first percentile. Blood tests revealed that I was only producing "borderline acceptable" levels of growth hormone. "Growth hormone injections may be an option," Yale pediatric endocrinologist William Tamborlane told my parents. The prospect terrified me. "I don't care if I'm a midget! It's what's inside that counts!" I protested. "I'm not having a shot every day."

Further testing showed that my thyroid gland was malfunctioning, a definable and common condition called hypothyroidism. Tamborlane prescribed a pill (which I will take every day for the rest of my life), and my growth velocity picked up immediately. Still, I was told that I would never surmount the magical 5-foot threshold.

That's because most short children can place primary blame for their stature on the genetic lottery. "Want to be taller, Jenny?" I remember Tamborlane asking me as his eyes shifted between my slumping growth chart, my X-rays, and my mom and dad. I nodded eagerly. "Well, you should've picked different parents." He chuckled, while I considered the merits of a parentectomy. Today I'm 26 years old and my height has topped off at . . . 5 feet 1, thank you very much.

Fifteen years after I flirted with growth hormone treatment, biotech's baby has exploded into a $1.5 billion industry that has reached more than 200,000 children and sent many more to the doctor wondering if hGH is for them—including my brother Alex. When my mom called to tell me Alex was growth-hormone-deficient and would soon begin injections, I was skeptical. The prospect of having a shot every day had sent fear through my own little body, and now, as an overprotective big sister, I didn't want my brother's carefree childhood to be interrupted by such stress— and such a serious, understudied medical treatment—unless it was entirely necessary. Is being short so horrible that it should be medicalized and treated as an illness?

My thoughts were interrupted by my mom's voice, bringing me back to reality. "Nurses are coming over next week to show us how to administer the injection," she said. The decision had been made.

As the 6 train squeals under Manhattan's Upper East Side, Alex's Nikes sway three inches above the floor. My brother is a happy kid whose sprite profile doesn't resemble that of the typical round-faced growth-hormone-deficient cherub. He's silent now but only because his mouth is full of jellybeans. The train reaches our stop, and Alex places his sticky little hand in mine.

"Excuse me," he says politely as we jostle our way off.

A surprised middle-aged mom looks up from her book. "My, you are much more polite than *my* kindergartener," she says.

It's been about two weeks since Alex began his nightly injections. Before that, he might have flinched at this well-intentioned under-estimate of his age. But today, he squares himself a bit and responds with a certain pride: "I'm 9 years old," he says, "and I'm on Humatrope!"

It strikes me, not for the first time, just how important the drug has become to Alex. He yearns to be taller. As the youngest of six, he knows how to get noticed—our family joke is that he swallowed an amplifier—and what he lacks in stature he was dealt in personality. But at school, where tall kids hold the social scepter, his big personality is overlooked.

"Everyone says that it's what's inside that counts, and that makes me feel good," Alex says, "but if I was the tallest instead of the shortest, everything would just be better. People would sit with me at lunch, I'd have more friends, and people in my class wouldn't make fun of me and call me Little Everett. And I'd be a better soccer goalie. I think 6 feet would be good."

Studies show that half of short kids report being teased and three-quarters say they're treated younger than their age—but keep in mind that this is an awkward age to begin with. Starting at about age 10, grade-wide height discrepancies tend to widen dramatically, which just adds fuel to the broader stew of middle school insecurities most of us shudder to recall. This is the age at which families often become conscious of and concerned about growth issues—because discrepancies are suddenly so visually apparent.

When I was in fifth grade, the boys would chase me down the hall on their knees playing "catch the midget," and one of the tougher girls would taunt me: "You're so small I need a microscope to see you." But before feeling sorry for me, consider my classmate Kelly (Editor's note: Name has been changed), who was 5 feet 10, a full 2 feet taller than I was—a virtual fifth-grade giant. (Given social norms, it's appropriate to compare the experience of being a short boy to that of being a tall girl.) Kelly was tortured so badly throughout adolescence that at 18 she became bulimic. When her weight dropped to 115 pounds, she was hospitalized. "I thought it would make me smaller and more attractive," she recalled in a recent phone conversation. "It almost killed me."

Being a tall girl is so psychologically traumatic, in fact, that in the 1950s, doctors began giving tall girls estrogen as a growth suppressant. In high doses, the hormone stimulates cartilage maturation without causing an increase in height, which means the girls stop growing earlier. In Kelly's case, treatment was discussed, but doctors were confident, based on her bone development, that she wouldn't grow much taller than 6 feet. Good call: Today Kelly is only an inch taller than she was in fifth grade. And although no formal long-term studies have been done, tall girls treated with estrogen have reported increased incidences of miscarriage, endometriosis, infertility and ovarian cysts. Yet a survey taken last year reported that one-third of pediatric endocrinologists have offered the treatment at least once in the past five years.

Learning about the side effects of estrogen therapy only increased my apprehension about treating Alex with hGH. Armed with a small forest of research, I drove up to Yale–New Haven Children's Hospital to unload my worries on Dr. Myron Genel, Alex's pediatric endocrinologist.

With his white hair and white lab coat, Genel looks the prototypical old-school doctor, the kind you imagine making house calls with his little black medical kit. I take a sip of my coffee. "This won't stunt my growth, will it?" I joke. "Too late to worry about that," he replies.

I reach into my bag and pull out binders of research: diagrams of the growth process, historical time lines, and a folder labeled "risks," which is packed with studies. "How concerned should my family be about the risks?" I ask.

I wait for reassurance—or, in any case, for a defense of Alex's treatment. But Genel surprises me.

"We honestly don't know the long-term side effects, and I think that's a reason for real concern," he says. "We're using a hormone that promotes growth, and there are things whose growth we don't want to promote. IGF-1, for example, has been shown to play a role in the development of malignancies in tissue culture."

This I knew. Multiple studies of human serum specimens have shown that elevated levels of IGF-1 identify people at higher risk for developing breast, prostate and colon cancer, and tumor specimens, most studies show, have more IGF-1 receptors than normal adjacent cells. Although it's not yet known whether an abundance of IGF-1 actually causes malignancies or is merely associated with some other risk factor, it is a reason for concern because growth hormone is what stimulates the liver and tissues to produce IGF-1.

But Genel explains that he'll test Alex's IGF levels every three months to make sure they're in what's considered the normal range. "In theory, if we keep his growth factors at an acceptable level, he's not at risk," he says.

I scan my list of questions, typed up in order of progressing intensity, and zoom to the bottom. "Given the risks, what makes Alex a good candidate?"

Again his response surprises me—this time because it challenges my assumption that Alex is in fact a good candidate for treatment. "We can define those youngsters who make virtually no growth hormone, because they have a very typical presentation," he says. "And we can generally sort out those youngsters who make an ample amount of growth hormone.

"We have a very difficult time, however, defining youngsters like your brother, who make *some* growth hormone, but who possibly don't make enough."

He explains that although Alex's levels of IGF-1 are low and his height has gradually declined to the first percentile, he does produce some growth hormone.

"Your brother is a murky case, and there are enough questions about the safety and efficacy of this drug that I cannot say one way or another whether he should definitely receive treatment," he continues. "Frankly, I felt we could wait—but not very much longer—and gather information. It was a decision that your family made and, I suspect, Alex made."

Here is a manifestation of just how complicated and unpredictable the growth process is: It's impossible to measure hGH levels using a simple blood test. Because the hormone oscillates in the blood, constantly peaking and sinking, a hundred samples can yield a hundred different answers. So doctors must rely on growth-hormone-stimulation tests, where the patient is injected with an artificial agent that stimulates the pituitary gland to produce growth hormone. After the agent is injected, nurses sample the patient's blood every 30 minutes for 2 hours, hoping to catch the pituitary operating at full strength.

"These are artificial tests," Genel says. "None of them tell us anything about what a youngster does under normal circumstances. It only tells us that if you give them an artificial stimulus, the pituitary gland will release hormone."

Genel shows me my brother's test results: Alex produced readings ranging from 0.11 to 9.9 ng/ml. Though most doctors look for a top level of at least 10 as an indicator of healthy hormone production, Yale has a lower benchmark of 7 or greater. So by Yale's standards, Alex passed. My parents, I realize, have no idea that Alex may not be growth-hormone-deficient by some careful definition; they believe he is clinically deficient. Essentially, my little brother is an experiment.

Over dinner that night, my mother and father recall the day Alex's test results arrived in the mail. Startled by the low numbers, they assumed he was producing far too little growth hormone. They had no idea growth hormone production is so difficult to measure. "I'm a parent, not a scientist," my mom says. "I shouldn't have to know that." It's safe to take him off the drug, I tell them: "It's not too late to change your mind."

But despite the day's revelations, they decide to move forward with treatment. Alex's confidence has already soared since starting Humatrope; they don't have the heart to disappoint him. Besides, my parents say, they're concerned Alex will have fewer professional opportunities, and worry he won't find a woman to be with, if his height remains in the basement.

Such anxieties, of course, are hardly unique to my parents—and, in fact, a quick glance at the research would appear to back them up. A recent University of Florida study, for example, found that each extra inch of height amounted to $789 more a year in pay. So someone who is 6 feet would be expected, on average, to earn $5,523 more annually than someone who is 5 feet 5. Another study indicates that just 3 percent of Fortune 500 CEOs are shorter than 5 feet 7, and more than half are taller than 6 feet, though only 20 percent of the population is.

But it's not as simple an equation as these numbers make it seem, says Dr. David Sandberg, an associate professor of psychiatry and pediatrics at the University of Buffalo. Sandberg's studies have found that although short kids are teased and treated younger than their age, there is no evidence that making them 2.5 inches taller will make any difference in their quality of life. "Our lives are so much more complicated than one single factor," Sandberg says.

In clinical trials by Humatrope manufacturer Eli Lilly, children taking the drug grew on average 1 to 1.5 inches more than the placebo group; 62 percent of the kids tested grew more than 2 inches over their predicted adult height, and 31 percent gained more than 4 inches. This would land Alex, whose predicted height without growth hormone is about 5 feet 6, somewhere between 5 feet 7 and 5 feet 10.

Dr. Harvey Guyda, chair of the department of pediatrics at McGill University in Canada, questions the studies, especially given what he describes as a high dropout rate. In the Eli Lilly studies, he points out, only 28 percent of the placebo and 42 percent of the growth-hormone-therapy subjects completed the study; it seems reasonable to assume, he says, that the subjects who endured the study were the ones who demonstrated the most extreme growth.

"The mantra is that healthy, short kids are handicapped, abnormal, have all sorts of problems, and we have to do something," says Guyda, who testified against the FDA's approval of Humatrope for treating kids with ISS. "But there is no data to prove that these kids are any different from normal-stature children, and there is absolutely zero data that says when you give growth hormone to a kid who's said to have this psychosocial problem because he's short there's any benefit. Prove to me that a few extra inches is worth the cost of daily injections."

Financially alone, that cost, according to Guyda, amounts to $10,000 per centimeter for a growth-hormone-deficient kid, and somewhere between $22,000 and $43,000 per centimeter for kids with idiopathic short stature. For now, my parents' insurance company, Anthem Blue Cross and Blue Shield, has agreed to cover Alex's treatment, but not every short child has insurance or a pediatric endocrinologist to recommend treatment.

The not-surprising result is that any advantage hGH does confer will likely go to already advantaged patients: rich, white American males. (For every two girls who receive treatment, five boys do; this is at least partly explained by the fact that boys suffer more discrimination in relation to their short stature than girls do.)

A week before Alex's three-month checkup, I return to Yale, this time to meet with Tamborlane, my own pediatric endocrinologist, whom I haven't seen since my last appointment eight years ago. I'm especially interested in his opinion about Alex because Tamborlane, now the chief of pediatric endocrinology at Yale, voted for the approval of Humatrope to treat idiopathic short stature. We meet in the cafeteria, and although I'm not looking for a free checkup, he palpates my throat right there. "Thyroid feels healthy," he reports.

Tamborlane voted for the approval, he tells me, because the drug was already OK'd to treat some groups of children who produce plenty of growth hormone—children with Turner syndrome, a genetic abnormality; children born small for gestational age; and children with chronic renal insufficiency, a kidney disease. In each of these cases, hGH isn't treating the disease, it's treating the resulting undesirable physical characteristic—short stature. In kids with ISS, though, it's even more ambiguous because the disease, if there is one, is unknown.

I present Alex's case to Tamborlane, explaining my family's motivations and the uncertainty surrounding the diagnosis. I tell him that although I want Alex to have every advantage and the best possible quality of life, I'm concerned about the drug's unclear benefits and the potential long-term risks for kids who are short for reasons that aren't fully understood.

"If Alex were your son," I ask, "would you put him on hGH?"

Tamborlane leans back and pauses to consider the question.

"Given the uncertainties, probably not. I was a short, geeky kid at a football prep school, and I survived—maybe even gained something from it," he says. (He's now 5 feet 9.) "All signs say Alex would probably grow to a very livable height without the growth hormone."

In early November, we bring Alex to Yale for his first checkup. By now, the injection has become routine—slotted into a 9 P.M. Nickelodeon commercial break—and my family is already noticing changes in Alex's body. His muscle tone is visibly improved, and his pants are suddenly too short. In the waiting room, I jot down a few things to mention to the doctor: Alex's appetite is uncharacteristically voracious; his growth pains are intensifying; and his hair is dry and brittle.

The room used for measuring height and weight is wall-papered with drawings by patients with a variety of metabolic disorders. One depicts a small, sad-looking stick figure labeled "before" and a taller, much happier stick figure labeled "after." Alex stands to the left of this, back to the wall, grinning in anticipation of his "after." The nurse scribbles on his chart and ushers us into the examining room. Alex is anxious because while we swear he's grown at least 3 inches, we're not positive because we haven't measured him yet—psychologists recommend we don't measure Alex at home.

"124.8 cm," Genel announces finally. "That's just about 4 feet 1, about an inch and a half in three months." "Wow," says my mom, extrapolating 6 inches of growth a year.

"That's *all*?" says Alex. "All those shots for one measly inch?!"

Genel warns them not to take the results too literally. "These are *positive* results," he says to Alex. Then, turning to my mom: "But it's too early to attribute this response to the treatment."

Indeed, there's no telling what the results of Alex's treatment will be; even at $20,000 a year there are no guarantees. Some kids end up in the 60th percentile, while others never crawl above the fifth. I'm still left wondering why we're rolling the dice on a healthy kid, particularly when the benefits of a few extra inches are unproven and the risks are unknown. At the same time, I'm rooting for results—and we leave the doctor's office cautiously optimistic that the treatment is having an impact. We're further reassured three months later, in early February, when Alex's next official measurement comes in: He's 4 feet 2 and a quarter inches, a full 2.5 inches taller than he was six months earlier when he began treatment.

Topics for Thought and Discussion

1. If Everett had the final and only say about Alex's treatment, how would she choose? How do you know? What evidence in the text supports your analysis?
2. How does Everett use outside experts? How does she introduce them? Look carefully at a minimum of three introduced experts.
3. What do you think about treating shortness? How is this treatment related to other more radical genetic manipulation? How is it related to other kinds of physical manipulation, like face-lifts, or breast implants? If there is no danger involved, where would you come down on the question of intervening to create a more desirable body for oneself?
4. Discuss the role that height plays in your current life. Would you change your height (either up or down) if you could?

Suggestions for Writing

1. Interview the tallest person you know and the shortest. Describe their experiences. Would they change their height if they could? How does gender figure in their experiences? Age? Write an essay in which you summarize your findings.
2. Should we, or should we not, be free to have the kind of body we want? Write an essay in which you use Everett as a source in a more general argument about the pros and cons of scientifically manipulating our bodies.

Designer Babies
SHARON BEGLEY

Sharon Begley is the science editor of The Wall Street Journal *and was for twenty-five years a senior editor at* Newsweek *magazine. She is a prolific commentator and writer about science and its connection to society. The following essay appeared in* Newsweek *in 1998, just as concerns about cloning and genetic manipulation were beginning to heat up. As you read, consider how Begley establishes her tone and what that tone contributes to her essay (beginning, of course, with her choice of title).*

---- ◆ ----

It is only a matter of time. One day—a day probably no more distant than the first wedding anniversary of a couple who are now teenage sweethearts—a man and a woman will walk into an in vitro fertilization clinic and make scientific history. Their problem won't be infertility, the reason couples now choose IVF. Rather, they will be desperate for a very special child, a child who will elude a family curse. To create their dream child, doctors will fertilize a few of the woman's eggs with her husband's sperm, as IVF clinics do today. But then they will inject an artificial human chromosome, carrying made-to-order genes like pearls on a string, into the fertilized egg. One of the genes will carry instructions ordering cells to commit suicide. Then the doctors will place the embryo into the woman's uterus. If her baby is a boy, when he becomes an old man he, like his father and grandfather before him, will develop prostate cancer. But the cell-suicide gene will make his prostate cells self-destruct. The man, unlike his ancestors, will not die of the cancer. And since the gene that the doctors gave him copied itself into every cell of his body, including his sperm, his sons will beat prostate cancer, too.

Genetic engineers are preparing to cross what has long been an ethical Rubicon.[1] Since 1990, gene therapy has meant slipping a healthy gene into the cells of one organ of a patient suffering from a genetic disease. Soon, it may mean something much more momentous: altering a fertilized egg so that genes in all of a person's cells, including eggs or sperm, also carry a gene that scientists, not parents, bequeathed them. When the pioneers of gene therapy first requested government approval for their experiments in 1987, they vowed they would never alter patients' eggs or sperm. That was then. This is now. One of those pioneers, Dr. W. French Anderson of the University of Southern California, recently put the National Institutes of Health on notice. Within two or three years, he said, he would ask approval to use gene therapy on a fetus that has been diagnosed with a deadly inherited disease. The therapy would cure the fetus before it is born. But the introduced genes, though targeted at only blood or immune-system cells, might inadvertently slip into the child's egg (or sperm) cells, too. If that happens, the genetic change would affect that child's children unto the nth generation. "Life would enter a new phase," says biophysicist Gregory Stock of UCLA, "one in which we seize control of our own evolution."

Judging by the 70 pages of public comments NIH has received since Anderson submitted his proposal in September, the overwhelming majority of scientists and ethicists weighing in oppose gene therapy that changes the "germline" (eggs and sperm). But the opposition could be a boulevard wide and paper thin. "There is a great divide in the bioethics community over whether we should be opening up this Pandora's box," says science-policy scholar Sheldon Krimsky of Tufts University. Many bioethicists are sympathetic to using germline therapy to shield a child from a family disposition to cancer, or atherosclerosis or other illnesses with a strong genetic component. As James Watson, president of the Cold Spring Harbor Laboratory and codiscoverer of the double-helical structure of DNA, said at a recent UCLA conference, "We might as well do what we finally can to take the threat of Alzheimer's or breast cancer away from a family." But something else is suddenly making it OK to discuss the once forbidden possibility of germline engineering: molecular biologists now

---

[1] A river in Italy. When Caeser crossed it with his army in 49 B.C.E., he initiated a civil war.

think they have clever ways to circumvent ethical concerns that engulf this sci-fi idea.

There may be ways, for instance, to design a baby's genes without violating the principle of informed consent. This is the belief that no one's genes—not even an embryo's—should be altered without his or her permission. Presumably few people would object to being spared a fatal disease. But what about genes for personality traits, like risk-taking or being neurotic? If you like today's blame game—it's Mom's fault that you inherited her temper—you'll love tomorrow's: she intentionally stuck you with that personality quirk. But the child of tomorrow might have the final word about his genes, says UCLA geneticist John Campbell. The designer gene for, say, patience could be paired with an on-off switch, he says. The child would have to take a drug to activate the patience gene. Free to accept or reject the drug, he retains informed consent over his genetic endowment.

There may also be ways to make an end run around the worry that it is wrong to monkey with human evolution. Researchers are experimenting with tricks to make the introduced gene self-destruct in cells that become eggs or sperm. That would confine the tinkering to one generation. Then, if it became clear that eliminating genes for, say, mental illness also erased genes for creativity, that loss would not become a permanent part of man's genetic blueprint. (Of course, preventing the new gene's transmission to future generations would also defeat the hope of permanently lopping off a diseased branch from a family tree.) In experiments with animals, geneticist Mario Capecchi of the University of Utah has designed a string of genes flanked by the molecular version of scissors. The scissors are activated by an enzyme that would be made only in the cells that become eggs or sperm. Once activated, the genetic scissors snip out the introduced gene and, presto, it is not passed along to future generations. "What I worry about," says Capecchi, "is that if we start messing around with [eggs and sperm], at some point— since this is a human enterprise—we're going to make a mistake. You want a way to undo that mistake. And since what may seem terrific now may seem naive in 20 years, you want a way to make the genetic change reversible."

There is no easy technological fix for another ethical worry, however: with germline engineering only society's "haves" will control their genetic traits. It isn't hard to foresee a day like that painted in last year's film *Gattaca*, where only the wealthy can afford to genetically engineer their children with such "killer applications" as intelligence, beauty, long life or health. "If you are going to disadvantage even further those who are already disadvantaged," says bioethicist Ruth Macklin of Albert Einstein College of Medicine, "then that does raise serious concerns." But perhaps not enough to keep designer babies solely in Hollywood's imagination. For one thing, genetic therapy as done today (treating one organ of one child or adult) has been a bitter disappointment. "With the exception of a few anecdotal cases," says USC's Anderson, "there is no evidence of a gene-therapy protocol that helps." But germline therapy might actually be easier. Doctors would not have to insinuate the new gene into millions of lung cells in, say, a cystic fibrosis patient. They could manipulate only a single cell—the fertilized egg—and still have the gene reach every cell of the person who develops from that egg.

How soon might we design our children? The necessary pieces are quickly falling into place. The first artificial human chromosome was created last year. By 2003 the Human Genome Project will have decoded all 3 billion chemical letters that spell out our 70,000 or so genes. Animal experiments designed to show that the process will not create horrible mutants are underway. No law prohibits germline engineering. Although NIH now refuses to even consider funding proposals for it, the rules are being updated. And where there is a way, there will almost surely be a will: none of us, says USC's Anderson, "wants to pass on to our children lethal genes if we can prevent it—that's what's going to drive this." At the UCLA symposium on germline engineering, two thirds of the audience supported it. Few would argue against using the technique to eradicate a disease that has plagued a family for generations. As Tuft's Krimsky says, "We know where to start." The harder question is this: do we know where to stop?

Topics for Thought and Discussion

1. Does Begley's essay take a side in this issue? Collect your evidence by looking carefully at the word and argument choices Begley makes as she writes this article.

2. At the end of her essay, Begley says that "where there is a way, there will almost surely be a will." This overturns a common catch-phrase, and begs a larger question: Should we pursue this technology? Is the argument that we *can* do it the same as the argument that we *should* do it?

3. At one point, Begley calls the ability to engineer our offspring the ability to "monkey with human evolution." What are the dangers inherent in "monkeying" with evolution? If it is dangerous, why might it be so?

4. The technology to engineer the germ-line seems to offer great promise and great risk. Can you think of other technologies that have offered similar promise and risk? Can you generalize about whether those technologies historically have been beneficial or dangerous? Or is the jury still out on most of them?

Suggestions for Writing

1. On a sheet of paper, make a list of the potential benefits of germline engineering and a list of potential dangers. Be as detailed as possible.
2. Weighing the advantages against the disadvantages, pick a side in the debate over—as Begley calls it—designing our children.
3. Use this essay to generalize about science. Is there a line across which scientists should not go? Or do scientists have an obligation to always push forward, regardless of the potential consequences?

The Year of the Clone?

Peter Singer

Peter Singer is an important and controversial bioethicist, concerned particularly with the ethics of biological systems. Currently the DeCamp Professor of Bioethics at the University Center for Human Values at Princeton University, Singer is best known for his book, Animal Liberation *(1975), which helped spark the modern animal rights movement. Singer, however, is also a formidable voice on the relationship between human beings and their world. Though Singer's conclusions about topics such as abortion, infanticide, and bestiality have caused considerable controversy—particularly in religious circles—he is known as a careful and methodical thinker and writer. He is a prolific writer as well, and in addition to* Animal Liberation, *his books include* Practical Ethics *(1979),* How Are We to Live? Ethics in an Age of Self-Interest *(1995),* Rethinking Life and Death: The Collapse of Our Traditional Ethics *(1996),* Writings on an Ethical Life *(2000),* One World: The Ethics of Globalization *(2002), and* The President of Good and Evil: The Ethics of George W. Bush *(2004), among others. The following article appeared in* Free Inquiry *in 2001. As you read, consider how Singer structures his argument to deal with this extremely controversial topic.*

---- ✦ ----

In January Panos Zavos, a professor of reproductive physiology at the University of Kentucky, announced that he was teaming up with Italian gynecologist Severino Antinori to try to produce the first cloned human being within the next year or two. To those who have followed Antinori's career, this should not come as a great surprise. Back in October 1998, Antinori said that he wanted to be the first scientist to clone a human being. Knowledgeable people then were doubtful that anything would happen soon. Today, they are still skeptical that Antinori will be able to pull off the feat in the foreseeable future.

Zavos and Antinori are not the only ones currently trying to clone a human being. The Raelians, a sect whose founder claims to have had contact with aliens, are working with an American couple whose baby died in infancy to help them have a genetic carbon copy of their lost child.

Graeme Bulfield, chief executive of Edinburgh, Scotland's Roslin Institute, where Dolly the sheep was cloned, has said that he would be "absolutely flabbergasted" if human cloning were done in his lifetime. Flabbergasted he may yet be. Let's leave the Raelians out of it and focus on the scientists with proven credentials in reproductive medicine.

Antinori has a record of pushing the boundaries back in the area of reproductive medicine. In 1994, he helped a sixty-two-year-old woman become the oldest woman recorded to have a child as a result of the use of new reproductive technology. But that was, technically speaking, a relatively simple task compared to cloning a human being. Until Ian Wilmut and his colleagues produced Dolly the sheep, the consensus was that it was impossible to produce a clone from an adult mammal. ("Cloning" in the sense of splitting an embryo, thus creating twins, happens in nature and can be done in the laboratory, too, but it does not raise the same issues as cloning in the sense of making a genetic carbon copy of a more developed human being.)

Now we know that cloning from an adult mammal can be done, but the question is whether anyone would have enough human volunteers to succeed in pulling it off. Bulfield has estimated that it would take 400 eggs and fifty surrogate mothers to produce a cloned human being—not to mention about $150 million. It seems doubtful that Zavos and Antinori can assemble such resources, both human and financial. (The Raelians claim that they have fifty women volunteering to act as egg donors and surrogate mothers, but their budget is nowhere near $150 million.)

Suppose, though, that someone did manage to produce a cloned human child. They would, of course, achieve headlines for themselves, an accomplishment at which Antinori and the Raelians have already demonstrated considerable skill. But would they have harmed anyone? Would anything significant really have changed? Let's take these two questions separately.

If a human being were cloned, who would be harmed? The most obvious answer is: the being who was cloned. There are real questions about the likely health of a clone. There have been suggestions that Dolly's cells are in some respects not behaving like the cells of a four-year-old sheep, but rather like the cells of a sheep that is six years older—the age of the sheep from which Dolly was cloned. If that were the case, then a human being cloned from, say, a fifty-year-old adult would have a sadly diminished life expectancy. It now seems that this may not be the case, but other concerns have emerged. At the University of Hawaii, Dr. Ryuzo Yanagimachi cloned mice and found that some of them became extremely obese, despite not being given any more food than normal mice. Other abnormalities have also been detected. Cows cloned at Texas A&M University have had abnormal hearts and lungs. If these problems are also likely to occur in humans, it would be ethically irresponsible to go ahead with a human clone.

Suppose, however, that these fears turn out to be groundless, and somehow we can be sure that cloned humans will not have a higher rate of abnormalities than humans produced in the usual way. Then would the life of a cloned human be significantly worse than the life of the rest of us? Only, I imagine, in the constant media attention. Otherwise, being a clone of, say, a child who had died, and whom the grieving parents were wishing to "recreate" would not be very different from being one of a pair of identical twins, one of whom had died. (Although one would, evidently, have parents with a rather unusual attachment to a dead child.)

Even if it could be argued that a cloned child would face psychological burdens, how serious would these be? Given that, if cloning were prohibited, this particular child would not have existed at all, would the burdens be so terrible that he or she would wish that cloning had been prohibited? That seems very unlikely. If not, then it is not possible to argue that cloning ought to be prohibited for the sake of the cloned child.

If not for the child, then for whose sake would we be acting if we were to prohibit cloning? Obviously not for the sake of the couple who wanted to have the cloned child, and not for the sake of the scientists willing to assist them. Does society need protecting from clones? Yes, if we are talking about whole armies of clones of popular rock stars or sports heroes. That could lead to a worrying loss of genetic diversity. But no, if only a small number of people will want to have children who are clones. That is much the most likely prospect, especially as long as cloning remains a very expensive and complicated procedure, with a higher than normal risk of abnormalities. Since that seems bound to be the case for a long time to come, we do not need to waste too much thought on how to deal with the would-be cloners. If they can assure us of their ability to produce normal human beings, then let them go ahead. In the larger scheme of things, it will not make all that much difference to the shape of human society in the twenty-first century.

Topics for Thought and Discussion

1. What is Singer's purpose with this essay? How does he accomplish this purpose?
2. Describe Singer's conclusion. He seems to put his thesis into his conclusion. What is it? How effective is this technique?
3. Summarize Singer's primary arguments for why (and under what circumstances) cloning should be allowed to go forward.
4. Do you agree with Singer's argument? Can you think of elements of this debate that he does not address?

Suggestions for Writing

1. Imagine a world in which Singer's prediction comes true. There are clones, but very few of them. What is this world like? How would our world change? What would life be like for the clones? Write a paper or a short story that investigates this world.
2. Write a letter to Singer in which you either agree or disagree with his argument. Answer his points, and provide your own.

Stripped for Parts

JENNIFER KAHN

Jennifer Kahn is a contributing editor of Wired *magazine and a frequent writer about science for a variety of national magazines. Trained as an astrophysicist, she has become an award-winning science writer. The following essay first appeared in* Wired *magazine in 2003. As you read, consider how Kahn establishes tone—particularly the impact of her opening line—and how that tone contributes to the purposes of her essay.*

——————————— ✦ ———————————

The television in the dead man's room stays on all night. Right now the program is *Shipmates*, a reality-dating drama that's barely audible over the hiss of the ventilator. It's 4 A.M. and I've been here for six hours, sitting in the corner while three nurses fuss intermittently over a set of intravenous drips. They're worried about the dead man's health.

To me, he looks fine. His face is slack but flush, he breathes steadily, and his heart beats like a clock, despite the fact that his lungs have recently begun to leak fluid. The nurses roll the body from side to side periodically so that the liquid doesn't pool. At one point, a white plastic vest designed to clear the lungs inflates and begins to vibrate violently—as if some invisible person has seized the dead man by the shoulders and is trying to shake him awake. The rest of the time, the nurses consult monitors and watch for signs of cardiac arrest. When someone scratches the bottom of the dead man's foot, it twitches.

None of this is what I expected from an organ transplant. When I arrived last night at this Northern California hospital I was prepared to see a fast-paced surgery culminating in renewal: the mortally ill patient restored to glorious health. In all my preliminary research on transplants, the dead man was rarely mentioned. Even doctors I spoke with avoided the subject, and popular accounts I came across ducked the matter of provenance altogether. In the movies, for instance, surgeons tended to say it would take time to "find" a heart—as though one had been hidden behind a tree or misplaced along with the car keys. Insofar as corpses came up, it was only in anxious reference to the would-be recipient whose time was running out.

In the dead man's room, a different calculus is unfolding. Here the organ is the patient, and the patient a mere container, the safest place to store body parts until surgeons are ready to use them. It can be more than a day from the time a donor dies until his organs are harvested—the surgery alone takes hours, not to mention the time needed to do blood tests, match tissue, and fly in special surgical teams for the evisceration. And yet, a heart lasts at most six hours outside the body, even after it has been kneaded, flushed with preservatives, and packed in a cooler. Organs left on ice too long tend to perform poorly in their new environment, and doctors are picky about which viscera they're willing to work with. Even an ailing cadaver is a better container than a cooler.

These conditions create a strange medical specialty. Rather than extracting this man's vitals right away, the hospital contacts the California Transplant Donor Network, which dispatches a procurement team to begin "donor maintenance": the process of artificially supporting a dead body until recipients are ready. When the parathyroid gland stops regulating calcium, key to keeping the heart pumping, the team sends the proper amount down an intravenous drip. When blood pressure drops, they add vasoconstrictors, which contract the blood vessels. Normally the brain would compensate for a decrease in blood pressure, but with it out of commission, the three-nurse procurement team must take over.

In this case, the eroding balance will have to be sustained for almost 24 hours. The goal is to fool the body into believing that it's alive and well, even as everything is falling apart. As one crew member concedes, "It's unbelievable that all this stuff is being done to a dead person."

Unbelievable and, to me, somehow barbaric. Sustaining a dead body until its organs can be harvested is a tricky process requiring the latest in medical technology. But it's also a distinct anachronism in an era when medicine is becoming less and less invasive. Fixing blocked coronary arteries, which not long ago required prying a patient's chest open with a saw and spreader, can now be accomplished with a tiny stent delivered to the heart on a slender wire threaded up the leg. Exploratory surgery has given way to robot cameras and high-resolution imaging. Already, we are eyeing the tantalizing summit of gene therapy, where diseases are cured even before they do damage. Compared with such microscale cures, transplants—which consist of salvaging entire organs from a heart-beating cadaver and sewing them into a different body—seem crudely mechanical, even medieval.

"To let an organ reach a state where the only solution is to cut it out is not progress; it's a failure of medicine," says pathologist Neil Theise of NYU. Theise, who was the first researcher to demonstrate that stem cells can become liver cells in humans, argues that the future of transplantation lies in regeneration. Within five years, he estimates, we'll be able to instruct the body to send stem cells to the liver from the store that exists in bone marrow, hopefully countering the effects of a disease like hepatitis A or B and letting the body heal itself. And numerous researchers are forging similar paths. One outspoken surgeon, Richard Satava from the University of Washington, says that medicine is only now catching on to the fundamental lesson of modern industry, which is that when our car alternator breaks, we get a brand new one. Transplantation, he argues, is a dying art.

Few researchers predict that human-harvested organs will become obsolete anytime soon, however; one cardiovascular pathologist, Charles Murry, says we'll still be using them a century from now. But it's reasonable to expect—and hope for—an alternative. "I don't think anybody enjoys recovering organs," Murry says frankly. "You tell yourself it's for a good cause, which it is, a very good cause, but you're still butchering a human."

Intensive care is not a good place to spend the evening. Tonight, the ward has perhaps 12 patients, including a woman who moans constantly and a deathly pale man who reportedly jumped out the window of a moving Greyhound bus. The absence of clocks and the always-on lights create a casino-like timelessness. In the staff lounge, which smells of stale pizza, a lone nurse corners me and describes watching a man bleed to death ("He was conscious. He knew what was happening"), and announces, sotto voce, that she knows of South American organ brokers who charge $60,000 for a heart, then swap it for a baboon's.

Although I don't admit it to the procurement team, I've grown attached to the dead man. There's something vulnerable about his rumpled hair and middle-aged body, naked save a waist-high sheet. Under the hospital lights, everything is exposed: the muscular arms gone flabby above the elbow; the legs, wiry and lean, foreshortened under a powerful torso. It's the body of a man in his fifties, simultaneously bullish and elfin. One foot, the right, peeps out from the sheet, and for a brief moment I want to hold it and rub the toes that must be cold—a hopeless gesture of consolation.

Organ support is about staving off entropy. In the moments after death, a cascade of changes sweeps over the body. Potassium diminishes and salt accumulates, drawing fluid into cells. Sugar builds up in the blood. With the pituitary system offline, the heart fills with lactic acid like the muscles of an exhausted runner. Free radicals circulate unchecked and disrupt other cells, in effect causing the body to rust. The process quickly becomes irreversible. As cell membranes grow porous, a "death gene" is activated and damaged cells begin to self-destruct. All this happens in minutes.

When transplant activists talk about an organ shortage, it's usually to lament how few people are willing to donate. This is a valid worry, but it eclipses an important point, which is that the window for retrieving a viable organ is staggeringly small. Because of how fast the body degrades once the heart stops, there's no way to recover an organ from someone who dies at home, in a car, in an ambulance, or even while on the operating table. In fact, the only situation that really lends itself to harvest is brain death, which means finding an otherwise healthy patient whose brain activity has ceased but whose heart continues to beat—right up until the moment it's taken out. In short, victims of stroke or severe head injury. These cases are so rare (approximately 0.5 percent of all deaths in the US) that even if everybody in America were to become a donor, they wouldn't clear the organ wait lists.

This is partly a scientific problem. Cell death remains poorly understood, and for years now, cadaveric transplants have lingered on a research plateau. While immunosuppressants have improved incrementally, transplants proceed much as they did 20 years ago. Compared with a field like psychopharmacology, the procedure has come to a near-standstill.

But there are cultural factors as well. Medicine has always reserved its glory for the living. Even among transplant surgeons, a hierarchy exists: Those who put organs into living patients have a higher status than those who extract them from the dead. One anesthesiologist confesses that his peers don't like to work on cadaveric organ recoveries. (Even brain-dead bodies require sedation, since spinal reflexes can make a corpse "buck" in surgery.) "You spend all this time monitoring the heartbeat, the blood pressure," the anesthesiologist explains. "To just turn everything off when you're done and walk out. It's bizarre."

Although the procurement team will stay up all night, I break at 4:30 A.M. for a two-hour nap on an empty bed in the ICU. The nurse removes a wrinkled top sheet but leaves the bottom one. Doctors sleep like this all the time, I know, catnapping on gurneys, but I can't shake the feeling of climbing onto my deathbed. The room is identical to the one I've been sitting in for the past eight hours, and I'd prefer to sleep almost anywhere else—in the nurses lounge or even on the small outside balcony. Instead, I lie down in my clothes and pull the sheet up under my arms.

For a while I read a magazine, then finally close my eyes, hoping I won't dream.

By morning, little seems to have changed, except that the commotion of chest X-rays and ultrasounds has left the dead man's hair more mussed. On both sides of his bed, vital stats scroll across screens: oxygen ratios, pulse, blood volumes.

All of this vigilance is good, of course: After all, transplants save lives. Every year, thousands of people who would otherwise die survive with organs from brain-dead donors; sometimes, doctors say, a patient's color will visibly change on the operating table once a newly attached liver begins to work. Still—and with the possible exception of kidneys—transplants have never quite lived up to their initial promise. In the early 1970s, few who received new organs lasted even a year, and most died within weeks. Even today, 22 percent of heart recipients die in less than four years, and 12 percent reject a new heart within the first few months. Those who survive are usually consigned to a lifetime regime of costly immunosuppressive drugs, some with debilitating side effects. Recipients of artificial hearts traditionally fare the worst, alongside those who receive transplants from animals. Under the circumstances, it took a weird kind of perseverance for doctors operating in 1984 to suggest sewing a walnut-sized baboon heart into a human baby. And there was grief, if not surprise, when the patient died of a morbid immune reaction just 21 days later.

By the time we head into surgery, the patient has been dead for more than 24 hours, but he still looks pink and healthy. In the operating room, all the intravenous drips are still flowing, convincing the body that everything's fine even as it's cleaved in half.

Although multiorgan transfer can involve as many as five teams in the OR at once, this time there is only one: a four-man surgical unit from Southern California. They've flown in to retrieve the liver, but because teams sometimes swap favors, they'll also remove the kidneys for a group of doctors elsewhere—saving them a last-minute, late-night flight. One of the doctors has brought a footstool for me to stand on at the head of the operating table, so that I can see over the sheet that hangs between the patient's head and body. I've been warned that the room will smell bad during the "opening," like flesh and burning bone—an odor that has something in common with a dentist's drill. Behind me, the anesthesiologist checks the dead man's mask and confirms that he's sedated. The surgery will take four hours, and the doctors have arranged for the score of Game Five of the World Series to be phoned in at intervals.

I've heard that transplant doctors are the endurance athletes of medicine, and the longer I stand on the stool, the better I understand the comparison. Below me, the rib cage has been split, and I can see the heart, strangely yellow, beating inside a cave of red muscle. It doesn't beat forward, as I expect, but knocks anxiously back and forth like a small animal trapped in a cage. Farther down, the doctors rummage under the slough of intestines as though through a poorly organized toolbox. When I tell the anes-thesiologist that the heart is beautiful, he says that livers are the transplants to watch. "Hearts are slash and burn," he shrugs, adjusting a dial. "No finesse."

Two hours pass, and the surgeons make progress. Despite the procurement team's best efforts, however, most of the organs have already been lost. The pancreas was deemed too old before surgery. One lung was bad at the outset, and the other turned out to be too big for the only matching recipients—a short list given the donor's rare blood type. At 7 this morning, the heart went bust after someone at the receiving hospital suggested a shot of thyroid hormone, shown in some studies to stimulate contractions—but even before then, the surgeon had had second thoughts. A 54-year-old heart can't travel far—and this one was already questionable—but the hospital may have thought this would improve its chances. Instead, the dead man's pulse shot to 140, and his blood began circulating so fast it nearly ruptured his arteries. Now the heart will go to Cryolife, a biosupply company that irradiates and freeze-dries the valves, then packages them for sale to hospitals in screw-top jars. The kidneys have remained healthy enough to be passed on—one to a man who will soon be in line for a pancreas, the other to a 42-year-old woman.

Both kidneys have been packed off in quart-sized plastic jars. Originally, the liver was going to a nearby hospital, but an ultrasound suggested it was hyperechoic, or fatty. On the second pass, it was accepted by a doctor in Southern California and ensconced in a bag of icy slurry.

The liver is enormous—it looks like a polished stone, flat and purplish—and with it gone, the body seems eerily empty, although the heart continues to beat. Watching this pumping vessel makes me oddly anxious. It's sped up slightly, as though sensing what will happen next. Below me, the man's face is still flushed. He's the one I wish would survive, I realize, even though there was never any chance of that. Meanwhile, the head surgeon has walked away. He's busy examining the liver and relaying a description over the phone to the doctor who will perform the attachment. Almost unnoticed, an aide clamps the arteries above and below the heart, and cuts. The patient's face doesn't move, but its pinkness drains to a waxy yellow. After 24 hours, the dead man finally looks dead.

Once all the organs are out, the tempo picks up in the operating room. The heart is packed in a cardboard box also loaded with the kidneys, which are traveling by Learjet to a city a few hundred miles away. Someday, I'm convinced, transporting organs in coolers will seem as strange and outdated as putting a patient in an iron lung. In the meantime, transplants will survive: a vehicle, like the dead man, to get us to a better place. As an assistant closes, sewing up the body so that it will be ready for its funeral, I get on the plane with the heart and the kidneys. They've become a strange, unhealthy orange in their little jars. But no one else seems worried. "A kidney almost always perks up," someone tells me, "once we get it in a happier environment."

Topics for Thought and Discussion

1. Reread Kahn's essay, making a list of metaphors she uses. Note when she uses them and what work they seem to do for her as she presents her information.
2. From the opening line of the essay, the dead man is a character in this "story." What role does he play? Why does Kahn develop and treat the dead man as she does? How does he serve her?
3. This essay is primarily an extended description of the process by which organs are kept healthy, harvested, and sent on to their recipients. Why does Kahn want you to know this? Why write this essay?
4. Kahn uses the term *barbaric* to describe the whole procedure she watches— from the tending to the dead man to the cutting out of his organs. In what ways is this a barbaric spectacle? Should we think of it another way, as well?

Suggestions for Writing

1. Write an essay in which you evaluate the techniques that Kahn uses in this essay. What are the various ways she makes this description vibrant?
2. Write a summary of this essay. How do you determine what is essential in an article like this one?
3. Write a process description using techniques you've identified in Kahn's essay. Try to find something to describe from your own experience that has the same edgy sense of taboo that Kahn's description has.

Bodies and Genes: Making Connections

1. Using Everett and Begley, discuss the utility and the desirability of manipulating and constructing the human body. What are the pros and cons? Is it different when we are discussing constructing someone else (a child, for instance) than it is when we decide to use technology to change something about ourselves?

2. Is there a difference between the kind of body manipulation discussed in this chapter, involving drugs and genes, and that discussed in Chapter 5 by John Hockenberry, involving machines and other hardware? Why or why not? Explain.

3. It seems a very small step from the technologies described by David Ewing Duncan and those discussed by Sharon Begley. Are the social issues raised by DNA testing the same as those raised by manipulating the genes of a child? Compare and contrast the social issues these two essays raise.

4. Singer argues that cloning ought to be allowed to go forward, and doesn't imagine it will have much effect on society. What is it about cloning that seems to particularly scare people? How, in its essential value, is cloning different from other types of reproduction? Using at least two other essays from this chapter as support, discuss cloning as a form of reproduction and as a social issue.

5. Science writing often relies heavily on description, and Jennifer Kahn's "Stripped for Parts" is a good example. Using that essay and at least two others from this chapter, evaluate how description, as a rhetorical strategy, is used by science writers.

Science and the Environment

This chapter asks you to consider the relationship between science and the natural world. The environmental movement of the second half of the twentieth century made us all aware of the importance to us of the natural environment, and fixed concern for the environment as a major social and political issue. None of us, now, believes that we can be entirely separate from the natural world, and most of us recognize that we are a part of the ecology of our particular place, and also a part of the ecosystem of the world. Our ways of living, and our actions and behaviors, impact not only us and our fellow human beings, but also the natural world within which we live, with all of its plants, animals, and complex nutrient, water, and chemical cycles. Regardless of how you approach the environment and environmentalism politically, you understand the importance of clean air, clean water, biodiversity, habitat protection, endangered wildlife protections, and the like. But being sympathetic to the environment, and understanding its importance, doesn't answer the question that lies at the heart of this chapter. The environment is important, but what is the relationship between science and the environment?

As we will see from the readings that make up this chapter, the relationship between science and the environment is a complex one. On one hand, science helps us describe the environment and understand it. We see this role of science in almost all of the essays that follow. In Elizabeth Kolbert's "Ice Memory," we see climatologists and physicists attempting to explain the geological history of Earth and its climate by drilling into the massive Greenland ice sheet. In Jared Diamond's "Easter Island's End," we see archaeologists, paleobotanists, historians, and biologists uncovering the mystery of Easter Island's civilization and its demise. Nicholas D. Kristof relies on climatologists and computer modeling to warn us about global warming; Alan Weisman makes heavy use of scientists of all types as he sets himself the task of describing what would happen to the world if humans were to suddenly disappear. Science, then, is extremely useful in understanding the environment and describing it. And as we see in many of the essays in this chapter, science also can be very useful in identifying problems, threats, and sources of environmental concern for us as individuals and for us as a species.

But science is not simply a passive tool that we can use to better understand the world. If science gives us the knowledge to avoid catastrophe (as Jared Diamond tells us at the end of "Easter Island's End," the advantage that we have that the Easter Islanders did not is that we know what happened to them), it also often seems to be contributing to the catastrophes that stalk us. "Warm, Warmer, Warmest," "Easter Island's End," "Thinking Like a Mountain," "The Earth Without People," and "Ice Memory" present us with worlds that are in some danger simply because of increasing damage caused by technology and industry, which are the results of science. Jonathan Rauch gives us yet another role for science in "Will Frankenfood Save the Planet?" Rauch argues that science, through biotechnology, has a very specific and active role to play in feeding and ultimately "saving" the world.

Science, then, seems to have a complicated and somewhat uneasy relationship with the environment. On one hand, it gives us the ability to understand and solve the problems that we have. On the other, it is perhaps the ultimate cause of much of the environmental trouble we face.

That is the tension that underlies this chapter, and the one that you ultimately must resolve for yourself, for your generation, for your species, and for your world. Science will be a part of our interchange with the natural environment. How we use it, these authors seem to say, will determine our success—or our failure.

Thinking Like a Mountain
ALDO LEOPOLD

Aldo Leopold (1887–1948), one of the founders of the modern environmental movement, was an important thinker and writer about the environment in the first half of the twentieth century. Leopold worked for twenty years for the U.S. Forest Service before moving to the University of Wisconsin at Madison, where he was chair of the Department of Wildlife Management. Leopold introduced the idea of a land ethic, and insisted on the ecological interconnection between the environment and humanity. He is best known for his book A Sand County Almanac *(1948), which had a wide impact on the environmental movement and on nature writing in general. The following essay is from this seminal book, appearing in 1948. As you read this essay, consider what it means to "think like a mountain."*

◆

A deep chesty bawl echoes from rimrock to rimrock, rolls down the mountain, and fades into the far blackness of the night. It is an outburst of wild defiant sorrow, and of contempt for all the adversities of the world.

Every living thing (and perhaps many a dead one as well) pays heed to that call. To the deer it is a reminder of the way of all flesh, to the pine a forecast of midnight scuffles and of blood upon the snow, to the coyote a promise of gleanings to come, to the cowman a threat of red ink at the bank, to the hunter a challenge of fang against bullet. Yet behind these obvious and immediate hopes and fears there lies a deeper meaning, known only to the mountain itself. Only the mountain has lived long enough to listen objectively to the howl of a wolf.

Those unable to decipher the hidden meaning know nevertheless that it is there, for it is felt in all wolf country, and distinguishes that country from all other land. It tingles in the spine of all who hear wolves by night, or who scan their tracks by day. Even without sight or sound of wolf, it is implicit in a hundred small events: the midnight whinny of a pack horse, the rattle of rolling rocks, the bound of a fleeing deer, the way shadows lie under the spruces. Only the ineducable tyro can fail to sense the presence or absence of wolves, or the fact that mountains have a secret opinion about them.

My own conviction on this score dates from the day I saw a wolf die. We were eating lunch on a high rimrock, at the foot of which a turbulent river elbowed its way. We saw what we thought was a doe fording the torrent, her breast awash in white water. When she climbed the bank toward us and shook out her tail, we realized our error: it was a wolf. A half-dozen others, evidently grown pups, sprang from the willows and all joined in a welcoming melee of wagging tails and playful maulings. What was literally a pile of wolves writhed and tumbled in the center of an open flat at the foot of our rimrock.

In those days we had never heard of passing up a chance to kill a wolf. In a second we were pumping lead into the pack, but with more excitement than accuracy: how to aim a steep downhill shot is always confusing. When our rifles were empty, the old wolf was down, and a pup was dragging a leg into impassable slide-rocks.

We reached the old wolf in time to watch a fierce green fire dying in her eyes. I realized then, and have known ever since, that there was something new to me in those eyes—something known only to her and to the mountain. I was young then, and full of trigger-itch; I thought that because fewer wolves meant more deer, that no wolves would mean hunters' paradise. But after seeing the green fire die, I sensed that neither the wolf nor the mountain agreed with such a view.

Since then I have lived to see state after state extirpate its wolves. I have watched the face of many a newly wolfless mountain, and seen the south-facing slopes wrinkle with a maze of new deer trails. I have seen every edible bush and seedling browsed, first to anaemic desuetude, and then to death. I have seen every edible tree defoliated to the height of a saddlehorn. Such a mountain looks as if someone had given God a new pruning shears, and forbidden Him all other exercise. In the end the starved bones of the hoped-for deer herd, dead of its own too-much, bleach with the bones of the dead sage, or molder under the high-lined junipers.

I now suspect that just as a deer herd lives in mortal fear of its wolves, so does a mountain live in mortal fear of its deer. And perhaps with better cause, for while a buck pulled down by wolves can be replaced in two or three years, a range pulled down by too many deer may fail of replacement in as many decades.

So also with cows. The cowman who cleans his range of wolves does not realize that he is taking over the wolf's job of trimming the herd to fit the range. He has not learned to think like a mountain. Hence we have dustbowls, and rivers washing the future into the sea.

We all strive for safety, prosperity, comfort, long life, and dullness. The deer strives with his supple legs, the cowman with trap and poison, the statesman with pen, the most of us with machines, votes, and dollars, but it all comes to the same thing: peace in our time. A measure of success in this is all well enough, and perhaps is a requisite to objective thinking, but too much safety seems to yield only danger in the long run. Perhaps this is behind Thoreau's dictum: In wildness is the salvation of the world. Perhaps this is the hidden meaning in the howl of the wolf, long known among mountains, but seldom perceived among men.

Topics for Thought and Discussion

1. One of the things that made Leopold's writing so influential to the early environmental movement was his ability to make a point while providing lush and moving description. Look carefully at the preceding essay and identify some examples of effective description. What makes it effective? What techniques does Leopold use?
2. Describe the interrelationship that Leopold sees between the wolves, the deer, the plants, and the mountain. Where do human beings fit into this web?
3. How relevant is Leopold's experience to your life? Which parts of this essay seem foreign—or dated—and which seem still important, or relevant, to you?
4. What does it mean to "think like a mountain"?

Suggestions for Writing

1. Describe a place that you love, with the purpose of teaching us something important about the web of connections of which it is a part. You may choose a natural environment or some other type of place.
2. Identify something else that we should think like and write an essay, or a position statement, from the point of view of this thing. What does the world look like from this point of view? What can you teach us about the world by writing from this point of view?

Ice Memory

ELIZABETH KOLBERT

Elizabeth Kolbert is a staff writer for The New Yorker *and before that, a columnist, writer, and bureau chief for the* New York Times. *Though she focuses particularly on politics in the New York area, and her recent book,* The Prophet of Love: And Other Tales of Power and Deceit *(2004) is a collection of essays about individuals involved in New York politics, the following essay demonstrates Kolbert's abilities as a writer and reporter of scientific topics as well. "Ice Memory" first appeared in* The New Yorker *in 2002. Many science writers use their own experience as a rhetorical strategy to get their audiences involved with larger scientific topics, and Kolbert does the same. As you read, note how she makes the transition between her own adventures in Greenland and the science that becomes the focus of this essay.*

——————————— ✦ ———————————

Ice, like water, flows, and so the North Greenland Ice-core Project, or North GRIP, lies in the center of the island, along a line known as the ice divide. This is a desolate spot eight degrees north of the Arctic Circle, but, thanks to the New York Air National Guard, not actually all that difficult to reach. The research station is open from mid-May to mid-August, and every season the Guard provides some half-dozen flights to it, using specially ski-equipped LC-130s. The planes, also outfitted with small rockets, can land directly on the ice, which stretches for hundreds of miles in every direction. (To the extent that there is a military justification for the flights, it is to keep pilots in practice; however, the main purpose of practicing seems to be to make the flights—an arrangement whose logic I could never quite fathom.) This past June, I flew up to North GRIP on a plane that was carrying several thousand feet of drilling cable, a group of glaciologists, and Denmark's then minister of research, a stout, red-haired woman named Birthe Weiss. Like the rest of us, the Minister had to sit in the hold, wearing military-issue earplugs.

One of the station's field directors, J. P. Steffensen, greeted us when we disembarked. We were dressed in huge insulated boots and heavy snow gear. Steffensen had on a pair of old sneakers, a filthy parka that was flapping open, and no gloves. Tiny icicles hung from his beard. First, he delivered a short lecture on the dangers of dehydration: "It sounds like a complete contradiction in terms—you're standing on three thousand metres of water but it's extremely dry, so make sure that you have to go and pee." Then he briefed us on camp protocol. North GRIP has two computerized toilets, from Sweden, but men were kindly requested to relieve themselves out on the ice, at a spot designated by a little red flag.

Steffensen, a Dane, runs North GRIP along with his wife, Dorthe Dahl-Jensen, whom he met on an earlier Greenland expedition. Together with a few dozen fellow-scientists—mostly Danes, but also Icelanders, Swedes, Germans, and Swiss, among others—they have spent the past six summers drilling a five-inch-wide hole from the top of the ice sheet down to the bedrock, ten thousand feet below. Their reason for wanting to do this is an interest in ancient climates. My reason for wanting to watch is perhaps best described as an interest—partly lurid, but also partly pragmatic—in apocalypse.

Over the past decade or so, there has been a shift—inevitably labelled a "paradigm shift"—in the way scientists regard the Earth's climate. The new view goes under the catchphrase "abrupt climate change," although it might more evocatively be called neo-catastrophism, after the old, Biblically inspired theories of flood and disaster. Behind it lies no particular theoretical insight— scientists have, in fact, been hard-pressed to come up with a theory to make sense of it—but it is supported by overwhelming empirical evidence, much of it gathered in Greenland. The Greenland ice cores have shown that it is a mistake to regard our own, relatively benign experience of the climate as the norm. By now, the adherents of neo-catastrophism include virtually every climatologist of any standing.

Abrupt climate changes occurred long before there was human technology, and therefore have nothing directly to do with what we refer to as global warming. Yet the discovery that for most of the past hundred thousand years the Earth's climate has been in flux, changing not gradually, or even incrementally, but violently and without warning, can't help but cast the global-warming debate in new terms. It is still possible to imagine that the Earth will slowly heat up, and that the landscape and the weather will gradually evolve in response. But it is also possible that the change will come, as it has in the past, in the form of something much worse.

Greenland, the world's largest island, is nearly four times the size of France—eight hundred and forty thousand square miles— and except for its southern tip lies above the Arctic Circle. The first Europeans to make a stab at settling it were the Norse, under the leadership of Erik the Red, who, perhaps deliberately, gave the island its misleading name. In the year 985, he arrived with twenty-five ships and nearly seven hundred followers. (Erik had left Norway when his father was exiled for killing a man, and then was himself exiled from Iceland for killing several more.) The Norse established two settlements, the Eastern Settlement, which was actually in the south, and the Western Settlement, which was to the north of that. For roughly four hundred years, they managed to scrape by, hunting, raising livestock, and making occasional logging expeditions to the coast of Canada. But then something went wrong. The last written record of them is an Icelandic affidavit regarding the marriage of Thorstein

Ólafsson and Sigríður Björnsdóttir, which took place in the Eastern Settlement on the "Second Sunday after the Mass of the Cross" in the autumn of 1408.

These days, the island has fifty-six thousand inhabitants, most of them Inuit, and almost a quarter live in the capital, Nuuk, about four hundred miles up the western coast. Since the late 1970s, Greenland has enjoyed a measure of home rule, but the Danes, who consider the island a province, still spend the equivalent of three hundred and forty million dollars a year to support it. The result is a thin and not entirely convincing First World veneer. Greenland has almost no agriculture or industry or, for that matter, roads. Following Inuit tradition, private ownership of land is not allowed, although it is possible to buy a house, an expensive proposition in a place where even the sewage pipes have to be insulated.

More than eighty percent of Greenland is covered by ice. Locked into this enormous glacier is eight percent of the Earth's freshwater supply: enough, were it to melt, to raise sea levels around the world by more than twenty feet. Except for researchers in the summer, no one lives on the ice, or even ventures out onto it very often. (The edges are riddled with crevasses large enough to swallow a dog sled, or, should the occasion arise, a five-ton truck.)

Like all glaciers, the Greenland ice sheet is made up entirely of accumulated snow. The most recent layers are thick and airy, while the older layers are thin and dense, which means that to drill down through the ice is to descend backward in time, at first gradually and then much more rapidly. A hundred and thirty-eight feet down, there is snow dating from the American Civil War; some twenty-five hundred feet down, snow from the days of Plato; and, five thousand three hundred and fifty feet down, from the time when prehistoric painters were decorating the caves of Lascaux. At the very bottom, there is snow that fell on Greenland before the last ice age, which began more than a hundred thousand years ago.

As the snow is compressed, its crystal structure changes to ice. (Two thousand feet down, there is so much pressure on the ice that a sample drawn to the surface will, if mishandled, fracture, and in some cases even explode.) But in most other respects the snow remains unchanged, a relic of the climate that first formed it. In the Greenland ice there is volcanic ash from Krakatau, lead pollution from ancient Roman smelters, and dust blown in from Mongolia on ice-age winds. Every layer also contains tiny bubbles of trapped air, each of them a sample of a past atmosphere.

All across the Earth, there are, of course, traces of climate history—buried in lake sediments, deposited in ancient beetle casings, piled up on the floor of the oceans. The distinguishing feature of the Greenland ice, and what separates it from other ice, including ice extracted from the Antarctic, is its extraordinary resolution.

Even in summer, when the sun never sets, the snow doesn't melt in central Greenland, though during a clear day some of the top layer will evaporate. Then at night—or what passes for night—this moisture will refreeze. The immediate effect is lovely to behold: one morning, I was wandering around North GRIP at about five o'clock, and I saw the hoarfrost growing in lacy patterns underfoot. As the summer snow gets buried under winter snow, it maintains its distinctive appearance; in a snow pit, summer layers show up as both coarser and airier than winter ones. It turns out that even after thousands of years the difference between summer snow and winter snow can be distinguished. Thus, simply by counting backward it is possible to date each layer of ice and also the climatological information embedded in it.

The North Greenland Ice-core Project consists of six cherry-red tents arrayed around a black geodesic dome that was purchased, mail order, from Minnesota. In front of the dome, someone has planted the standard jokey symbol of isolation, a milepost that shows Kangerlussuaq, the nearest town, to be nine hundred kilometres away. Nearby stands the standard jokey symbol of the cold, a plywood palm tree. The view on all sides is exactly the same: an utterly flat stretch of white which could be described as sublime or, alternatively, as merely bleak.

Beneath the camp, an eighty-foot-long tunnel leads down to what is known as the drilling room. This chamber has been hollowed out of the ice, and inside the temperature never rises above fourteen degrees. A few years ago, foot-thick pine beams were added to reinforce the ceiling, but the weight of the snow piling up on top has grown so great that the beams have splintered. Because of the way the ice moves, the chamber, which is lit by overhead lights and filled with electronic equipment, is not just being buried but is also slowly shrinking and at the same time sinking.

Drilling begins at North GRIP every morning at eight. The first task of the day is to lower the drill, a twelve-foot-long tube with big metal teeth on one end, down to the bottom of the borehole. Once in position, the drill can be set spinning so that an ice cylinder gradually forms within it. This, in turn, can be pulled up to the surface by means of a steel cable.

The first time I went down to watch the process, a glaciologist from Iceland and another from Germany were manning the controls. At the depth they had reached—nine thousand six hundred and eighty feet—it took an hour for the drill just to descend. During that period, there was not much for the two men to do except monitor the computer, which sat on a little heating pad, and listen to Abba. The ice near the bottom of the hole was warmer than expected, and it had been breaking badly. "The word 'stuck' is not in our vocabulary," the Icelander, Thorsteinn Thorsteinsson, told me, with a nervous giggle. Eventually, the drillers managed to pull out a short piece of core—about two feet—to show Birthe Weiss, who arrived in the chamber wearing a red snowsuit. To me, it looked a lot like a two-foot-long cylinder of ordinary ice, except that it was heavily scored around the edges. It was made up of snow that had fallen a hundred and five thousand years ago, Thorsteinsson said. Weiss exclaimed something in Danish and seemed suitably impressed.

After a piece of core comes up, it is packed in a plastic tube, put in an insulated crate, and shipped out on the next LC-130 to Kangerlussuaq. From there, it is flown to Denmark, where it is stored in a refrigerated vault at the University of Copenhagen, to be cut up later for analysis. Inevitably, more researchers want a piece of the core than there are pieces to give out. A small library of papers has been written on the various gases and dust particles and radioactive by-products that have been trapped in the ice. These papers have shown that the concentration of greenhouse gases in the atmosphere has fluctuated over time, and that these fluctuations have occurred roughly in tandem with changes in the climate. But the crucial insight has to do with the ice itself.

Water occurs naturally in several isotopic forms, depending on the hydrogen and oxygen atoms that joined together to make it. Typically, hydrogen has one proton and an atomic weight of 1, but when its nucleus also contains a neutron and it has an atomic weight of 2, it produces heavy water, which is used in nuclear reactors. Oxygen generally has eight neutrons and an atomic weight of 16, but it also comes in another stable version, with two extra neutrons and an atomic weight of 18. In any given water sample, the lighter 16-O atoms will vastly outnumber the heavier 18-O atoms, but by how much, exactly, is variable. In the early 1960s, Willi Dansgaard, a Danish chemist, proved that the ratio between the two in rainwater was related to the temperature. Dansgaard took samples of rain from around the world and demonstrated that, by running them through a mass spectrometer, he could in most cases arrive at the average temperature of the spot where they had fallen. Subsequently, he showed that this same technique could be applied to ice and, in particular, to the Greenland ice sheet.

Going back over the past ten thousand years, the Greenland 18-O record shows lots of bumps and squiggles. There is, for example, a slight but perceptible increase in temperature in the early years of the Middle Ages, which leads to what has become known as the Medieval Warm Period, when the English planted vineyards and the Norse established their Greenland settlements. And there's a dip some six or seven hundred years later, corresponding to the Little Ice Age, which killed off the vineyards and, most likely, led to the demise of the Greenland Norse. But the variation is limited. Between the Medieval Warm Period and the Little Ice Age, Greenland's average temperature fell by only a few degrees. Its average temperature today, meanwhile, is not very different from what it was ten millennia ago, when our ancestors stopped doing whatever it was that they had been doing and learned to plant crops.

It's hard to look much farther back in the record, however, without feeling a little queasy. About twenty thousand years ago, the Earth was still in the grip of the last ice age. During this period, called the Wisconsin by American scientists, ice sheets covered nearly a third of the world's landmass, reaching as far south as New York City.

The transition out of the Wisconsin is preserved in great detail in the Greenland ice. What the record shows is that it was a period of intense instability. The temperature did not rise slowly, or even steadily; instead, the climate flipped several times from temperate conditions back into those of an ice age, and then back again. Around fifteen thousand years ago, Greenland abruptly warmed by sixteen degrees in fifty years or less. In one particularly traumatic episode some twelve thousand years ago, the mean temperature in Greenland shot up by fifteen degrees in a single decade.

If we go back farther still, the picture is no more comforting. Even as much of Europe and North America lay buried under glaciers, the temperature in Greenland was oscillating wildly, sometimes in spikes of ten degrees, sometimes in spikes of twenty. In an effort to convey the erratic nature of these changes, Richard Alley, a geophysicist who is leading a National Academy of Sciences panel on abrupt climate change, has compared the climate to a light switch being toyed with by an impish three-year-old. (The panel recently issued a report warning of the possibility of "large, abrupt, and unwelcome" climate changes.) He has also likened it to a freakish carnival ride. "Dozens of rapid changes litter the record of the last hundred thousand years," he observed. "If you can possibly imagine the spectacle of some really stupid person (or, better, a mannequin) bungee jumping off the side of a moving roller-coaster car, you can begin to picture the climate."

The first Greenland ice core was drilled in the mid-1960s, at a U.S. military installation called Camp Century. The goal was not to challenge established views of the Earth's climate. Rather, the core was an instance of what Thomas Kuhn, in his famous essay "The Structure of Scientific Revolutions," called "normal science"—although it would perhaps be unfair to label anything associated with Camp Century as normal.

Built in 1959 in the northwestern corner of Greenland, the camp was a semi-secret research station for a very cold war. It featured a tunnel eleven hundred feet long and twenty-six feet wide, called Main Street, which led to dormitories, a ten-bed hospital, a mess hall, a skating rink, and a store that sold perfume to send back home—all under the ice. (A favorite camp joke was that there was a girl behind every tree.) Powering the enterprise was a portable nuclear reactor. "In an era in which it has become fashionable to describe the democratic countries as soft or lazy, the fantastic ice city is a wholesome answer to such nonsensical clichés," one particularly patriotic visitor reported. (The camp, which closed after a decade in operation, has since been obliterated by the movement of the ice.)

The U.S. Army Corps of Engineers led the camp's ice-coring effort. The Americans managed to drill their way right down to the bottom of the ice sheet, but when they were finished they didn't quite know what to do with the core they had produced. It fell to Chester Langway, a glaciologist who was working for the Corps's Cold Regions Research and Engineering Laboratory, to figure something out. Langway is now semi-retired and operates a small antique store on Cape Cod. He recalled travelling all around the country, attempting to drum up interest. "Some people looked at it and they said, 'That's just ice,' which it's not," he told me. Eventually, he and Dansgaard got in touch, and together the two men made the first study of the core.

At the time, one of the central questions in climate research was how ice ages began and how they ended. One theory, first worked out in detail in the nineteen-twenties by a Serbian astrophysicist named Milutin Milankovitch, was that glaciers advance and retreat in response to slight, periodic changes in the Earth's orbit. These changes alter the distribution of sunlight at various latitudes during various seasons, and Milankovitch predicted that the strongest effects would be observed at intervals of nineteen thousand, twenty-three thousand, forty-one thousand, and a hundred thousand years.

Dansgaard and Langway's study of the Camp Century core confirmed these so-called Milankovitch cycles but also gave evidence of the climate's carnival-ride-like reversals. This evidence was dismissed by many as an idiosyncrasy of the polar ice. Sigfus Johnsen was a student of Dansgaard's who worked with him on the Camp Century core, and he happened to be travelling to North GRIP at the same time I was. Johnsen is now sixty-one, with wispy white hair and pale-blue eyes, and looks like a slightly dissolute Santa. He told me that the scientists working on the Camp Century core weren't sure themselves what to make of what they had found. "It was too incredible, something we didn't expect at all," he said.

It took fifteen years for anyone to drill another Greenland core. Largely because of Dansgaard and Langway's friendship, this second core was a European-American collaboration. It was drilled at an American radar base, Dye 3, a spot chosen for budgetary rather than scientific reasons, and from the outset everyone involved in the project knew that the location was a problem. Dye 3 was so close to the coast that the oldest layers of ice had mostly flowed out to sea. Nevertheless, the core confirmed all the most significant Camp Century results, demonstrating that findings which had seemed anomalous were at least reproducible. When the Dye 3 results were published, in the early 1980s, they set off what is perhaps best described as an ice rush, and the spirit of international coöperation quickly broke down. The Europeans decided to drill a new core where the ice is most stable, along the ice divide, and the Americans decided to do the same thing some twenty miles away.

Theorists are still struggling to catch up with the data from those two cores, the first of which was completed in 1992 and the second a year later. No known external force, or even any that has been hypothesized, seems capable of yanking the temperature back and forth as violently, and as often, as these cores have shown to be the case. Somehow, the climate system—through some vast and terrible feedback loop—must, it is now assumed, be capable of generating its own instabilities. The most popular hypothesis is that the oceans are responsible. Currents like the Gulf Stream transfer heat in huge quantities from the tropics toward the poles, and if this circulation pattern could somehow be shut off—by, say, a sudden influx of freshwater—it would have a swift and dramatic impact. Computer modellers have tried to reproduce such a shutdown, with some success. But once the ocean circulation comes to a halt, modellers have had a hard time getting it to start up again. "We are in a state now where the more we know, the more it becomes clear how little we really understand about the system," the oceanographer Jochem Marotzke told me.

For at least half a million years, and probably a lot longer, warm periods and ice ages have alternated according to a fairly regular, if punishing, pattern: ten thousand years of warmth, followed by ninety thousand years of cold. The current warm period, the Holocene, is now ten thousand years old, and, all things being equal—which is to say had we not interfered with the pattern by burning fossil fuels—we should now be heading toward another ice age.

As a continuous temperature record, the Greenland ice gives out at about a hundred and fifteen thousand years ago, at a moment in the climate cycle roughly analogous to our own—the end of the last interglacial period, which the Europeans call the Eemian and the Americans the Sangamon. What this part of the record suggests is disputed. The European core seemed to indicate that the period ended with a cataclysm even worse than the wild temperature swings that occurred at the end of the Wisconsin. During this cold snap, temperatures appear to have plunged from warmer than they are today to the coldest levels of the ice age, all within a matter of a few decades, and then to have climbed back up again, equally dramatically, a century or so later. The Europeans euphemistically dubbed this instant Eemian ice age Event One.

The Americans, however, determined that at the bottom of their core the ice had folded in on itself as it flowed, making accurate interpretation impossible. The two groups got together for a conference in Wolfeboro, New Hampshire, in 1995, and agreed on virtually everything except for Event One. Steffensen, North GRIP's field leader, recalls that the Europeans, who had rushed to publish their results, were crestfallen to have them discredited. He remembers going down to the hotel bar in Wolfeboro with some colleagues and thinking, The Eemian is dead; we have to bury it. Then, he told me, "We had a few drinks, and it came back to life."

The driving purpose behind North GRIP is to drill a core that will finally provide a clean record of the last interglacial period and validate Event One. Doing so would obviously be significant for several reasons: retrospectively, it would show temperature instabilities in yet another part of the climate cycle, and prospectively it would seem to suggest a cataclysm in our own not too distant future. "In the first place, if we find this it will scare the hell out of us," Sigfus Johnsen told me. But getting back to the Eemian remains a daunting technical challenge. In the summer of 1997, after the drillers at North GRIP had reached nearly a mile deep, the drill got stuck and could not be retrieved. The next summer, they had to start all over again. They were almost two miles down when, in July, 2000, the drill got stuck again. At that point, they poured antifreeze down the hole, and eventually managed to yank the drill back up, but by then the weather was turning, and they had to close the station for the season. When I arrived, last June, they had finally finished bailing out the antifreeze and resumed drilling. Still, things were not going well. Something—presumably geothermal heat from some previously undetected "hot spot"—was warming the ice from below, making drilling extremely difficult.

Everyone I met at North GRIP was quite open about saying he believed—and hoped—that Event One had indeed taken place. Apparently, the prospect of having spent six summers up on the ice with essentially nothing to show for it was more disturbing than any fate that might lie in store for the planet. I found myself feeling torn as well. On the one hand, Event One did not sound like much to look forward to. On the other, it did seem to offer a certain perverse consolation: global warming versus Event One—either way, things were bound to end badly. I proposed this idea to Steffensen. Unimpressed, he pointed out that, if you believed the climate to be inherently unstable, the last thing you'd want to do is conduct a vast unsupervised experiment on it, and he went on to explain that it would be wrong to think of global warming and Event One as alternatives. It is entirely possible, if apparently paradoxical, that global warming could produce a precipitous cooling, at least in Europe and parts of North America, by, say, shutting down the Gulf Stream. It is also possible that it could push the climate into an unstable mode, leading, especially in the upper latitudes, to a period of wild temperature swings of the sort that characterized the end of the last ice age. Finally, it is possible that we have changed the atmosphere so much—carbon-dioxide levels are approaching those of the age of the dinosaurs—that we will enter a new climate phase altogether. During the Cretaceous period, there were no major ice sheets, or ice ages, and much of the planet was covered with steamy swamps. To the extent that the historical record is any guide, the result of any climate change is unlikely to be a happy one. Steffensen recited to me an old Danish saying, whose pertinence I didn't entirely understand, but which nevertheless stuck with me. He translated it as "Pissing in your pants will only keep you warm for so long."

Life at North GRIP, if not exactly comfortable, is at least well supplied. Lunch the day I arrived was a fish stew prepared in a delicate tomato base. In the midafternoon, there was coffee and cake; then, in the evening, cocktails, which were served in a chamber hollowed out of the snowpack, to relieve pressure on the drilling room. The German driller had provided a recipe for *Glühwein*, and everyone—scientists, graduate students, the Danish minister and her entourage, and the crew from the Air National Guard—was standing around in the dark, in cold-weather gear, drinking. ("Why do all the Danes I meet seem to come from Copenhagen?" I heard one of the pilots ask a young glaciologist.) For dinner, although I wasn't really hungry, I had a lamb chop in cream sauce, topped with diced leeks. At around midnight, the drillers finally emerged from under the ice. It was broad daylight outside, and inside the geodesic dome there was still a crowd drinking beer and smoking cigars.

As with so many recent discoveries about natural history, what seems, in the end, most surprising about the Greenland cores is exactly what might have seemed, at the outset, not to require any explanation at all. How is it that we happen to live in this, climatologically speaking, best of all possible times? On statistical grounds, it certainly seems improbable that the only period in the climate record as stable as our own *is* our own. And it seems, if anything, even more improbable that climatologists should make the discovery that we are living in this period of exceptional stability at the very moment when, by their own calculations, it is likely nearing an end.

But to approach the problem in this way is to fail to realize the extent to which we are ourselves a product of the climate record. Scientists were once puzzled by the evidence in lake sediments of the return of Arctic flowers to northern Europe at a time when the ice age had been over for more than a thousand years. Now those lake sediments seem to provide exemplary evidence of how the climate shifted and shifted again during that period. The reappearance of cold-loving beetles in the British Isles and the resurgence of tiny, cold-tolerant foraminifers in the North Atlantic can also be interpreted in these terms. And so, too, arguably, can the rise of human civilization and, by extension, the progress of climatology.

One night, I was sitting in the geodesic dome at North GRIP with Steffensen. He was coming to the end of a month on the ice, and had the weatherbeaten look of someone who has spent too long at sea. "If you look at the paleoclimatic output of ice cores, it has really changed the picture of the world, our view of past climates, and of human evolution," he said, while, next to us, a group of graduate students played board games and listened to the soundtrack from "Buena Vista Social Club." "Now you're able to put human evolution into a climatic framework. You can ask, Why did human beings not make civilization fifty thousand years ago? You know that they had just as big brains as we have today. When you put it in a climatic framework, you can say, Well, it was the ice age. And also this ice age was so climatically unstable that each time you had the beginning of a culture they had to move. Then comes the present interglacial—ten thousand years of very stable climate. The perfect conditions for agriculture. If you look at it, it's amazing. Civilizations in Persia, in China, and in India start at the same time, maybe six thousand years ago. They all developed writing and they all developed religion and they all built cities, all at the same time, because the climate was stable. I think that if the climate would have been stable fifty thousand years ago it would have started then. But they had no chance."

The only way into North GRIP is through Kangerlussuaq, and it is the only way out as well. The name means "very long fjord," and Kangerlussuaq does indeed lie at the end of a hundred-and-eighty-mile-long fjord, which opens out into the Davis Strait. The setting is spectacular—snow-covered mountains rising out of a glacial plain. The town itself, however, is mostly poured concrete and corrugated iron, the remains of a now defunct American Air Force base that was called Sonderstrom, or, for short, Sondy. The night I arrived, I was invited to dinner at the town's best restaurant, at the airport. I missed the hors d'oeuvres, which had included whale skin, but arrived in time for the entrée, which was reindeer. When I left, at about 9 P.M., I saw a musk ox on the hillside just beyond the terminal.

The edge of the ice sheet lies some ten miles away, and it can be seen—a ghostly white blur in the distance—by climbing just about any hill. After returning from North GRIP, I had a few days to spend in Kangerlussuaq, and one afternoon I hitched a ride out to the ice with some glaciologists who were also awaiting flights home. We took a dirt road that had been built by Volkswagen, and someone put Pink Floyd on the truck's CD player. Almost as soon as we got out of town, we were in the wild, cutting through fields of tiny purple Arctic rhododendron.

The Volkswagen road goes all the way up onto the ice sheet and ends a hundred miles later at a test track. (Rumor has it that there is also a three-star hotel and restaurant in a modular building that was trucked out to the site.) We stopped far short of that, at a fast-running river, brown with silt. The ice sheet rose up beyond it, like a wall, two hundred feet high. It was a startling shade of blue. One of the glaciologists explained that the color was an effect of the ice's peculiar density. Up at North GRIP, a set of poles that are slowly drifting apart mark the glacier's flow; at the edge of the ice, the same process produces more dramatic results. As we were talking, a huge section of the wall tore free and crashed into the river, sprinkling us with ice chips.

Although it was a clear blue day, a chill wind was blowing off the glacier, and, after we had all finished taking pictures, we climbed back into the truck. Soon we passed a small herd of reindeer that had come down to drink at a half-frozen lake, and then, a little later, the remains of a recent reindeer hunt—a pile of hooves with the fur still on them. The only other signs of human life we encountered were some ancient Inuit graves, or cairns; traditionally, Greenlanders buried their dead under mounds of rocks, a concession to the fact that most of the year the ground is frozen solid.

Humans are a remarkably resourceful species. We have spread into every region of the globe that is remotely habitable, and some, like Greenland, that aren't even that. The fact that we have managed this feat in an era of exceptional climate stability does not diminish the accomplishment, but it does make it seem that much more tenuous. As we drove back to Kangerlussuaq, listening to Pink Floyd—"Hey you, out there in the cold / Getting lonely, getting old / Can you feel me?"—I found myself thinking again about the Greenland Norse. They had arrived on the island at a moment of uncharacteristically benign weather, but they wouldn't have had any way of knowing this. Then the weather turned, and they were gone.

Topics for Thought and Discussion

1. In this article, Kolbert uses an interesting combination of immediate description (of facilities, of music, of landscape, of people), history (of science, of humans, of climate), and storytelling. Choose one of these techniques and describe how Kolbert uses it, why, and what work it does for her.

2. What is "abrupt climate change" and "neo-catastrophism"? How are these terms related to Kolbert's admitted interest in apocalypse?

3. At the end of the article, Kolbert describes a drive out along the Volkswagen road to a river at the base of the ice sheet, and this description serves as a transition into her conclusion. Why does she choose to end in this way? How are the details of that trip somehow appropriate as a way to usher us into her final thoughts?

4. In many ways Kolbert uses the Norse settlement of Greenland as an analogy for humanity in general. Explain how this analogy works.

Suggestions for Writing

1. Write a short paper in which you weave history, description, and storytelling together into a single essay, using Kolbert's technique as a model.
2. Using Kolbert's article as a source, construct a thesis for an argument paper. What kinds of arguments might you get out of the material Kolbert has given you? Once you have a thesis, make a list of potential arguments and arrange them in two columns on your page—one side supporting your position, the other opposed. Note that your argument does not have to be explicitly about climate change. It might be focused on some other element of human behavior, history, or even writing technique.

Warm, Warmer, Warmest
NICHOLAS D. KRISTOF

Nicholas D. Kristof is a columnist for the New York Times. *He has been with the* Times *since 1984, and has been Hong Kong bureau chief, Beijing bureau chief, and Tokyo bureau chief. He won a Pulitzer Prize in 1990 (with his wife, Sheryl WuDunn) for his coverage of the Tiannamen Square democracy movement. He is the author of two books:* China Wakes: The Struggle for the Soul of a Rising Power *(1995), and* Thunder from the East: Portrait of a Rising Asia *(2000), both written with Sheryl WuDunn. His columns engage with political, social, and international issues. The following essay appeared in his column in the* New York Times *in 2006. Note particularly the text structure of this essay. Why do you think the paragraphs are so short?*

———————— ✦ ————————

One of the hottest environmental battles has been over oil drilling in the coastal plain of the Arctic National Wildlife Refuge, but the sad reality is that much of the Arctic plain will probably be lost anyway in this century to rising sea levels.

That should be our paramount struggle: to stop global warming. It threatens not only the Arctic plain, but also low-lying areas around the world with 100 million inhabitants. And it could be accelerating because of the three scariest words in climate science: positive feedback loops.

Bear with me now: a positive feedback loop occurs when a small change leads to an even larger change of the same type. For example, a modest amount of warming melts ice in northern climates. But the bare ground absorbs three times as much heat as ground covered by snow or ice, so the change amplifies the original warming. Even more ice melts, more heat is absorbed, and the spiral grows.

That feedback loop is well understood and part of climate models, but others aren't.

For example, perhaps the biggest single source of uncertainty about whether Lower Manhattan will be underwater in 2100 has to do with the glaciers of Greenland. If Greenland's ice sheet melted completely, that alone—over centuries—would raise the oceans by 23 feet. And those glaciers are dumping much more water into the oceans than they did a decade ago, according to two satellite surveys just published, but the studies disagree on the amounts.

Positive feedback seems to be at work. As a glacier melts a little, the water trickles down to the rock and lubricates the glacier's slide toward the sea. So, because of this and other effects, some of Greenland's glaciers are now, in glacial terms, rocketing toward the sea at 7.5 miles a year.

Here's another positive loop. The Arctic permafrost may hold 14 percent of the world's carbon, but as it melts, some of its carbon dioxide and methane are released, adding to the amount of greenhouse gases. So more permafrost melts.

Likewise, millions of years ago, warming oceans with vast amounts of methane in their depths had great episodes of methane belching, which added to the greenhouse effect then. I don't expect the oceans to burp in the same massive way tomorrow, but if they did, no one would know how to fit those unmannerly oceans into a climate model.

Part of the challenge in modeling climate is that we're already off the charts with greenhouse gases like nitrous oxide, carbon dioxide, and methane. "We've driven them out of the range that has existed for the last one million years," noted James Hansen, NASA's top climate expert. "And the climate has not fully responded to changes that have already occurred."

In fairness, there are also negative feedback loops, which could dampen change. For example, warmer temperatures could mean more snow over Antarctica, implying an initial buildup of the Antarctic ice sheet. The added ice could slow global warming and rising sea levels. But a new study just published in Science Express says that the Antarctic ice sheet is already thinning significantly—raising more alarms and casting doubt on that negative feedback. In any case, it's clear that negative feedback loops in climatology are much less common than positive loops, which amplify change and leave our climate both unstable and vulnerable to human folly.

Still with me?

Look, I know that climate science can be—here's a shock—boring! But it's better for us to slog through it now than for coming generations to slog through the rising waters of, say, Manhattan. It may be more exciting to thump the table about Iraq or torture—or even the preservation of the Arctic National Wildlife Refuge—and those are all hugely important. But global warming may ultimately be the greatest test we face as stewards of our planet. And so far we're failing catastrophically.

"Historians of science will be brutal on us," said Jerry Mahlman, a climate expert at the National Center for Atmospheric Research. "We are right now in a state of deep denial about how severe the problem is. Political people are saying, 'Well, it's not on my watch.' They're ducking for cover, because who's going to tell the American people?"

We know what to do: energy conservation, gas taxes and carbon taxes, more renewable energy sources like wind and solar power, and new (and safe) nuclear power plants. But our political system is paralyzed in the face of what may be the single biggest challenge to our planet.

"Are we an intelligent species or not?" Dr. Mahlman asked. "Right now, the evidence is against it."

Topics for Thought and Discussion

1. Kristof often writes about political issues. In this essay, how does he use science, and in what ways is science, in the case of global warming, also a political issue?

2. Explain positive feedback loops and their importance to climate science. According to Kristof, why are positive feedback loops so dangerous? How do positive feedback loops raise the stakes in America's current approach to global warming?

3. Kristof argues that "we know what to do" about global warming. Do we? If so, why do you think we are not doing it? Why does Kristof think we are not doing it?

Suggestions for Writing

1. In a short essay, evaluate our society's response to global warming. Why have we responded as we have? What are the forces that drive us? In the course of your essay, defend or attack our collective response.

2. Referring specifically to this article, write an essay in which you describe the implicit request that Kristof is making of his audience. According to your reading, what is he asking you to do?

3. Global warming has become a political issue as well as a scientific one. Research what has been written about the issue in the last year. What seem to be the primary issues? Who is on what side? Write an argumentative paper in which you take a stand on the issue.

Will Frankenfood Save the Planet?

Jonathan Rauch

Jonathan Rauch is a widely published commentator on contemporary culture, science, and politics, and his articles have appeared in a wide variety of national and international publications. He is a senior writer and columnist for National Journal *magazine in Washington, a correspondent for* The Atlantic Monthly, *and a writer-in-residence at the Brookings Institution, a leading Washington think-tank. In addition to his prolific work in periodicals, he is also the author of many books, including* The Outnation: A Search for the Soul of Japan *(1992),* Kindly Inquisitors: The New Attacks on Free Thought *(1993),* Government's End: Why Washington Stopped Working *(1999), and most recently,* Gay Marriage: Why It Is Good for Gays, Good for Straights, and Good for America *(2004). The following essay appeared in* The Atlantic *in 2003. As you read this article, consider Rauch's take on the relationship between politics, science, and the environment.*

✦

That genetic engineering may be the most environmentally beneficial technology to have emerged in decades, or possibly centuries, is not immediately obvious. Certainly, at least, it is not obvious to the many U.S. and foreign environmental groups that regard biotechnology as a bête noire.[1] Nor is it necessarily obvious to people who grew up in cities, and who have only an inkling of what happens on a modern farm. Being agriculturally illiterate

---

[1] French for "black beast." The term has come to refer to a topic or person that is especially disliked or avoided.

myself, I set out to look at what may be, if the planet is fortunate, the farming of the future.

It was baking hot that April day. I traveled with two Virginia state soil-and-water-conservation officers and an agricultural-extension agent to an area not far from Richmond. The farmers there are national (and therefore world) leaders in the application of what is known as continuous no-till farming. In plain English, they don't plough. For thousands of years, since the dawn of the agricultural revolution, farmers have ploughed, often several times a year; and with ploughing has come runoff that pollutes rivers and blights aquatic habitat, erosion that wears away the land, and the release into the atmosphere of greenhouse gases stored in the soil. Today, at last, farmers are working out methods that have begun to make ploughing obsolete.

At about one-thirty we arrived at a 200-acre patch of farmland known as the Good Luck Tract. No one seemed to know the provenance of the name, but the best guess was that somebody had said something like "You intend to farm this? Good luck!" The land was rolling, rather than flat, and its slopes came together to form natural troughs for rainwater. Ordinarily this highly erodible land would be suitable for cows, not crops. Yet it was dense with wheat—wheat yielding almost twice what could normally be expected, and in soil that had grown richer in organic matter, and thus more nourishing to crops, even as the land was farmed. Perhaps most striking was the almost complete absence of any chemical or soil runoff. Even the beating administered in 1999 by Hurricane Floyd, which lashed the ground with nineteen inches of rain in less than twenty-four hours, produced no significant runoff or erosion. The land simply absorbed the sheets of water before they could course downhill.

At another site, a few miles away, I saw why. On land planted in corn whose shoots had only just broken the surface, Paul Davis, the extension agent, wedged a shovel into the ground and dislodged about eight inches of topsoil. Then he reached down and picked up a clump. Ploughed soil, having been stirred up and turned over again and again, becomes lifeless and homogeneous, but the clump that Davis held out was alive. I immediately noticed three squirming earthworms, one grub, and quantities of tiny white insects that looked very busy. As if in greeting, a worm defecated. "Plant-available food!" a delighted Davis exclaimed.

This soil, like that of the Good Luck Tract, had not been ploughed for years, allowing the underground ecosystem to return. Insects and roots and microorganisms had given the soil an elaborate architecture, which held the earth in place and made it a sponge for water. That was why erosion and runoff had been reduced to practically nil. Crops thrived because worms were doing the ploughing. Crop residue that was left on the ground, rather than ploughed under as usual, provided nourishment for the soil's biota and, as it decayed, enriched the soil. The farmer saved the fuel he would have used driving back and forth with a heavy plough. That saved money, and of course it also saved energy and reduced pollution. On top of all that, crop yields were better than with conventional methods.

The conservation people in Virginia were full of excitement over no-till farming. Their job was to clean up the James and York Rivers and the rest of the Chesapeake Bay watershed. Most of the sediment that clogs and clouds the rivers, and most of the fertilizer runoff that causes the algae blooms that kill fish, comes from farmland. By all but eliminating agricultural erosion and runoff—so Brian Noyes, the local conservation-district manager, told me—continuous no-till could "revolutionize" the area's water quality.

Even granting that Noyes is an enthusiast, from an environmental point of view no-till farming looks like a dramatic advance. The rub—if it is a rub—is that the widespread elimination of the plough depends on genetically modified crops.

It is only a modest exaggeration to say that as goes agriculture, so goes the planet. Of all the human activities that shape the environment, agriculture is the single most important, and it is well ahead of whatever comes second. Today about 38 percent of the earth's land area is cropland or pasture—a total that has crept upward over the past few decades as global population has grown. The increase has been gradual, only about 0.3 percent a year; but that still translates into an additional Greece or Nicaragua cultivated or grazed every year.

Farming does not go easy on the earth, and never has. To farm is to make war upon millions of plants (weeds, so-called) and animals (pests, so-called) that in the ordinary course of things would crowd out or eat or infest whatever it is a farmer is growing. Crop monocultures, as whole fields of only wheat or corn or any other single plant are called, make poor habitat and are vulnerable to disease and disaster. Although fertilizer runs off and pollutes water, farming without fertilizer will deplete and eventually exhaust the soil. Pesticides can harm the health of human beings and kill desirable or harmless bugs along with pests. Irrigation leaves behind trace elements that can accumulate and poison the soil. And on and on.

The trade-offs are fundamental. Organic farming, for example, uses no artificial fertilizer, but it does use a lot of manure, which can pollute water and contaminate food. Traditional farmers may use less herbicide, but they also do more ploughing, with all the ensuing environmental complications. Low-input agriculture uses fewer chemicals but more land. The point is not that farming is an environmental crime—it is not—but that there is no escaping the pressure it puts on the planet.

In the next half century the pressure will intensify. The United Nations, in its midrange projections, estimates that the earth's human population will grow by more than 40 percent, from 6.3 billion people today to 8.9 billion in 2050. Feeding all those people, and feeding their billion or so hungry pets (a dog or a cat is one of the first things people want once they move beyond a subsistence lifestyle), and providing the increasingly protein-rich diets that an increasingly wealthy world will expect—doing all of that will require food output to at least double, and possibly triple.

But then the story will change. According to the UN's midrange projections (which may, if anything, err somewhat on the high side), around 2050 the world's population will more or less level off. Even if the growth does not stop, it will slow. The crunch will be over. In fact, if in 2050 crop yields are still increasing, if most of the world is economically developed, and if population pressures are declining or even reversing—all of which seems reasonably likely—then the human species may at long last be able to feed itself, year in and year out, without putting any additional net stress on the environment. We might even be able to grow everything we need while reducing our agricultural footprint: returning cropland to wilderness, repairing damaged soils, restoring ecosystems, and so on. In other words, human agriculture might be placed on a sustainable footing forever: a breathtaking prospect.

The great problem, then, is to get through the next four or five decades with as little environmental damage as possible. That is where biotechnology comes in.

One day recently I drove down to southern Virginia to visit Dennis Avery and his son, Alex. The older Avery, a man in late middle age with a chinstrap beard, droopy eyes, and an intent, scholarly manner, lives on ninety-seven acres that he shares with horses, chickens, fish, cats, dogs, bluebirds, ducks, transient geese, and assorted other creatures. He is the director of global food issues at the Hudson Institute, a conservative think tank; Alex works with him, and is trained as a plant physiologist. We sat in a sunroom at the back of the house, our afternoon conversation punctuated every so often by dog snores and rooster crows. We talked for a little while about the Green Revolution, a dramatic advance in farm productivity that fed the world's burgeoning population over the past four decades, and then I asked if the challenge of the next four decades could be met.

"Well," Dennis replied, "we have tripled the world's farm output since 1960. And we're feeding twice as many people from the same land. That was a heroic achievement. But we have to do what some think is an even more difficult thing in this next forty years, because the Green Revolution had more land per person and more water per person—"

"—and more potential for increases," Alex added, "because the base that we were starting from was so much lower."

"By and large," Dennis went on, "the world's civilizations have been built around its best farmland. And we have used most of the world's good farmland. Most of the good land is already heavily fertilized. Most of the good land is already being planted with high-yield seeds. [Africa is the important exception.] Most of the good irrigation sites are used. We can't triple yields again with the technologies we're already using. And we might be lucky to get a fifty percent yield increase if we froze our technology short of biotech."

"Biotech" can refer to a number of things, but the relevant application here is genetic modification: the selective transfer of genes from one organism to another. Ordinary breeding can cross related varieties, but it cannot take a gene from a bacterium, for instance, and transfer it to a wheat plant. The organisms resulting from gene transfers are called "transgenic" by scientists—and "Frankenfood" by many greens.

Gene transfer poses risks, unquestionably. So, for that matter, does traditional crossbreeding. But many people worry that transgenic organisms might prove more unpredictable. One possibility is that transgenic crops would spread from fields into forests or other wild lands and there become environmental nuisances, or worse. A further risk is that transgenic plants might cross-pollinate with neighboring wild plants, producing "superweeds" or other invasive or destructive varieties in the wild. Those risks are real enough that even most biotech enthusiasts—including Dennis Avery, for example—favor some government regulation of transgenic crops.

What is much less widely appreciated is biotech's potential to do the environment good. Take as an example continuous no-till farming, which really works best with the help of transgenic crops. Human beings have been ploughing for so long that we tend to forget why we started doing it in the first place. The short answer: weed control. Turning over the soil between plantings smothers weeds and their seeds. If you don't plough, your land becomes a weed garden—unless you use herbicides to kill the weeds. Herbicides, however, are expensive, and can be complicated to apply. And they tend to kill the good with the bad.

In the mid-1990s the agricultural-products company Monsanto introduced a transgenic soybean variety called Roundup Ready. As the name implies, these soybeans tolerate Roundup, an herbicide (also made by Monsanto) that kills many kinds of weeds and then quickly breaks down into harmless ingredients. Equipped with Roundup Ready crops, farmers found that they could retire their ploughs and control weeds with just a few applications of a single, relatively benign herbicide—instead of many applications of a complex and expensive menu of chemicals. More than a third of all U.S. soybeans are now grown without ploughing, mostly owing to the introduction of Roundup Ready varieties. Ploughless cotton farming has likewise received a big boost from the advent of bio-engineered varieties. No-till farming without biotech is possible, but it's more difficult and expensive, which is why no-till and biotech are advancing in tandem.

In 2001 a group of scientists announced that they had engineered a transgenic tomato plant able to thrive on salty water—water, in fact, almost half as salty as seawater, and fifty times as salty as tomatoes can ordinarily abide. One of the researchers was quoted as saying, "I've already transformed tomato, tobacco, and canola. I believe I can transform any crop with this gene"—just the sort of Frankenstein hubris that makes environmentalists shudder. But consider the environmental implications. Irrigation has for millennia been a cornerstone of agriculture, but it comes at a price. As irrigation water evaporates, it leaves behind traces of salt, which accumulate in the soil and gradually render it infertile. (As any Roman legion knows, to destroy a nation's agricultural base you salt the soil.) Every year the world loses about 25 million acres—an area equivalent to a fifth of California—to salinity; 40 percent of the world's irrigated land, and 25 percent of America's, has been hurt to some degree. For decades traditional plant breeders tried to create salt-tolerant crop plants, and for decades they failed.

Salt-tolerant crops might bring millions of acres of wounded or crippled land back into production. "And it gets better," Alex Avery told me. The transgenic tomato plants take up and sequester in their leaves as much as six or seven percent of their weight in sodium. "Theoretically," Alex said, "you could reclaim a salt-contaminated field by growing enough of these crops to remove the salts from the soil."

His father chimed in: "We've worried about being able to keep these salt-contaminated fields going even for decades. We can now think about centuries."

One of the first biotech crops to reach the market, in the mid-1990s, was a cotton plant that makes its own pesticide. Scientists incorporated into the plant a toxin-producing gene from a soil bacterium known as *Bacillus thuringiensis*. With Bt cotton, as it is called, farmers can spray much less, and the poison contained in the plant is delivered only to bugs that actually eat the crop. As any environmentalist can tell you, insecticide is not very nice stuff—especially if you breathe it, which many Third World farmers do as they walk through their fields with backpack sprayers.

Transgenic cotton reduced pesticide use by more than two million pounds in the United States from 1996 to 2000, and it has reduced pesticide sprayings in parts of China by more than half. Earlier this year the Environmental Protection Agency approved a genetically modified corn that resists a beetle larva known as rootworm. Because rootworm is American corn's most voracious enemy, this new variety has the potential to reduce annual pesticide use in America by more than 14 million pounds. It could reduce or eliminate the spraying of pesticide on 23 million acres of U.S. land.

All of that is the beginning, not the end. Bioengineers are also working, for instance, on crops that tolerate aluminum, another major contaminant of soil, especially in the tropics. Return an acre of farmland to productivity, or double yields on an already productive acre, and, other things being equal, you reduce by an acre the amount of virgin forest or savannah that will be stripped and cultivated. That may be the most important benefit of all.

Of the many people I have interviewed in my twenty years as a journalist, Norman Borlaug must be the one who has saved the most lives. Today he is an unprepossessing eighty-nine-year-old man of middling height, with crystal-bright blue eyes and thinning white hair. He still loves to talk about plant breeding, the discipline that won him the 1970 Nobel Peace Prize: Borlaug led efforts to breed the staples of the Green Revolution. (See "Forgotten Benefactor of Humanity," by Gregg Easterbrook, an article on Borlaug in the January 1997 *Atlantic*.) Yet the renowned plant breeder is quick to mention that he began his career, in the 1930s, in forestry, and that forest conservation has never been far from his thoughts. In the 1960s, while he was working to improve crop yields in India and Pakistan, he made a mental connection. He would create tables detailing acres under cultivation and average yields—and then, in another column, he would estimate how much land had been saved by higher farm productivity. Later, in the 1980s and 1990s, he and others began paying increased attention to what some agricultural economists now call the Borlaug hypothesis: that the Green Revolution has saved not only many human lives but, by improving the productivity of existing farmland, also millions of acres of tropical forest and other habitat—and so has saved countless animal lives.

From the 1960s through the 1980s, for example, Green Revolution advances saved more than 100 million acres of wild lands in India. More recently, higher yields in rice, coffee, vegetables, and other crops have reduced or in some cases stopped forest-clearing in Honduras, the Philippines, and elsewhere. Dennis Avery estimates that if farming techniques and yields had not improved since 1950, the world would have lost an additional 20 million or so square miles of wildlife habitat, most of it forest. About 16 million square miles of forest exists today. "What I'm saying," Avery said, in response to my puzzled expression, "is that we have saved every square mile of forest on the planet."

Habitat destruction remains a serious environmental problem; in some respects it is the most serious. The savannahs and tropical forests of Central and South America, Asia, and Africa by and large make poor farmland, but they are the earth's storehouses of biodiversity, and the forests are the earth's lungs. Since 1972 about 200,000 square miles of Amazon rain forest have been cleared for crops and pasture; from 1966 to 1994 all but three of the Central American countries cleared more forest than they left standing. Mexico is losing more than 4,000 square miles of forest a year to peasant farms; sub-Saharan Africa is losing more than 19,000.

That is why the great challenge of the next four or five decades is not to feed an additional three billion people (and their pets) but to do so without converting much of the world's prime habitat into second- or third-rate farmland. Now, most agronomists agree that some substantial yield improvements are still to be had from advances in conventional breeding, fertilizers, herbicides, and other Green Revolution standbys. But it seems pretty clear that biotechnology holds more promise—probably much more. Recall that world food output will need to at least double and possibly triple over the next several decades. Even if production could be increased that much using conventional technology, which is doubtful, the required amounts of pesticide and fertilizer and other polluting chemicals would be immense. If properly developed, disseminated, and used, genetically modified crops might well be the best hope the planet has got.

If properly developed, disseminated, and used. That tripartite qualification turns out to be important, and it brings the environmental community squarely, and at the moment rather jarringly, into the picture.

Not long ago I went to see David Sandalow in his office at the World Wildlife Fund, in Washington, D.C. Sandalow, the organization's executive vice-president in charge of conservation programs, is a tall, affable, polished, and slightly reticent man in his forties who holds degrees from Yale and the University of Michigan Law School.

Some weeks earlier, over lunch, I had mentioned Dennis Avery's claim that genetic modification had great environmental potential. I was surprised when Sandalow told me he agreed. Later, in our interview in his office, I asked him to elaborate. "With biotechnology," he said, "there are no simple answers. Biotechnology has huge potential benefits and huge risks, and we need to address both as we move forward. The huge potential benefits include increased productivity of arable land, which could relieve pressure on forests. They include decreased pesticide usage. But the huge risks include severe ecological disruptions—from gene flow and from enhanced invasiveness, which is a very antiseptic word for some very scary stuff."

I asked if he thought that, absent biotechnology, the world could feed everybody over the next forty or fifty years without ploughing down the rain forests. Instead of answering directly he said, "Biotechnology could be part of our arsenal if we can overcome some of the barriers. It will never be a panacea or a magic bullet. But nor should we remove it from our tool kit."

Sandalow is unusual. Very few credentialed greens talk the way he does about biotechnology, at least publicly. They would readily agree with him about the huge risks, but they wouldn't be caught dead speaking of huge potential benefits—a point I will come back to. From an ecological point of view, a very great deal depends on other environmentalists' coming to think more the way Sandalow does.

Biotech companies are in business to make money. That is fitting and proper. But developing and testing new transgenic crops is expensive and commercially risky, to say nothing of politically controversial. When they decide how to invest their research-and-development money, biotech companies will naturally seek products for which farmers and consumers will pay top dollar. Roundup Ready products, for instance, are well suited to U.S. farming, with its high levels of capital spending on such things as herbicides and automated sprayers. Poor farmers in the developing world, of course, have much less buying power. Creating, say, salt-tolerant cassava suitable for growing on hardscrabble African farms might save habitat as well as lives—but commercial enterprises are not likely to fall over one another in a rush to do it.

If earth-friendly transgenics are developed, the next problem is disseminating them. As a number of the farmers and experts I talked to were quick to mention, switching to an unfamiliar new technology—something like no-till—is not easy. It requires capital investment in new seed and equipment, mastery of new skills and methods, a fragile transition period as farmer and ecology re-adjust, and an often considerable amount of trial and error to find out what works best on any given field. Such problems are only magnified in the Third World, where the learning curve is steeper and capital cushions are thin to nonexistent. Just handing a peasant farmer a bag of newfangled seed is not enough. In many cases peasant farmers will need one-on-one attention. Many will need help to pay for the seed, too.

Finally there is the matter of using biotech in a way that actually benefits the environment. Often the technological blade can cut either way, especially in the short run. A salt-tolerant or drought-resistant rice that allowed farmers to keep land in production might also induce them to plough up virgin land that previously was too salty or too dry to farm. If the effect of improved seed is to make farming more profitable, farmers may respond, at least temporarily, by bringing more land into production. If a farm becomes more productive, it may require fewer workers; and if local labor markets cannot provide jobs for them, displaced workers may move to a nearby patch of rain forest and burn it down to make way for subsistence farming. Such transition problems are solvable, but they need money and attention.

In short, realizing the great—probably unique—environmental potential of biotech will require stewardship. "It's a tool," Sara Scherr, an agricultural economist with the conservation group Forest Trends, told me, "but it's absolutely not going to happen automatically."

So now ask a question: Who is the natural constituency for earth-friendly biotechnology? Who cares enough to lobby governments to underwrite research—frequently unprofitable research—on transgenic crops that might restore soils or cut down on pesticides in poor countries? Who cares enough to teach Asian or African farmers, one by one, how to farm without ploughing? Who cares enough to help poor farmers afford high-tech, earth-friendly seed? Who cares enough to agitate for programs and reforms that might steer displaced peasants and profit-seeking farmers away from sensitive lands? Not politicians, for the most part. Not farmers. Not corporations. Not consumers.

At the World Resources Institute, an environmental think tank in Washington, the molecular biologist Don Doering envisions transgenic crops designed specifically to solve environmental problems: crops that might fertilize the soil, crops that could clean water, crops tailored to remedy the ecological problems of specific places. "Suddenly you might find yourself with a virtually chemical-free agriculture, where your cropland itself is filtering the water, it's protecting the watershed, it's providing habitat," Doering told me. "There is still so little investment in what I call design-for-environment." The natural constituency for such investment is, of course, environmentalists.

But environmentalists are not acting as such a constituency today. They are doing the opposite. For example, Greenpeace declares on its Web site: "The introduction of genetically engineered (GE) organisms into the complex ecosystems of our environment is a dangerous global experiment with nature and evolution . . . GE organisms must not be released into the environment. They pose unacceptable risks to ecosystems, and have the potential to threaten biodiversity, wildlife and sustainable forms of agriculture."

Other groups argue for what they call the Precautionary Principle, under which no transgenic crop could be used until proven benign in virtually all respects. The Sierra Club says on its Web site,

> In accordance with this Precautionary Principle, we call for a moratorium on the planting of all genetically engineered crops and the release of all GEOs [genetically engineered organisms] into the environment, *including those now approved*. [italics added] Releases should be delayed until extensive, rigorous research is done which determines the long-term environmental and health impacts of each GEO and there is public debate to ascertain the need for the use of each GEO intended for release into the environment.

Under this policy the cleaner water and healthier soil that continuous no-till farming has already brought to the Chesapeake Bay watershed would be undone, and countless tons of polluted runoff and eroded topsoil would accumulate in Virginia rivers and streams while debaters debated and researchers researched. Recall David Sandalow: "Biotechnology has huge potential benefits and huge risks, and we need to address both as we move forward." A lot of environmentalists would say instead, *"before* we move forward." That is an important difference, particularly because the big population squeeze will happen not in the distant future but over the next several decades.

For reasons having more to do with politics than with logic, the modern environmental movement was to a large extent founded on suspicion of markets and artificial substances. Markets exploit the earth; chemicals poison it. Biotech touches both hot buttons. It is being pushed forward by greedy corporations, and it seems to be the very epitome of the unnatural. Still, I hereby hazard a prediction. In ten years or less, most American environmentalists (European ones are more dogmatic) will regard genetic modification as one of their most powerful tools. In only the past ten years or so, after all, environmentalists have reversed field and embraced market mechanisms—tradable emissions permits and the like—as useful in the fight against pollution. The environmental logic of biotechnology is, if anything, even more compelling. The potential upside of genetic modification is simply too large to ignore—and therefore environmentalists will not ignore it. Biotechnology will transform agriculture, and in doing so will transform American environmentalism.

Topics for Thought and Discussion

1. Describe the overall structure of Rauch's argument. What are the main sections of his text and what does each do? How would you describe the structure of his essay?
2. At one point Rauch says that "from an ecological point of view, a very great deal depends on other environmentalists coming to" embrace biotech. What does he mean? Why does so much depend upon environmentalists?
3. Is Rauch's argument more about genetically modified organisms or about environmentalists? Explain your answer.
4. Explain the implications of Rauch's title.

Suggestions for Writing

1. Make a list of the benefits Rauch sees in "Frankenfood." Be as complete as possible.
2. Read Mark Shapiro's article "Sowing Disaster" (*The Nation*, October 28, 2002). Write an essay in which you take a stand on genetically engineered crops. Write an argumentative thesis, and support your argument with evidence from Shapiro's and Rauch's essays.

Easter Island's End

JARED DIAMOND

*Jared Diamond is one of the premier thinkers writing today. A deco-
rated scientist working in a wide variety of fields, Diamond's ability
to synthesize many branches of science and history has enabled him
to address big questions of human evolution and society. Currently
holding several appointments at UCLA, Diamond is also a contributing editor for* Discover Magazine *and director of the U.S. Division of
the World Wildlife Fund. Diamond is also known to the public for his
award-winning books, including* Guns, Germs, and Steel *(1997),
which won the Pulitzer Prize for nonfiction and Britain's Science
Book Prize (among other awards);* The Third Chimpanzee: The
Evolution and Future of the Human Animal *(1992), which won
Britain's Science Book Prize;* Why Is Sex Fun?: The Evolution of
Human Sexuality *(1997); and most recently,* Collapse: How Societies Choose to Fail or Succeed *(2004). The following essay, first
published in* Discover Magazine *in 1995, demonstrates Diamond's
engaging style, and also shows him grappling with the ideas that
would later become his book* Collapse. *As you read, consider the central analogy that Diamond is drawing between Easter Island and the
earth. How does it work? Is it legitimate?*

---- ✦ ----

A mong the most riveting mysteries of human history are those
posed by vanished civilizations. Everyone who has seen the
abandoned buildings of the Khmer, the Maya, or the Anasazi[1] is
immediately moved to ask the same question: Why did the societies that erected those structures disappear?

Their vanishing touches us as the disappearance of other animals, even the dinosaurs, never can. No matter how exotic those
lost civilizations seem, their framers were humans like us. Who is
to say we won't succumb to the same fate? Perhaps someday New
York's skyscrapers will stand derelict and overgrown with vegetation, like the temples at Angkor Wat and Tikal.[2]

Among all such vanished civilizations, that of the former
Polynesian society on Easter Island remains unsurpassed in

---

[1]The Khmer were in what is today Southeast Asia, the Maya in Central America,
and the Anasazi in the Southwestern United States.
[2]Sites of famous ruins of the Khmer civilization in Cambodia and of the Mayan
in Guatemala.

mystery and isolation. The mystery stems especially from the island's gigantic stone statues and its impoverished landscape, but it is enhanced by our associations with the specific people involved: Polynesians represent for us the ultimate in exotic romance, the background for many a child's, and an adult's, vision of paradise. My own interest in Easter was kindled over 30 years ago when I read Thor Heyerdahl's fabulous accounts of his Kon-Tiki voyage.

But my interest has been revived recently by a much more exciting account, one not of heroic voyages but of painstaking research and analysis. My friend David Steadman, a paleontologist, has been working with a number of other researchers who are carrying out the first systematic excavations on Easter intended to identify the animals and plants that once lived there. Their work is contributing to a new interpretation of the island's history that makes it a tale not only of wonder but of warning as well.

Easter Island, with an area of only 64 square miles, is the world's most isolated scrap of habitable land. It lies in the Pacific Ocean more than 2,000 miles west of the nearest continent (South America), 1,400 miles from even the nearest habitable island (Pitcairn). Its subtropical location and latitude—at 27 degrees south, it is approximately as far below the equator as Houston is north of it—help give it a rather mild climate, while its volcanic origins make its soil fertile. In theory, this combination of blessings should have made Easter a miniature paradise, remote from problems that beset the rest of the world.

The island derives its name from its "discovery" by the Dutch explorer Jacob Roggeveen, on Easter (April 5) in 1722. Roggeveen's first impression was not of a paradise but of a wasteland: "We originally, from a further distance, have considered the said Easter Island as sandy; the reason for that is this, that we counted as sand the withered grass, hay, or other scorched and burnt vegetation, because its wasted appearance could give no other impression than of a singular poverty and barrenness."

The island Roggeveen saw was a grassland without a single tree or bush over ten feet high. Modern botanists have identified only 47 species of higher plants native to Easter, most of them grasses, sedges, and ferns. The list includes just two species of small trees and two of woody shrubs. With such flora, the islanders Roggeveen encountered had no source of real firewood to warm themselves during Easter's cool, wet, windy winters. Their native animals included nothing larger than insects, not even a single species of native bat, land bird, land snail, or lizard. For domestic animals, they had only chickens.

European visitors throughout the eighteenth and early nineteenth centuries estimated Easter's human population at about 2,000, a modest number considering the island's fertility. As Captain James Cook recognized during his brief visit in 1774, the islanders were Polynesians (a Tahitian man accompanying Cook was able to converse with them). Yet despite the Polynesians' well-deserved fame as a great seafaring people, the Easter Islanders who came out to Roggeveen's and Cook's ships did so by swimming or paddling canoes that Roggeveen described as "bad and frail." Their craft, he wrote, were "put together with manifold small planks and light inner timbers, which they cleverly stitched together with very fine twisted threads. . . . But as they lack the knowledge and particularly the materials for caulking and making tight the great number of seams of the canoes, these are accordingly very leaky, for which reason they are compelled to spend half the time in bailing." The canoes, only ten feet long, held at most two people, and only three or four canoes were observed on the entire island.

With such flimsy craft, Polynesians could never have colonized Easter from even the nearest island, nor could they have traveled far offshore to fish. The islanders Roggeveen met were totally isolated, unaware that other people existed. Investigators in all the years since his visit have discovered no trace of the islanders' having any outside contacts: not a single Easter Island rock or product has turned up elsewhere, nor has anything been found on the island that could have been brought by anyone other than the original settlers or the Europeans. Yet the people living on Easter claimed memories of visiting the uninhabited Sala y Gomez reef 260 miles away, far beyond the range of the leaky canoes seen by Roggeveen. How did the islanders' ancestors reach that reef from Easter, or reach Easter from anywhere else?

Easter Island's most famous feature is its huge stone statues, more than 200 of which once stood on massive stone platforms lining the coast. At least 700 more, in all stages of completion, were abandoned in quarries or on ancient roads between the quarries and the coast, as if the carvers and moving crews had thrown down their tools and walked off the job. Most of the erected statues were carved in a single quarry and then somehow transported as far as six miles—despite heights as great as 33 feet and weights up to 82 tons. The abandoned statues, meanwhile, were as much as 65 feet tall and weighed up to 270 tons. The stone platforms were equally gigantic: up to 500 feet long and 10 feet high, with facing slabs weighing up to 10 tons.

Roggeveen himself quickly recognized the problem the statues posed: "The stone images at first caused us to be struck with astonishment," he wrote, "because we could not comprehend how it was possible that these people, who are devoid of heavy thick timber for making any machines, as well as strong ropes, nevertheless had been able to erect such images." Roggeveen might have added that the islanders had no wheels, no draft animals, and no source of power except their own muscles. How did they transport the giant statues for miles, even before erecting them? To deepen the mystery, the statues were still standing in 1770, but by 1864 all of them had been pulled down, by the islanders themselves. Why then did they carve them in the first place? And why did they stop?

The statues imply a society very different from the one Roggeveen saw in 1722. Their sheer number and size suggest a population much larger than 2,000 people. What became of everyone? Furthermore, that society must have been highly organized. Easter's resources were scattered across the island: the best stone for the statues was quarried at Rano Raraku near Easter's northeast end; red stone, used for large crowns adorning some of the statues, was quarried at Puna Pau, inland in the southwest; stone carving tools came mostly from Aroi in the northwest. Meanwhile, the best farmland lay in the south and east, and the best fishing grounds on the north and west coasts. Extracting and redistributing all those goods required complex political organization. What happened to that organization, and how could it ever have arisen in such a barren landscape?

Easter Island's mysteries have spawned volumes of speculation for more than two and a half centuries. Many Europeans were incredulous that Polynesians—commonly characterized as mere savages—could have created the statues or the beautifully constructed stone platforms. In the 1950s, Heyerdahl argued that Polynesia must have been settled by advanced societies of American Indians, who in turn must have received civilization across the Atlantic from more advanced societies of the Old World. Heyerdahl's raft voyages aimed to prove the feasibility of such prehistoric transoceanic contacts. In the 1960s the Swiss writer Erich von Däniken, an ardent believer in Earth visits by extraterrestrial astronauts, went further, claiming that Easter's statues were the work of intelligent beings who owned ultramodern tools, became stranded on Easter, and were finally rescued.

Heyerdahl and Von Däniken both brushed aside overwhelming evidence that the Easter Islanders were typical Polynesians derived from Asia rather than from the Americas and that their culture (including their statues) grew out of Polynesian culture. Their language was Polynesian, as Cook had already concluded. Specifically, they spoke an eastern Polynesian dialect related to Hawaiian and Marquesan, a dialect isolated since about A.D. 400, as estimated from slight differences in vocabulary. Their fishhooks and stone adzes resembled early Marquesan models. Last year DNA extracted from 12 Easter Island skeletons was also shown to be Polynesian. The islanders grew bananas, taro, sweet potatoes, sugarcane, and paper mulberry—typical Polynesian crops, mostly of Southeast Asian origin. Their sole domestic animal, the chicken, was also typically Polynesian and ultimately Asian, as were the rats that arrived as stowaways in the canoes of the first settlers.

What happened to those settlers? The fanciful theories of the past must give way to evidence gathered by hardworking practitioners in three fields: archeology, pollen analysis, and paleontology. Modern archeological excavations on Easter have continued since Heyerdahl's 1955 expedition. The earliest radiocarbon dates associated with human activities are around A.D. 400 to 700, in reasonable agreement with the approximate settlement date of 400 estimated by linguists. The period of statue construction peaked around 1200 to 1500, with few if any statues erected thereafter. Densities of archeological sites suggest a large population; an estimate of 7,000 people is widely quoted by archeologists, but other estimates range up to 20,000, which does not seem implausible for an island of Easter's area and fertility.

Archeologists have also enlisted surviving islanders in experiments aimed at figuring out how the statues might have been carved and erected. Twenty people, using only stone chisels, could have carved even the largest completed statue within a year. Given enough timber and fiber for making ropes, teams of at most a few hundred people could have loaded the statues onto wooden sleds, dragged them over lubricated wooden tracks or rollers, and used logs as levers to maneuver them into a standing position. Rope could have been made from the fiber of a small native tree, related to the linden, called the hauhau. However, that tree is now extremely scarce on Easter, and hauling one statue would have required hundreds of yards of rope. Did Easter's now barren landscape once support the necessary trees?

That question can be answered by the technique of pollen analysis, which involves boring out a column of sediment from a swamp or pond, with the most recent deposits at the top and relatively more ancient deposits at the bottom. The absolute age of each layer can be dated by radiocarbon methods. Then begins the hard work: examining tens of thousands of pollen grains under a microscope, counting them, and identifying the plant species that produced each one by comparing the grains with modern pollen from known plant species. For Easter Island, the bleary-eyed scientists who performed that task were John Flenley, now at Massey University in New Zealand, and Sarah King of the University of Hull in England.

Flenley and King's heroic efforts were rewarded by the striking new picture that emerged of Easter's prehistoric landscape. For at least 30,000 years before human arrival and during the early years of Polynesian settlement, Easter was not a wasteland at all. Instead, a subtropical forest of trees and woody bushes towered over a ground layer of shrubs, herbs, ferns, and grasses. In the forest grew tree daisies, the rope-yielding hauhau tree, and the toromiro tree, which furnishes a dense, mesquite-like firewood. The most common tree in the forest was a species of palm now absent on Easter but formerly so abundant that the bottom strata of the sediment column were packed with its pollen. The Easter Island palm was closely related to the still-surviving Chilean wine palm, which grows up to 82 feet tall and 6 feet in diameter. The tall, unbranched trunks of the Easter Island palm would have been ideal for transporting and erecting statues and constructing large canoes. The palm would also have been a valuable food source, since its Chilean relative yields edible nuts as well as sap from which Chileans make sugar, syrup, honey, and wine.

What did the first settlers of Easter Island eat when they were not glutting themselves on the local equivalent of maple syrup? Recent excavations by David Steadman, of the New York State Museum at Albany, have yielded a picture of Easter's original animal world as surprising as Flenley and King's picture of its plant world. Steadman's expectations for Easter were conditioned by his experiences elsewhere in Polynesia, where fish are overwhelmingly the main food at archeological sites, typically accounting for more than 90 percent of the bones in ancient Polynesian garbage heaps. Easter, though, is too cool for the coral reefs beloved by fish, and its cliff-girded coastline permits shallow-water fishing in only a few places. Less than a quarter of the bones in its early garbage heaps (from the period 900 to 1300) belonged to fish; instead, nearly one-third of all bones came from porpoises.

Nowhere else in Polynesia do porpoises account for even 1 percent of discarded food bones. But most other Polynesian islands offered animal food in the form of birds and mammals, such as New Zealand's now extinct giant moas and Hawaii's now extinct flightless geese. Most other islanders also had domestic pigs and dogs. On Easter, porpoises would have been the largest animal available— other than humans. The porpoise species identified at Easter, the common dolphin, weighs up to 165 pounds. It generally lives out at sea, so it could not have been hunted by line fishing or spearfishing from shore. Instead, it must have been harpooned far offshore, in big seaworthy canoes built from the extinct palm tree.

In addition to porpoise meat, Steadman found, the early Polynesian settlers were feasting on seabirds. For those birds, Easter's remoteness and lack of predators made it an ideal haven as a breeding site, at least until humans arrived. Among the prodigious numbers of seabirds that bred on Easter were albatross, boobies, frigate birds, fulmars, petrels, prions, shearwaters, storm petrels, terns, and tropic birds. With at least 25 nesting species, Easter was the richest seabird breeding site in Polynesia and probably in the whole Pacific.

Land birds as well went into early Easter Island cooking pots. Steadman identified bones of at least six species, including barn owls, herons, parrots, and rail. Bird stew would have been seasoned with meat from large numbers of rats, which the Polynesian colonists inadvertently brought with them; Easter Island is the sole known Polynesian island where rat bones outnumber fish bones at archeological sites. (In case you're squeamish and consider rats inedible, I still recall recipes for creamed laboratory rat that my British biologist friends used to supplement their diet during their years of wartime food rationing.)

Porpoises, seabirds, land birds, and rats did not complete the list of meat sources formerly available on Easter. A few bones hint at the possibility of breeding seal colonies as well. All these delicacies were cooked in ovens fired by wood from the island's forests.

Such evidence lets us imagine the island onto which Easter's first Polynesian colonists stepped ashore some 1,600 years ago, after a long canoe voyage from eastern Polynesia. They found themselves in a pristine paradise. What then happened to it? The pollen grains and the bones yield a grim answer.

Pollen records show that destruction of Easter's forests was well under way by the year 800, just a few centuries after the start of human settlement. Then charcoal from wood fires came to fill the sediment cores, while pollen of palms and other trees and woody shrubs decreased or disappeared, and pollen of the grasses that replaced the forest became more abundant. Not long after 1400 the palm finally became extinct, not only as a result of being chopped down but also because the now ubiquitous rats prevented its regeneration: of the dozens of preserved palm nuts discovered in caves on Easter, all had been chewed by rats and could no longer germinate. While the hauhau tree did not become extinct in Polynesian times, its numbers declined drastically until there weren't enough left to make ropes from. By the time Heyerdahl visited Easter, only a single, nearly dead toromiro tree remained on the island, and even that lone survivor has now disappeared. (Fortunately, the toromiro still grows in botanical gardens elsewhere.)

The fifteenth century marked the end not only for Easter's palm but for the forest itself. Its doom had been approaching as people cleared land to plant gardens; as they felled trees to build canoes, to transport and erect statues, and to burn; as rats devoured seeds; and probably as the native birds died out that had pollinated the trees' flowers and dispersed their fruit. The overall picture is among the most extreme examples of forest destruction anywhere in the world: the whole forest gone, and most of its tree species extinct.

The destruction of the island's animals was as extreme as that of the forest: without exception, every species of native land bird became extinct. Even shellfish were overexploited, until people had to settle for small sea snails instead of larger cowries. Porpoise bones disappeared abruptly from garbage heaps around 1500; no one could harpoon porpoises anymore, since the trees used for constructing the big seagoing canoes no longer existed. The colonies of more than half of the seabird species breeding on Easter or on its offshore islets were wiped out.

In place of these meat supplies, the Easter Islanders intensified their production of chickens, which had been only an occasional food item. They also turned to the largest remaining meat source available: humans, whose bones became common in late Easter Island garbage heaps. Oral traditions of the islanders are rife with cannibalism; the most inflammatory taunt that could be snarled at an enemy was "The flesh of your mother sticks between my teeth." With no wood available to cook these new goodies, the islanders resorted to sugarcane scraps, grass, and sedges to fuel their fires.

All these strands of evidence can be wound into a coherent narrative of a society's decline and fall. The first Polynesian colonists found themselves on an island with fertile soil, abundant food, bountiful building materials, ample lebensraum,[3] and all the prerequisites for comfortable living. They prospered and multiplied.

---

[3] A German word meaning "living space," referring to territory a nation deems necessary for economic well-being.

After a few centuries, they began erecting stone statues on platforms, like the ones their Polynesian forebears had carved. With passing years, the statues and platforms became larger and larger, and the statues began sporting ten-ton red crowns—probably in an escalating spiral of one-upmanship, as rival clans tried to surpass each other with shows of wealth and power. (In the same way, successive Egyptian pharaohs built ever-larger pyramids. Today Hollywood movie moguls near my home in Los Angeles are displaying their wealth and power by building ever more ostentatious mansions. Tycoon Marvin Davis topped previous moguls with plans for a 50,000-square-foot house, so now Aaron Spelling has topped Davis with a 56,000-square-foot house. All that those buildings lack to make the message explicit are ten-ton red crowns.) On Easter, as in modern America, society was held together by a complex political system to redistribute locally available resources and to integrate the economies of different areas.

Eventually Easter's growing population was cutting the forest more rapidly than the forest was regenerating. The people used the land for gardens and the wood for fuel, canoes, and houses—and, of course, for lugging statues. As forest disappeared, the islanders ran out of timber and rope to transport and erect their statues. Life became more uncomfortable—springs and streams dried up, and wood was no longer available for fires.

People also found it harder to fill their stomachs, as land birds, large sea snails, and many seabirds disappeared. Because timber for building seagoing canoes vanished, fish catches declined and porpoises disappeared from the table. Crop yields also declined, since deforestation allowed the soil to be eroded by rain and wind, dried by the sun, and its nutrients to be leeched from it. Intensified chicken production and cannibalism replaced only part of all those lost foods. Preserved statuettes with sunken cheeks and visible ribs suggest that people were starving.

With the disappearance of food surpluses, Easter Island could no longer feed the chiefs, bureaucrats, and priests who had kept a complex society running. Surviving islanders described to early European visitors how local chaos replaced centralized government and a warrior class took over from the hereditary chiefs. The stone points of spears and daggers, made by the warriors during their heyday in the 1600s and 1700s, still litter the ground of Easter today. By around 1700, the population began to crash toward between one-quarter and one-tenth of its former number. People took to living in caves for protection against their enemies.

Around 1770 rival clans started to topple each other's statues, breaking the heads off. By 1864 the last statue had been thrown down and desecrated.

As we try to imagine the decline of Easter's civilization, we ask ourselves, "Why didn't they look around, realize what they were doing, and stop before it was too late? What were they thinking when they cut down the last palm tree?"

I suspect, though, that the disaster happened not with a bang but with a whimper. After all, there are those hundreds of abandoned statues to consider. The forest the islanders depended on for rollers and rope didn't simply disappear one day—it vanished slowly, over decades. Perhaps war interrupted the moving teams; perhaps by the time the carvers had finished their work, the last rope snapped. In the meantime, any islander who tried to warn about the dangers of progressive deforestation would have been overridden by vested interests of carvers, bureaucrats, and chiefs, whose jobs depended on continued deforestation. Our Pacific Northwest loggers are only the latest in a long line of loggers to cry, "Jobs over trees!" The changes in forest cover from year to year would have been hard to detect: yes, this year we cleared those woods over there, but trees are starting to grow back again on this abandoned garden site here. Only older people, recollecting their childhoods decades earlier, could have recognized a difference. Their children could no more have comprehended their parents' tales than my eight-year-old sons today can comprehend my wife's and my tales of what Los Angeles was like 30 years ago.

Gradually trees became fewer, smaller, and less important. By the time the last fruit-bearing adult palm tree was cut, palms had long since ceased to be of economic significance. That left only smaller and smaller palm saplings to clear each year, along with other bushes and treelets. No one would have noticed the felling of the last small palm.

By now the meaning of Easter Island for us should be chillingly obvious. Easter Island is Earth writ small. Today, again, a rising population confronts shrinking resources. We too have no emigration valve, because all human societies are linked by international transport, and we can no more escape into space than the Easter Islanders could flee into the ocean. If we continue to follow our present course, we shall have exhausted the world's major fisheries, tropical rain forests, fossil fuels, and much of our soil by the time my sons reach my current age.

Every day newspapers report details of famished countries— Afghanistan, Liberia, Rwanda, Sierra Leone, Somalia, the former

Yugoslavia, Zaire—where soldiers have appropriated the wealth or where central government is yielding to local gangs of thugs. With the risk of nuclear war receding, the threat of our ending with a bang no longer has a chance of galvanizing us to halt our course. Our risk now is of winding down, slowly, in a whimper. Corrective action is blocked by vested interests, by well-intentioned political and business leaders, and by their electorates, all of whom are perfectly correct in not noticing big changes from year to year. Instead, each year there are just somewhat more people, and somewhat fewer resources, on Earth.

It would be easy to close our eyes or to give up in despair. If mere thousands of Easter Islanders with only stone tools and their own muscle power sufficed to destroy their society, how can billions of people with metal tools and machine power fail to do worse? But there is one crucial difference. The Easter Islanders had no books and no histories of other doomed societies. Unlike the Easter Islanders, we have histories of the past—information that can save us. My main hope for my sons' generation is that we may now choose to learn from the fates of societies like Easter's.

Topics for Thought and Discussion

1. Diamond's essay is constructed, ultimately, around a single central analogy. Explain it. Does the analogy seem fair?
2. The story that Diamond tells about Easter Island is in many ways a detective story. Describe the various branches of science that Diamond uses to uncover the truth about Easter. What might this suggest about the interconnection of scientific disciplines in human society?
3. What is Diamond's purpose in this essay? Does he tell us his purpose outright, or does he imply it, expecting us to understand and to act?

Suggestions for Writing

1. Write an essay in which you look into the future, and using Easter Island and Jared Diamond's analysis of it as a model, imagine what one small piece of the world (a piece that you already know well) is like. In your vision, what forces ultimately form your world and make it the way it is?
2. One of the dangers of arguing by analogy is that the two things we compare are not enough the same to allow us to draw the conclusions we draw. Write an evaluation of Diamond's analogy, and using his essay as material, answer the question: "How like Easter Island is the earth, and does Easter give us a model of the earth's future?"

3. Write an essay in which you describe your response to reading Diamond's essay (what you felt, what you thought, what you did), and compare it to how Diamond hopes you will react (his purpose, and what he hopes you will think, feel, and do).

Earth Without People
Alan Weisman

Alan Weisman is a journalist, nonfiction writer, and award-winning radio producer and writer. His articles have been published widely in a variety of magazines, and have appeared on National Public Radio and Public Radio International. He is the author of a number of books, including La Frontera: The United States Border with Mexico *(1986),* Gaviotas: A Village to Reinvent the World *(1998), the memoir* An Echo in My Blood: The Search for a Family's Hidden Past *(1999) and* The World Without Us *(2007). Weisman has an affinity for place, and for the physical world. In the following article, first published in* Discover Magazine *in 2005, he describes in physical terms what would happen to Earth were people to suddenly disappear. As you read, think about how Weisman uses description.*

──────── ✦ ────────

Given the mounting toll of fouled oceans, overheated air, missing topsoil, and mass extinctions, we might sometimes wonder what our planet would be like if humans suddenly disappeared. Would Superfund sites revert to Gardens of Eden? Would the seas again fill with fish? Would our concrete cities crumble to dust from the force of tree roots, water, and weeds? How long would it take for our traces to vanish? And if we could answer such questions, would we be more in awe of the changes we have wrought, or of nature's resilience?

A good place to start searching for answers is in Korea, in the 155-mile-long, 2.5-mile-wide mountainous Demilitarized Zone, or DMZ, set up by the armistice ending the Korean War. Aside from rare military patrols or desperate souls fleeing North Korea, humans have barely set foot in the strip since 1953. Before that, for 5,000 years, the area was populated by rice farmers who carved the land into paddies. Today those paddies have become barely discernible, transformed into pockets of marsh, and the new occupants of these lands arrive as dazzling white squadrons of red-crowned cranes that glide over the bulrushes in perfect formation, touching down so lightly that they detonate no land mines. Next to whooping cranes, they are the rarest such birds on Earth. They winter in the DMZ alongside the endangered white-naped cranes, revered in Asia as sacred portents of peace.

If peace is ever declared, suburban Seoul, which has rolled ever northward in recent decades, is poised to invade such tantalizing real estate. On the other side, the North Koreans are building an industrial megapark. This has spurred an international coalition of scientists called the DMZ Forum to try to consecrate the area for a peace park and nature preserve. Imagine it as "a Korean Gettysburg and Yosemite rolled together," says Harvard University biologist Edward O. Wilson, who believes that tourism revenues could trump those from agriculture or development.

As serenely natural as the DMZ now is, it would be far different if people throughout Korea suddenly disappeared. The habitat would not revert to a truly natural state until the dams that now divert rivers to slake the needs of Seoul's more than 20 million inhabitants failed—a century or two after the humans had gone. But in the meantime, says Wilson, many creatures would flourish. Otters, Asiatic black bears, musk deer, and the nearly vanquished Amur leopard would spread into slopes reforested with young daimyo oak and bird cherry. The few Siberian tigers that still prowl the North Korean–Chinese borderlands would multiply and fan across Asia's temperate zones. "The wild carnivores would make short work of livestock," he says. "Few domestic animals would remain after a couple of hundred years. Dogs would go feral, but they wouldn't last long: They'd never be able to compete."

If people were no longer present anywhere on Earth, a worldwide shakeout would follow. From zebra mussels to fire ants to crops to kudzu, exotics would battle with natives. In time, says Wilson, all human attempts to improve on nature, such as our painstakingly bred horses, would revert to their origins. If horses survived at all, they would devolve back to Przewalski's horse, the only true wild horse, still found in the Mongolian steppes. "The plants, crops, and animal species man has wrought by his own hand would be wiped out in a century or two," Wilson says. In a few thousand years, "the world would mostly look as it did before humanity came along—like a wilderness."

The new wilderness would consume cities, much as the jungle of northern Guatemala consumed the Mayan pyramids and megalopolises of overlapping city-states. From A.D. 800 to 900, a combination of drought and internecine warfare over dwindling farmland brought 2,000 years of civilization crashing down. Within 10 centuries, the jungle swallowed all.

Mayan communities alternated urban living with fields sheltered by forests, in contrast with today's paved cities, which are more like man-made deserts. However, it wouldn't take long for nature to undo even the likes of a New York City. Jameel Ahmad, civil engineering department chair at Cooper Union College in New York City, says repeated freezing and thawing common in months like March and November would split cement within a decade, allowing water to seep in. As it, too, froze and expanded, cracks would widen. Soon, weeds such as mustard and goosegrass would invade. With nobody to trample seedlings, New York's prolific exotic, the Chinese ailanthus tree, would take over. Within five years, says Dennis Stevenson, senior curator at the New York Botanical Garden, ailanthus roots would heave up sidewalks and split sewers.

That would exacerbate a problem that already plagues New York—rising groundwater. There's little soil to absorb it or vegetation to transpire it, and buildings block the sunlight that could evaporate it. With the power off, pumps that keep subways from flooding would be stilled. As water sluiced away soil beneath pavement, streets would crater.

Eric Sanderson of the Bronx Zoo Wildlife Conservation Society heads the Mannahatta Project, a virtual re-creation of pre-1609 Manhattan. He says there were 30 to 40 streams in Manhattan when the Dutch first arrived. If New Yorkers disappeared, sewers would clog, some natural watercourses would reappear, and others would form. Within 20 years, the water-soaked steel columns that support the street above the East Side's subway tunnels would corrode and buckle, turning Lexington Avenue into a river.

New York's architecture isn't as flammable as San Francisco's clapboard Victorians, but within 200 years, says Steven Clemants, vice president of the Brooklyn Botanic Garden, tons of leaf litter would overflow gutters as pioneer weeds gave way to colonizing native oaks and maples in city parks. A dry lightning strike, igniting decades of uncut, knee-high Central Park grass, would spread flames through town.

As lightning rods rusted away, roof fires would leap among buildings into paneled offices filled with paper. Meanwhile, native Virginia creeper and poison ivy would claw at walls covered with lichens, which thrive in the absence of air pollution. Wherever foundations failed and buildings tumbled, lime from crushed concrete would raise soil pH, inviting buckthorn and birch. Black locust and autumn olive trees would fix nitrogen, allowing more goldenrods, sunflowers, and white snakeroot to move in along with apple trees, their seeds expelled by proliferating birds. Sweet carrots would quickly devolve to their wild form, unpalatable Queen Anne's lace, while broccoli, cabbage, brussels sprouts, and cauliflower would regress to the same unrecognizable broccoli ancestor.

Unless an earthquake strikes New York first, bridges spared yearly applications of road salt would last a few hundred years before their stays and bolts gave way (last to fall would be Hell Gate Arch, built for railroads and easily good for another thousand years). Coyotes would invade Central Park, and deer, bears, and finally wolves would follow. Ruins would echo the love song of frogs breeding in streams stocked with alewives, herring, and mussels dropped by seagulls. Missing, however, would be all fauna that have adapted to humans. The invincible cockroach, an insect that originated in the hot climes of Africa, would succumb in unheated buildings. Without garbage, rats would starve or serve as lunch for peregrine falcons and red-tailed hawks. Pigeons would genetically revert back to the rock doves from which they sprang.

It's unclear how long animals would suffer from the urban legacy of concentrated heavy metals. Over many centuries, plants would take these up, recycle, redeposit, and gradually dilute them. The time bombs left in petroleum tanks, chemical plants, power plants, and dry-cleaning plants might poison the earth beneath them for eons. One intriguing example is the former Rocky Mountain Arsenal next to Denver International Airport. There a chemical weapons plant produced mustard and nerve gas, incendiary bombs, napalm, and after World War II, pesticides. In 1984 it was considered by the arsenal commander to be the most contaminated spot in the United States. Today it is a national wildlife refuge, home to bald eagles that feast on its prodigious prairie dog population.

However, it took more than $130 million and a lot of manhours to drain and seal the arsenal's lake, in which ducks once died minutes after landing and the aluminum bottoms of boats sent to fetch their carcasses rotted within a month. In a world with no one left to bury the bad stuff, decaying chemical containers would slowly expose their lethal contents. Places like the Indian Point nuclear power plant, 35 miles north of Times Square, would dump radioactivity into the Hudson long after the lights went out.

Old stone buildings in Manhattan, such as Grand Central Station or the Metropolitan Museum of Art, would outlast every modern glass box, especially with no more acid rain to pock their marble. Still, at some point thousands of years hence, the last stone walls—perhaps chunks of St. Paul's Chapel on Wall Street, built in 1766 from Manhattan's own hard schist—would fall. Three times in the past 100,000 years, glaciers have scraped New York clean, and they'll do so again. The mature hardwood forest would be mowed down. On Staten Island, Fresh Kills's four giant mounds of trash would be flattened, their vast accumulation of stubborn PVC plastic and glass ground to powder. After the ice receded, an unnatural concentration of reddish metal—remnants of wiring and plumbing—would remain buried in layers. The next tool-maker to arrive or evolve might discover it and use it, but there would be nothing to indicate who had put it there.

Before humans appeared, an oriole could fly from the Mississippi to the Atlantic and never alight on anything other than a tree-top. Unbroken forest blanketed Europe from the Urals to the English Channel. The last remaining fragment of that primeval European wilderness—half a million acres of woods straddling the border between Poland and Belarus, called the Bialowieza Forest—provides another glimpse of how the world would look if we were gone. There, relic groves of huge ash and linden trees rise 138 feet above an understory of hornbeams, ferns, swamp alders, massive birches, and crockery-size fungi. Norway spruces, shaggy as Methuselah, stand even taller. Five-century-old oaks grow so immense that great spotted woodpeckers stuff whole spruce cones in their three-inch-deep bark furrows. The woods carry pygmy owl whistles, nutcracker croaks, and wolf howls. Fragrance wafts from eons of mulch.

High privilege accounts for such unbroken antiquity. During the 14th century, a Lithuanian duke declared it a royal hunting preserve. For centuries it stayed that way. Eventually, the forest was subsumed by Russia and in 1888 became the private domain of the czars. Occupying Germans took lumber and slaughtered game during World War I, but a pristine core was left intact, which in 1921 became a Polish national park. Timber pillaging resumed briefly under the Soviets, but when the Nazis invaded, nature fa-natic Hermann Göring decreed the entire preserve off limits. Then, following World War II, a reportedly drunken Josef Stalin agreed one evening in Warsaw to let Poland retain two-fifths of the forest.

To realize that all of Europe once looked like this is startling. Most unexpected of all is the sight of native bison. Just 600 remain in the wild, on both sides of an impassable iron curtain erected by the Soviets in 1980 along the border to thwart escapees to Poland's renegade Solidarity movement. Although wolves dig under it, and roe deer are believed to leap over it, the herd of the largest of Europe's mammals remains divided, and thus its gene pool.

Belarus, which has not removed its statues of Lenin, has no specific plans to dismantle the fence. Unless it does, the bison may suffer genetic degradation, leaving them vulnerable to a disease that would wipe them out.

If the bison herd withers, they would join all the other extinct megafauna that even our total disappearance could never bring back. In a glass case in his laboratory, paleoecologist Paul S. Martin at the University of Arizona keeps a lump of dried dung he found in a Grand Canyon cave, left by a sloth weighing 200 pounds. That would have made it the smallest of several North American ground sloth species present when humans first appeared on this continent. The largest was as big as an elephant and lumbered around by the thousands in the woodlands and deserts of today's United States. What we call pristine today, Martin says, is a poor reflection of what would be here if *Homo sapiens* had never evolved.

"America would have three times as many species of animals over 1,000 pounds as Africa does today," he says. An amazing megafaunal menagerie roamed the region: Giant armadillos resembling armor-plated autos; bears twice the size of grizzlies; the hoofed, herbivorous toxodon, big as a rhinoceros; and saber-toothed tigers. A dozen species of horses were here, as well as the camel-like litoptern, giant beavers, giant peccaries, woolly rhinos, mammoths, and mastodons. Climate change and imported disease may have killed them, but most paleontologists accept the theory Martin advocates: "When people got out of Africa and Asia and reached other parts of the world, all hell broke loose." He is convinced that people were responsible for the mass extinctions because they commenced with human arrival everywhere: first, in Australia 60,000 years ago, then mainland America 13,000 years ago, followed by the Caribbean islands 6,000 years ago, and Madagascar 2,000 years ago.

Yet one place on Earth did manage to elude the intercontinental holocaust: the oceans. Dolphins and whales escaped for the simple reason that prehistoric people could not hunt enough giant marine mammals to have a major impact on the population. "At least a dozen species in the ocean Columbus sailed were bigger than his biggest ship," says marine paleoecologist Jeremy Jackson of the Smithsonian Tropical Research Institute in Panama. "Not only mammals—the sea off Cuba was so thick with 1,000-pound green turtles that his boats practically ran aground on them." This was a world where ships collided with schools of whales and where sharks were so abundant they would swim up rivers to prey on cattle. Reefs swarmed with 800-pound goliath grouper, not just today's puny aquarium species. Cod could be fished from the sea in baskets. Oysters filtered all the water in Chesapeake Bay every five days. The planet's shores teemed with millions of manatees, seals, and walrus.

Within the past century, however, humans have flattened the coral reefs on the continental shelves and scraped the sea grass beds bare; a dead zone bigger than New Jersey grows at the mouth of the Mississippi; all the world's cod fisheries have collapsed. What Pleistocene humans did in 1,500 years to terrestrial life, modern man has done in mere decades to the oceans—"almost," Jackson says. Despite mechanized overharvesting, satellite fish tracking, and prolonged butchery of sea mammals, the ocean is still bigger than we are. "It's not like the land," he says. "The great majority of sea species are badly depleted, but they still exist. If people actually went away, most could recover."

Even if global warming or ultraviolet radiation bleaches the Great Barrier Reef to death, Jackson says, "It's only 7,000 years old. New reefs have had to form before. It's not like the world is a constant place." Without people, most excess industrial carbon dioxide would dissipate within 200 years, cooling the atmosphere. With no further chlorine and bromine leaking skyward, within decades the ozone layer would replenish, and ultraviolet damage would subside. Eventually, heavy metals and toxins would flush through the system; a few intractable PCBs might take a millennium.

During that same span, every dam on Earth would silt up and spill over. Rivers would again carry nutrients seaward, where most life would be, as it was long before vertebrates crawled onto the shore. Eventually, that would happen again. The world would start over.

Topics for Thought and Discussion

1. Choose a paragraph from this essay and look carefully at it as an example of description. How does Weisman use sensory detail (invoking the five senses)? What words from your paragraph seem to carry the most authority and power? Generalize about Weisman's word choice from the paragraph you've chosen.
2. What is the purpose, for Weisman, of discussing the Korean Demilitarized Zone and the Bialowieza Forest?
3. This article is primarily description, but is it also an argument? Would you say this article is more likely to support the environmental movement, or argue against it? Explain.
4. What is the result of considering the world without people? How does it make you feel? What does it make you think about? Does it make people seem more or less important, more or less powerful? Is this a useful exercise?

Suggestions for Writing

1. Choose an element, or a description, from Weisman's article that fired your imagination and expand and develop it. You may write a descriptive essay, or you may integrate your description into a short story.
2. Write an essay in which you discuss, in environmental terms, the position human beings should—and do—occupy in the world. You may use Weisman's article as evidence.

Science and the Environment: Making Connections

1. Aldo Leopold became an environmentalist after his experiences in the wilderness; Jonathon Rauch accuses environmental organizations of being blindly opposed to science and technology; Nicholas Kristof uses science to warn against coming cataclysm; Jared Diamond uses science to uncover the fate of Easter Island and the rich flora and fauna and human civilization of that place. All of these articles, directly or indirectly, link concern for the environment with science, though they do not all assume the same relationship between the two. From your reading in this chapter, what would you say is the relationship between science and the environmental movement? Are the two partners or adversaries?
2. Using any three of the essays in this chapter, evaluate the relationship between science and the environment. Is science, in general, dangerous and damaging to the environment? Is it a tool by which the environment is made better? Describe this relationship as carefully and insightfully as you can.
3. What is the relationship between global warming and "neo-catastrophism"? Using Kolbert's essay ("Ice Memory") and Kristof's essay ("Warm, Warmer, Warmest"), evaluate the relationship between these two models of climate change. Is climate change now out of our hands, and what, according to these writers, should we do?
4. Leopold ("Thinking Like a Mountain") asks us to "think like a mountain." Using two other essays from this chapter, discuss what the natural environment might be thinking about people these days. In other words, from the point of view of the natural world, what are the roles that humans play?
5. Many of the essays in this chapter issue warnings. Generalize about those warnings. Then, using specific examples from at least three essays, address them.

Frontiers

This chapter will introduce you to some of the ideas and issues on the frontier of today's science, and through these essays, will seek to provide you with a sense of where we are going and what the world of our future might look like. One way or another, this chapter will ask you to think about robots and evolution, about cyborgs and time machines, about space exploration and human engineering. It will ask you to think about where science itself is going, and where, in the end, science is taking us.

But these issues, as racy as they may seem, are really no different from any of the other science you have read about in the other chapters of this book. All science, after all, is in some ways about the frontier. The most basic research into nerve regeneration, into what killed the dinosaurs, into genetic manipulation, is by its nature designed to push forward, past what we already know, past the signposts erected by earlier scientists, and into new territory. Our chapters on "Bodies and Genes," "Science and the Environment," and "Human Behavior" have provided you with example after example of the frontier of science. That is the job of science: to push knowledge forward and help us understand the world better. If you have read through the other chapters in this book, you already have a pretty good idea of where the frontier of science is. It is all around us, in every field imaginable. The world and what we know about it, and what we can do in it, are changing fast; we know it, and expect it. As Fred Guterl notes in the essay that ends this chapter, "Pondering the Future's Future," "these days we've learned how to ride the rocket of innovation."

This chapter, then, rather than taking you into something radically different from what you've seen in other chapters, will instead give you a sense of where science itself is going, while at the same time introducing you to some of the bold and (admittedly) recognizable issues that will mark the future in profound ways for all of us. Will we get to the point where we can no longer tell the difference between humans and robots (as Dan Ferber suggests in "The Man Who Mistook His Girlfriend for a Robot")? How will we define *human* when technology has become a part of our bodies? For the disabled, as John Hockenberry points out ("The Next Brainiacs"), that moment is already here. Should we develop and use drugs that have the potential to improve our performance in all areas of our lives (James Vlahos's "Will Drugs Make Us Smarter and Happier")? Should we send humans into space (Tyson's "Launching the Right Stuff"), and can we really build a time machine (Davies's "How to Build a Time Machine")? And finally, what is the role of science in our lives and our future, and how will the ways we do science affect the future of the future (Guterl's "Pondering the Future's Future")?

Fred Guterl reports that the great science fiction writer Arthur C. Clarke, the author of dozens of books set in the future (most famously, perhaps, *2001: A Space Odyssey*), has said he seldom predicts the future; he merely extrapolates from the present. The essays in this chapter should give you material for extrapolation as you, too, think about where science is taking us, and what the world will be like for us, in one, ten, or fifty years. But your job, too, as you read these essays, is to consider not only the science, but also the ways that science will have to fit into our larger cultural lives. As science moves forward, society must accommodate it, integrate it, and make decisions about how to use it. That integration—and those decisions—will be largely up to you.

The Man Who Mistook His Girlfriend for a Robot

DAN FERBER

Dan Ferber is a freelance writer whose work has appeared in science and medical periodicals around the country. A contributing editor for Popular Science *and correspondent for* ScienceNow, *he is a member of the National Association of Science Writers, the Society of Environmental Journalists, and the National Writers Union.*

The following article appeared in Popular Science *in 2003. As you read this article, notice how Ferber defines and critiques "the uncanny valley."*

———————— ✦ ————————

It's the fourth day of a scientific conference in Denver—four busy February days in a huge rabbit-warren convention center with long hallways and fluorescent lighting and serious scientists giving serious PowerPoint presentations in darkened auditoriums; four days of breakthroughs and advances—nanotech to biotech, anthropology to zoology, the whole mind-spinning stew. Four days, for the assembled journalists, of making sense of it all and banging out stories on the fly—and now comes word of what could be a light interlude: *Keep an eye out for the guy carrying the head.* Say what? *The robotic human head.* The press people for the American Association for the Advancement of Science, the conference's sponsor, say the demonstration's on for tomorrow morning.

For now, though: another darkened auditorium, another presentation, this one on biologically inspired intelligent robots, robots that emulate the form and function of real creatures. Yoseph Bar-Cohen of NASA's Jet Propulsion Laboratory, a roundish, gray-haired dynamo, gives a whirlwind tour of the possibilities, which he says are not far off—insect-like bots that walk and fly and crawl and hop, others that dive and swim. Cynthia Breazeal from the MIT Media Lab shows videos of the world's most lovable robot, the infant-like Kismet, looking up innocently at a woman who's practically cooing at it; Breazeal talks about how she gave Kismet emotions and why. Finally, there's David Hanson, a grad student in interactive arts and engineering at the University of Texas at Dallas. He's got thick dark hair, a square jaw, urban-hip artsy sideburns, and he's moving a bit jerkily in a nervous-but-trying-to-stay-calm sort of way. This, it turns out, is the guy with the head—but the head is out of commission today and he's just showing slides: a smiling urethane self-portrait, a tan bot named Andy-roid, a pirate robot with earring and eye patch. Overlook the fact that they're disembodied heads and they all look remarkably lifelike.

And that, it turns out, makes Hanson's heads unique. The humanoids that have made news the past few years—Asimo, Grace, Kismet—are fine robots all, talented, versatile, smart, friendly. Asimo, the plastic-suited Honda humanoid, walks on two legs and welcomes visitors to the factory that builds it. Carnegie Mellon's

Grace, a six-foot-tall conglomeration of metal parts on wheels topped with an animated computer-monitor face, registered itself for a conference last year, found its way to the right room, and gave a presentation. Kismet, the media darling of a few years back, looks people in the eye, smiles when they do, and learns just like a baby would, by watching and copying. Who wouldn't like these three? Other robots are being designed to work as nurses, tutors, servants and companions. But despite their talents, every one of these robots looks . . . well, like a robot. They're sometimes appealing in a cartoonish sort of way, but they're metallic, awkward, clunky.

Not Hanson's heads. And for that reason, the next morning at 10:30 sharp the reporters are waiting—a roomful of them—and TV cameras are here to capture the debut of Hanson's latest, most advanced model. Hanson, 33, walks in and sets something on a table. It's a backless head, bolted to a wooden platform, but it's got a face, a real face, with soft flesh-toned polymer skin and finely sculpted features and high cheekbones and big blue eyes. Hanson hooks it up to his laptop, fiddles with the wires. He's not saying much; it might be an awkward moment except for the fact that everyone else is too busy checking out the head to notice. Then Hanson taps a few keys and . . . it moves. It looks left and right. It smiles. It frowns, sneers, knits its brows anxiously. Now the questions start, and Hanson is in his element: The head's got 24 servomotors, he says, covering the major muscles in the human face. It's got digital cameras in its eyes, to watch the people watching it, and new software will soon let the head mimic viewers. Its name is K-Bot, and it's modeled after Kristen Nelson, his lab assistant. And K-Bot is a hit. In the weeks following the head's debut, stories appear in newspapers and television on six continents. Hanson receives an abundance of e-mails and phone calls: from scientists who want to collaborate, from companies that make prosthetics and surgical-training devices, from movie producers, from companies that make sex dolls. Androidworld.com, a Web site that serves up humanoid parts, software and news, places Hanson's robot at the top of its list of 22 head projects, enthusing: "WOW—this guy is clearly one of the top head builders in the WORLD."

For a 33-year-old UTD grad student, it's an extraordinary burst of attention. But at least in the short term, the whole thing plays out just the way the buzz had billed it: Hanson's K-Bot serves, for a moment, as a light interlude. No one asks why, of all the roboticists in the world, only Hanson appears to be attempting to build a robotic head that is indistinguishable in form and function from a human. No one points out that he is violating a decades-old taboo among robot designers. And no one asks him how he's going to do it—how he plans to cross to the other side of the Uncanny Valley.

David Hanson has the sort of mixed pedigree that might just be a prerequisite for tilting at robotic windmills. On his Web page, he identifies himself as a sculptor-roboticist.

He spent two years in the late '80s as an aimless physics major at the University of North Texas in Denton, where he pursued, as he puts it, "wild imaginative flights of fancy"—for example, turning his apartment into a "tropical paradise" (plants, parrots, tree frogs, a running stream) for a four-day party he and his friends called Disturbathon. "The high jinks," he says, "were top-notch." Such projects fueled an absenteeism habit; Hanson's grades suffered, which cost him his financial aid and forced him to leave school. Then, in 1992, he was accepted at the Rhode Island School of Design, one of the country's top art schools.

At RISD, Hanson alienated professors by building the Primordial Ooze Bath, an enormous installation in which art patrons crawled, slid, and swam about in gelatinous seaweed extract. Back during his years as a lonely, oddball teenager, Hanson had immersed himself in drawing and sci-fi—Philip K. Dick and Isaac Asimov were favorites—and at RISD he managed, after a fashion, to meld his two passions. He took an artificial-intelligence class at nearby Brown University, and in 1995 he focused an independent-study project on "out-of-body experiences," building a remotely operated humanoid head on a retractable five-foot stalk. The head, which he sculpted as a self-portrait, wheeled from room to room and chatted with people (via a remote operator). "The idea was always hanging in my mind of turning a sculpture into a smart sentient being," he says.

After graduation, Hanson worked as an artist for six years, ending up at Disney in Los Angeles, where he sculpted theme-park characters, researched new materials, and hobnobbed with animatronics experts. In 2000, he saw Bar-Cohen speak at a conference on high-tech materials; at the Jet Propulsion Lab, Bar-Cohen was developing electroactive polymers to use as artificial muscles in NASA robots. Inspired, Hanson showed Bar-Cohen his portfolio, and Bar-Cohen decided to take a flier on this talented, motivated Walt Disney artist; he asked Hanson to write a book chapter describing how a network of artificial muscles could animate a robot. In early 2002, Bar-Cohen again tapped the talents of his young protégé, now a grad student at UTD; Bar-Cohen was preparing a presentation to NASA bigwigs on the agency's emerging robotics technology when he realized he needed some visual oomph—so he sent Hanson a plastic model of a human skull and gave him a week to build a head. The evening Hanson got the skull, in April 2002, he grabbed a pair of calipers and struck out for a popular bar in an artsy Dallas warehouse district called Exposition Park. There he quickly scanned the room and spotted Kristen Nelson—a willowy blue-eyed brunette he knew casually—chatting with a guy at the bar. Hanson walked past once or twice, and they smiled at each other. Finally he walked up and said hello. "Can I measure your skull?" he asked.

Or maybe that's not exactly, or entirely, what Hanson asked. By the time of the AAAS conference and the unveiling of K-Bot in February, Hanson's robot-model instincts had borne fruit beyond his wildest hopes: He and Nelson were engaged. Not surprisingly, their "meet cute" story has seen its share of tellings and retellings; when the two recount the evening, they finish each other's sentences and expand upon each other's details. Hanson says he asked Nelson if he could measure her skull. She remembers it slightly differently:

"He asked, 'Can I make you into a robot?'"

Can he make her into a robot? Can he make a robot into her? Should he even try? A month before Hanson and Nelson launched into barroom banter, Hanson had discovered that the almost universal answer from roboticists to that last question would be a resounding no: David Hanson should not try to make his robot look too much like Kristen Nelson—because to do so would mean risking a tumble into the depths of the Uncanny Valley.

In the late '70s, a Japanese roboticist named Masahiro Mori published what would become a highly influential insight into the interplay between robotic design and human psychology. Mori's central concept holds that if you plot similarity to humans on the x-axis against emotional reaction on the y, you'll find a funny thing happens on the way to the perfectly lifelike android. Predictably, the curve rises steadily, emotional embrace growing as robots become more human-like. But at a certain point, just shy of true verisimilitude, the curve plunges down, through the floor of neutrality and into real revulsion, before rising again to a second peak of acceptance that corresponds with 100 percent human-like. This chasm—Mori's Uncanny Valley—represents the notion that something that's like a human but slightly off will make people recoil. Here there be monsters.

Breazeal, creator of Kismet, has, like many of her colleagues, taken both inspiration and warning from the Uncanny Valley.

Kismet's gentle expression and enormous baby-blue eyes are designed to get the robot as close as possible on the acceptance curve to Mori's first peak, but it's so indisputably still a robot that there's no chance of it toppling over the precipice. To relate socially to a machine, Breazeal says, people must accept it. A mechanical human face that doesn't look quite right is "disquieting," she says. A realistic face that doesn't move right would be "doubly creepy."

Breazeal was the first to let Hanson know he was setting off into this uncharted territory. Hanson met her at a conference in early 2002 and struck up a conversation about robotic heads. "She seemed to totally reject the notion of reproducing the human face," he says. "I felt a little bit sad that this hero of mine would hold a view that was so opposite to my own. But I did feel defiant as well. And I felt a certain pleasure, like I was onto something." The first head Hanson built for Bar-Cohen—Andy-roid— is, frankly, a rudimentary prototype. A mere four servos allow it to make just a handful of rather unconvincing expressions. Once he finished with that model, though, Hanson plunged heedlessly into a pursuit of robotic verisimilitude way beyond anything ever attempted. He pored over *Gray's Anatomy* and clicked obsessively through medical Web sites, noting the major human facial muscles, from the occipitofrontalis, which elevates the eyebrow and wrinkles the forehead, to the depressor anguli oris, which pulls the corners of the mouth down into a frown. He took in the pioneering work of psychologist Paul Ekman, who has classified thousands of facial expressions, specifying which combinations of individual facial muscles move in what manner to create each one; he pondered the mechanics of how specific muscles and tendons and ligaments work together to move portions of the face. He studied the facial form, composition, proportions and contours of everyone he knew; he spent hours in front of the mirror making faces.

He then experimented with plastic molds and materials, fitting the head from the inside with 24 servomotors, two microprocessors, anchors and nylon fishing line to tug on the skin. Then he wired the head and programmed the software to control it.

It was tough going. To get accurate, believable expressions, Hanson fiddled endlessly with the placement of the servomotors and the lines that tug the skin. The urethane skin of his early prototype heads was too stiff and heavy for the servomotors to move, and so he had invented a new polymer, which he dubbed F'rubber (foam + rubber **x** Fred MacMurray). Now, he and Nelson worked to perfect the F'rubber formula, mixing 970 combinations of ingredients in the bathroom of the apartment they'd moved into in Hollywood, until they found one polymer that was elastic and flexible and remarkably stable. A month before K-Bot's February debut, Hanson spent three to four hours a day for a week in a local hardware store, piecing together brass plumbing parts to make a movable neck for the robot. Clerks asked him repeatedly if he was all right. Ultimately, Hanson built K-Bot with $400 in parts from hobby, crafts and hardware stores, paid for by his student loans.

As Hanson's work progressed, it became ever more clear that making lifelike robot heads meant more than building a convincing surface and creating realistic facial expressions. So late last year he began to consider K-Bot's brain. The Internet led him to a Los Angeles company, Eyematic, which makes state-of-the-art computer-vision software that recognizes human faces and expressions. Hanson sought out co-founder and chief technology officer Hartmut Neven, who gave him a beta version of the software. Then, through a mutual acquaintance Hanson had met at a scientific conference, he approached Jochen Triesch, a cognitive scientist at the University of California, San Diego, who was using robot heads to test theories about the mental processes underlying vision and rudimentary social skills. Also at UCSD was Javier Movellan, who was working on technologies that would allow a social robot to tutor schoolchildren. Hanson began commuting regularly to UCSD from Hollywood, three hours each way by train. One day this spring, Hanson and I visited Movellan's UCSD lab, a sunny room crowded with books and art and people and computers. Movellan has asked Hanson to build him a head, and is hoping to give it social skills. He and Marian Bartlett, a cognitive scientist who co-directs the UCSD Machine Perception Lab, have collaborated in the development of software featuring an animated schoolteacher who helps teach children to read. The child reads text on the screen. The schoolteacher can recognize if the child looks frustrated, and soon will be able to respond verbally. The character also makes expressions that correspond to the story the child is reading. Movellan plans to program one of Hanson's heads to do what the teacher character does, then test it with children. The scientific question, Hanson says, is "whether people respond more powerfully to a three-dimensional embodied face versus a computer-generated face."

Inspired by this sort of practical use of his human-like robotic head, Hanson has taken to calling K-Bot "a face for social robotics," and says he's "throwing down a glove" for robotics engineers. This is why he has little patience for the Uncanny Valley: It's a concept that plays on fear rather than possibility, that asserts we should shy away from making robots look too human, rather than asking what positive benefits there might be to the truly lifelike robot. "Achieving the subtlety of human appearance is a challenge that should really be undertaken," he says. Only realistic heads will challenge AI researchers to integrate the various robot capabilities— adaptive vision, natural language processing and more—to create "integrated humanoid robotics," Hanson says.

A face robot like K-Bot could also help psychologists figure out exactly which facial movements convey one person's fear, sadness, anger or joy to the mind of another. Today, psychologists try to do that by seeing how people interpret the raised eyebrows, furrowed brows and other expressions of actors in video clips or animated characters, says psychologist Craig Smith of Vanderbilt University. But even actors have difficulty precisely manipulating their expressions, so the experiments aren't always completely controlled, and animated characters may be too unrealistic. A humanoid head that makes accurate facial expressions, in which every facial movement could be precisely controlled, would enable researchers to find out, in three dimensions and in real time, the purpose of specific facial muscles in communicating emotion, Smith says. That, he says, would solve a mystery that's "been a puzzle since Darwin."

Late on the afternoon of our visit to Movellan's lab, Hanson and Triesch sat in the courtyard of a campus coffee shop, a cool breeze rustling the eucalyptus trees. They'd been planning to write a scientific paper about Hanson's facial robots but hadn't decided how to focus it. "What if we write a paper on how to cross the Uncanny Valley?" Hanson suggested. Triesch stretched out his long legs, looked at Hanson, and nodded: "I think it would be great."

Soon the two were in Triesch's conference room, plotting the Uncanny Valley on a white marker board. Hanson pointed to the lip of the valley. "Mori says, 'Go here. Don't go further. Don't, no matter what you do, go further!'" he said. Triesch's brow furrowed. Realism can't be plotted on one axis, Hanson continued; it depends on shape, timing, movement and behavior. The idea, he said, is "really pseudoscientific, but people treat it like it's science." Indeed, despite its status as dogma, the Uncanny Valley is nothing more than a theory. "We have evidence that it's true, and evidence that it's not," says Sara Kiesler, a psychologist at Carnegie Mellon

University who studies human-robot interaction. She calls the debate "theological," with both sides arguing with firm convictions and little scientific evidence—and says that the back-and-forth is most intense when it comes to faces. "I'd like to test it," she says, "with talking heads."

In a pivotal 2001 paper in *Science*, Olaf Sporns of Indiana University in Bloomington and six other leading roboticists described a new breed of robots that navigate the world and learn on their own. The new bots, which include Sporns's Darwin V, have mobile bodies and sensors that let them perceive their environment, much as we do. They're endowed with a developmental program that starts learning at birth. And they need human caretakers to teach them what they need to know about the world. As Triesch, who programs his robots on similar principles, says, "We're getting more into raising robots like children."

It will take decades at least to raise robots that are as smart and independent as we are, but the work has begun. Robots that learn on their own, robots that walk, robots that socialize with people, are all now in various stages of development. "A realistic autonomous humanoid is the Holy Grail," Sporns says. And, on the far side of the Uncanny Valley, robots would have a realistic, emotionally expressive face—a face that challenges robot-brain builders to make smarter robots, a face that fools us into treating a machine as if it were human. A face a person could grow attached to.

In his 2002 book, *Flesh and Machines*, leading MIT roboticist Rodney Brooks, who oversaw Kismet's development, writes that "mankind's centuries-long quest to build artificial creatures is bearing fruit." We'll have different relationships with these machines than all earlier machines, he suggests. "The coming robotics revolution," Brooks writes, "will change the fundamental nature of our society."

On a cool, sunny day this past spring, Hanson, Nelson and I scrambled up and down the steep rises and canyons of Griffith Park, the ubiquitous Hollywood sign perched on a nearby hillside, the sky bright blue above the L.A. smog. We rested on a hilltop, where we could see for miles. Humans are facing an identity crisis, Hanson said—one that just a few people know about but many sense. "If we can mechanize what makes us human, that will make us feel like a mechanism," he said. Maybe that's what really lies behind the resistance to realistic humanoids, the reluctance to venture into the Uncanny Valley. And when we do cross over? At the February AAAS conference, someone asked Hanson his ultimate goal. A compassionate robot, he said: a peer, a friend. The goal, he said, is "letting it loose."

Topics for Thought and Discussion

1. Why does Ferber take time to describe Hansen and his undergraduate career? What does this information contribute to Ferber's essay and to your feeling about Hansen himself?
2. Describe the "Uncanny Valley." Sara Keisler describes the debate over the "Uncanny Valley" as a theological one, implying that it is based more on faith and belief than on science and evidence. With what side do you align yourself? Do you think that Mori is right about people's reaction to a near-human robot?
3. What are the advantages and disadvantages of a human-like robot? What does Hansen mean when he says that the goal is "letting it loose"?
4. Should we make a human-like robot?

Suggestions for Writing

1. Unleash your imagination and make two lists, one of the advantages and uses of a truly human-looking robot, and one of the disadvantages of such a robot. Answer the question: "Should we make such a robot?" Why or why not?
2. Think about the position that robots and artificial intelligence (AI) occupy in our culture today (look at films, novels, stories, advertising, etc.) and write a single paragraph that generalizes and sums up our culture's feelings about and responses to robots and AI.
3. Use the paragraph that you wrote for #2 above to construct an argumentative thesis. Write a paper in which you take a stand either with or against the dominant cultural position.

The Next Brainiacs
JOHN HOCKENBERRY

John Hockenberry is a multiple-award-winning broadcast and print journalist (four Emmys, three Peabodys) who has created and hosted radio and television news programs for National Public Radio, ABC, NBC, and MSNBC. He has been a frequent contributor to the New York Times, *the* Washington Post, The New Yorker, *and* Wired, *among others, as well as being the author of* Moving Violations: War Zones, Wheelchairs and Declarations of Independence, *a memoir of his life as a foreign correspondent (a finalist for the National Book Critics Circle Award in 1996), and* A River Out of Eden *(2001), a novel. The following essay first appeared in* Wired *in 2001. Note how Hockenberry uses himself as a subject in the essay.*

──────────── ✦ ────────────

When you think disability, think zeitgeist.[1] I'm serious. We live at a time when the disabled are on the leading edge of a broader societal trend toward the use of assistive technology. With the advent of miniature wireless tech, electronic gadgets have stepped up their invasion of the body, and our concept of what it means and even looks like to be human is wide open to debate. Humanity's specs are back on the drawing board, thanks to some unlikely designers, and the disabled have a serious advantage in this conversation. They've been using technology in collaborative, intimate ways for years—to move, to communicate, to interact with the world.

When you think disability, free yourself from the sob-story crap, all the oversize shrieking about people praying for miracles and walking again, or triumphing against the odds. Instead, think puppets. At a basic level, physical disability is really just a form of puppetry. If you've ever marveled at how someone can bring a smudged sock puppet to life or talked back to Elmo and Grover, then intellectually you're nearly there. Puppetry is the original brain-machine interface. It entertains because it shows you how this interface can be ported to different platforms.

If puppetry is the clever mapping of human characteristics onto a nonhuman object, then disability is the same mapping onto a still-human object. Making the body work regardless of physical deficit is not a challenge I would wish on anyone, but getting good at being disabled is like discovering an alternative platform. It's closer to puppetry than anything else I can think of. I should know: I've been at it for 25 years. I have lots of moving parts. Two of them are not my legs. When you think John Hockenberry, think wheelchair. Think alternative platform. Think puppet.

Within each class of disability, there are different forms of puppetry, different people and technologies interacting to solve various movement or communication problems. The goal, always, is to project a whole human being, to see the puppet as a character rather than a sock or a collection of marionette strings.

───────────────

[1]Zeitgeist is a German word meaning "spirit of the time." It is used to refer to the taste and outlook of a particular historical period.

When you meet Johnny Ray, it's a challenge to see the former drywall contractor and amateur musician trapped inside his body, but he's there. Ray, a 63-year-old from Carrollton, Georgia, suffered a brain-stem stroke in 1997, which produced what doctors call "locked-in syndrome": He has virtually no moving parts. Cognitively he's intact, but he can't make a motion to deliver that message or any other to the world.

Getting a puppet with no moving parts to work sounds like a task worthy of the Buddha, but a pioneering group of neuroscientists affiliated with Emory University in Atlanta has taken a credible stab at it. In a series of animal and human experiments dating back to 1990, Philip Kennedy, Roy Bakay, and a team of researchers have created a basic but completely functional alternative interface using electrodes surgically implanted in the brain. In 1996, their success with primates convinced the FDA to allow two human tests. The first subject, whose name was withheld to protect her privacy, was a woman in the terminal stages of ALS (Lou Gehrig's disease); she died two months after the procedure. The second was Johnny Ray.

Kennedy, who invented the subcranial cortical implant used in these operations, wanted to create a device that could acquire a signal from inside the brain—a signal robust enough to travel through wires and manipulate objects in the physical world. Making this happen involved creating new access points for the brain, in addition to the natural ones (defunct in Ray's case) that produce muscle motion. Bakay has since moved to Rush-Presbyterian-St. Luke's Medical Center in Chicago, where he's part of an institute devoted entirely to alternative brain-body interfaces. The soft-spoken doctor wouldn't describe anything he does as show business, but to me the results of his work sound like a real-world version of the nifty plug Neo/Keanu sported in *The Matrix*.

"We simply make a hole in the skull right above the ear, near the back end of the motor cortex, secure our electrodes and other hardware to the bone so they don't migrate, and wait for a signal," Bakay says. The implant is an intriguing hybrid of electronics and biology—it physically melds with brain tissue.

"We use a small piece of glass shaped like two narrow cones into which a gold electrical contact has been glued," Bakay says. "The space in the cones is filled with a special tissue culture, and the whole thing is placed inside the motor cortex." The tissue culture is designed to "attract" brain cells to grow toward the contact. When brain cells meet gold, the electrical activity of individual cells is detectable across the electrode. Gold wires carry signals back out of the skull, where they are amplified. This produces a far more sensitive and usable signal than you get from surface technology like the taped-on electrodes used in EEGs.

To get a broad sense of what the patient's brain is doing, neurologists perform magnetic resonance imaging and compare changes in the motor cortex with voltages monitored through the electrodes. Then the doctors get really clever. The patient is encouraged to think simple thoughts that correspond to distinct conditions and movements, like hot/cold or up/down. Gradually, the doctors extract and codify electrical patterns that change as a patient's thoughts change. If a patient can reproduce and trigger the signal using the same thought patterns, that signal can be identified and used to control, say, a cursor on a computer screen. The technique is very crude, but what Bakay and his colleagues have demonstrated is a truly alternative brain-body interface platform.

Ray's implant was installed in 1998, and he survived to start working with the signals, which were amplified and converted to USB input for a Dell Pentium box. In the tests that followed, Ray was asked to think about specific physical motions—moving his arms, for example. Kennedy and Bakay took the corresponding signal and programmed it to move the cursor. By reproducing the same brain pattern, Ray eventually was able to move the cursor at will to choose screen icons, spell, even generate musical tones.

That this was in fact an alternative platform, a true brain-machine interface, was demonstrated after months of tests, when Ray reported that the thoughts he used to trigger the electrode—imagined arm motions—were changing. He was now activating the electrode by thinking about facial movements, and as he manipulated the cursor, doctors could see his cheeks move and his eyes flutter. Kennedy and Bakay had predicted that Ray's focused mental activity might result in neurological changes, but to see actual facial movements was a surprise. It didn't mean that his paralysis was receding, rather that his brain had tapped into capabilities rendered dormant by the stroke. The results showed that Ray's thoughts about motion were triggering clusters of motor neurons.

How? Kennedy and Bakay presumed the implant had put various motion centers in Ray's brain back into play. Disconnected from the body/hardware they once controlled, these neurons now had a crude way to interact. Adapting to the new platform, Ray's brain was demonstrating a flexibility standard worthy of Java or Linux.

As the brain cells in and around Ray's implant did what he asked them to do, the imagined sensation of moving his body parts gradually disappeared altogether. One day when his skill at moving the cursor seemed particularly adept, the doctors asked Ray what he was feeling. Slowly, he typed "nothing."

Ray was interacting directly with the cursor in a way similar to how he might once have interacted with his hand. "People don't think, 'move hand' to move their hands unless they are small children just learning," Bakay explains. "Eventually the brain just eliminates these intermediate steps until the hand feels like a part of the brain." The description reminds me of how I've heard Isaac Stern describe his violin as an extension of his body. I think of my wheelchair the same way.

The fact that Ray's cursor is indistinguishable from almost any other prosthesis raises an important philosophical question: Because of the implant, is a Dell Pentium cursor now more a part of Johnny Ray than one of his own paralyzed arms?

The National Institutes of Health is interested enough in this technology to have provided $1.1 million in seed funding for an additional eight human tests that will continue over the coming year. Bakay hopes the next patients won't be as profoundly disabled as the first two. "The more kinds of applications we find for this," Bakay says, "the more we learn about it."

From my perspective as a wheelchair puppet, life is a question of optimizing the brain-machine interface. In the beginning, this was far from obvious to me. My spinal cord was injured in a car accident when I was 19—an utterly random occurrence in which a woman picked me up while I was hitchhiking and later fell asleep at the wheel. She died. But I emerged from her crumpled car, then from a hospital, and resumed my life. I looked for a way to describe what I was doing: Rehabilitation was a word for it. Courage was a word for it. Coping was a word for it. But none of those labels even approached the reality of what relearning physical life was all about.

Since then I've been improvising motion by merging available body functionality (arms, hands, torso, neck, head) with a small arsenal of customized machines (wheelchairs, grabbers, cordless phones, remote controls, broomsticks with a bent nail pounded into the end). At times I've seen my own quest for new physical ability in odd places—a musician seeking virtuosity, an athlete seeking perfection. I've become convinced that the process of fine-tuning one's mobility through practice and the use of tools is as old as humanity itself. I've come to believe it is identical to an infant's task of developing coordination while facing near-zero available functionality of legs, arms, and muscles.

There is no better puppet show than watching your own children teach themselves to walk. In my case, it involved watching Zoë and Olivia, my twin daughters. Their strategies were complicated improvisations that proceeded from observing the world around them. Olivia made especially good use of her hands and arms, grabbing tables, drawer handles, and the spokes on my wheelchair to pull herself upright, where she would stand in place for long periods of time, feeling the potential in her chubby little legs.

Zoë spent weeks on her stomach flapping like a seal, hoping somehow to launch spontaneously onto her feet. She did not see her legs as helpful, and to her credit, in our house walking was merely one of two major models for locomotion. One morning, well before she was 2 years old and long before she walked, I placed Zoë in my wheelchair and watched as she immediately grabbed the wheels and began to push herself forward as though she'd been doing it for years. She had even figured out how to use the different rotation rates of the rear wheels to steer herself. Zoë had grasped that the wheelchair was the most accessible motion platform for someone—in this case, an infant—who couldn't use her legs. She smiled as she looked at me, with an expression that said something like, "Give up the wheels, Mr. Chairhog."

Zoë and Olivia walk perfectly now, but their choices in those formative weeks were startlingly different. In both, the same brain-machine transaction was at work creating functionality from what was available. Engineers and designers have discovered that this is a process as distinctive as fingerprints. Every person solves problems in his or her own way, with a mix of technology and body improvisation. The variables are cultural and psychological, and precise outcomes are difficult to predict—but they determine what technology will work for which person. Think puppetry as a universal metaphor for the design of machines.

Jim Jatich has been a cyborg puppet for years now and is proud of it. A 53-year-old former engineering technician and draftsman from Akron, Ohio, Jatich is a quadriplegic who first donated his body to science back in 1978. A near-fatal diving accident the year before left him without use of his legs and hands, and with limited use of muscles in his arms and shoulders.

The computer term *expansion port* was unknown back in the late '70s, but Jatich's doctors at Case Western Reserve University in Cleveland arrived at the same idea. They imagined building an alternative path around Jatich's injured spinal cord to restore a local area network that could be controlled by his brain.

In a series of operations and therapies starting in 1986, Jatich became the first human to receive surgically implanted electrodes in his hands to mimic nerves by stimulating the muscles with tiny bursts of electricity. The process is known as functional electrical stimulation, or FES. By using a shoulder-mounted joystick to trigger patterns of electrical impulses, Jatich was able to open and close his hands. Others have since used the technology to move leg muscles and allow the exercise of paralyzed limbs.

Two years ago, a research assistant named Rich Lauer came to Jatich with the suggestion that he think about tapping into his brain directly. "This one sounded real crazy," Jatich says. "He claimed he had a way to see if I could control first a computer cursor and then maybe the muscles of my hand, just by thinking. I thought it was BS," he says with a wink. "You know, brain science."

Researchers placed a skullcap containing 64 electrodes on Jatich's head. These produced a waveform of his brain activity, though the signal was much weaker than the one obtained from Johnny Ray's cortical implants. Like Ray's doctors, the researchers asked Jatich to concentrate on simple but opposite concepts like up and down. They carefully observed the EEG for readable changes in brain patterns. They used software to measure the maximums and minimums in his overall brain wave and to calculate the moving averages in exactly the same way stock analysts try to pull signals from the jagged data noise of the stock market. A pattern was identified and fashioned as a switch: Above the average equaled on; below the average, off. With this switch they could control a cursor's direction and, as a hacker might say, they were "in."

While Jatich's doctors worked to optimize the software, he concentrated on a wall-size computer screen. Monitoring changes in his EEG and modifying the programming accordingly produced a kind of biofeedback. Gradually, like Johnny Ray, Jatich was able to move a flashing cursor to the middle of a projected line. The goal was to have the computer search for distinct, recallable brain-wave patterns that could be used to control any number of devices that could be connected to a chip.

Jatich says there was nothing portable about the equipment— he found the electrode skullcap cumbersome and the whole system a bit rickety. "Cell phones down the hall at the hospital would cause the thing to go blank every once in a while." But the enterprise did deliver a breakthrough he hadn't anticipated.

"When I got downstairs after the first couple of experiments," he says, "I was sitting outside, waiting for my ride, and it hit me. I had caused something to move just by using my mind alone. The tears streamed down my face, because it was the first time I had done that since I got injured." Jatich says he felt like "a kid being handed keys to a car for the first time."

Going from manually controlled FES to brain implants that bypass the spinal cord to produce muscle movement would represent a significant leap. But Ron Triolo, a professor of orthopedics and biomedical engineering at Case Western and a clinician at the Cleveland FES Center, thinks this is possible. He sees this leap as the possible fulfillment of FES's many, often outsize, promises for people with disabilities. The challenge is immense, but, as Triolo puts it, "Failure is closer to success than doing nothing. I've seen some of the preliminary work on cortical control and it's impressive. Clearly, it's going to pay off eventually."

Since Jatich's first implantable hand device was installed, the technology for nerve stimulation has advanced to the point where the reliable, long-lasting electrodes in both of his hands are barely visible, require practically zero maintenance, and have become more or less permanent parts of his body. For the last 15 years, he's used a shoulder joystick controller to move his right hand. Controlling his left hand is an IJAT, or implantable joint angle transducer, which employs a magnet and sensor attached to the bones of the wrist. Slight movements trigger complex hand-grasping motions. The computer mounted on the back of Jatich's wheelchair stores the software that helps produce as many as five different motions, which he can specify depending on whether he wants to hold a pencil and write or grasp a utensil and feed himself—capabilities he would not otherwise have at all.

Over the years, Jatich has gone from being a person completely dependent on others to having some degree of autonomy. His grasping ability means he can use a computer and feed himself, among other simple tasks. In the past few years, Jatich has been able to do some mechanical drawing, using his hand devices along with commercially available computer-aided design systems.

Thinking about taking the next step—an implant that might allow him to connect his brain, via computer, to his electrode-filled hands—excites him. "You could sure get a hell of a signal from the surface of the brain as compared to the electrodes in that ugly skullcap," Jatich says. He speaks as though he's talking about a science fair project and not the tissue under his own cranium. "I would have to think hard about it, but if they could deliver on their promises, it would be great. I would do it in a minute."

Suddenly, million-dollar grants are being thrown around to investigate the possibilities of direct interaction with the brain. While much of the study is geared toward finding ways to reopen avenues closed by massive paralysis, it also raises the possibility of creating alternative brain outlets to the world in addition to the ones we were born with. The FDA won't allow it yet, but there's no scientific barrier preventing some brave pioneer from adding a new ability—for instance, a brain-controlled wireless device to regulate climate and lighting in one's home. In November, British cybernetics professor Kevin Warwick plans to have a chip implanted next to his arm's central nerve bundle so he can experiment with sending and receiving digital signals.

"Deep brain stimulation" is the overarching term for the therapies in development, and specific projects are under way to address severe nervous system disorders like Parkinson's disease, TBI (traumatic brain injury), and other locked-in syndromes. The NIH has embarked on an aggressive program to develop cortical control devices as the first truly practical neuro-prostheses. This is a kind of low-bandwidth alternative to the field of spinal cord research focused on repairing injured spinal tissue and restoring the original brain-muscle connection.

Dubbed "the Cure" by its passionate supporters, savvy marketers, and fundraisers, this vision of spinal cord repair has a much higher profile and is far better financed than FES and other alternative-interface explorations. The Cure has Christopher Reeve as its cash-gushing poster boy. FES has Jim Jatich. Cortical implant technology has Johnny Ray. Certainly, anyone who wakes up with a spinal cord injury is inclined to hope for a cure above all other options. But one would expect medical research strategies to be more detached from the emotional trauma of disability. As someone who has lived in a wheelchair comfortably for a quarter century, it is hard to justify why the Cure would be so favored over its alternatives.

Rush-Presbyterian's Roy Bakay expresses some frustration that his efforts directly compete with the Cure movement for funding. "We can do things for people now, whereas spinal cord research isn't going to pay off for a very long time, if at all. I'm not saying that spinal cord research shouldn't be conducted, just that [deep-brain stimulation] may be a more immediate solution for getting the brain to interact with the outside world." Others report that Reeve's visibility has made it more difficult to find people willing to try new technology involving surgery or implants. "They say they want to keep their bodies in good shape for when the Cure happens," says Jatich, who often counsels people considering FES.

Reeve was injured in a 1995 horse-riding accident; he can't move anything below his neck and needs assistance to breathe. Despite declaring shortly after the accident that he would someday walk again, Reeve is not pro-Cure to the exclusion of all other options. He has carefully maintained that he supports any endeavor that might help people with disabilities. He has muted his personal predictions about walking again, though he is still dedicated to the

Cure. The movement Reeve helped create represents those who believe the body is the brain's best interface to the outside world. Certainly, there's nothing on the market to give the fully functioning body any serious competition. Yet for people without one, supplementing bodies with onboard technology to increase functionality is a way around the wait for a full cure.

It's a familiar trade-off: As every technology develops, there is the tension of using the interesting but cumbersome first-wave device versus waiting until the tech is small enough, convenient enough, or integrated enough with the body to bother with it. This trade-off has been debated within the disabled community for generations, and it is just starting to be reflected in the broader culture.

The field with perhaps the best track record in dealing with complicated brain-machine interfaces is communications technology for the sensory- and voice-impaired. It's also the area in which the trade-offs between functionality and ease of use are most critical. With computers, turning text into voice is considerably easier than making a device that operates with the ease and speed of speech.

"There is a real issue of gadget tolerance, and people have finite limits," says Frank DeRuyter, chief of speech pathology at Duke University Medical Center and a leader in the field of augmented communication. "Our smart systems need to be environmentally sensitive or they don't get used." DeRuyter has worked with all kinds of communications devices, from primitive boards—little more than alphabets and pictures used by noncommunicators to slowly construct sentences by pointing—to more sophisticated electronic speech-synthesis devices. All have their own advantages and disadvantages, which are ignored at a designer's peril.

DeRuyter describes how designers can be locked into narrow functionality traps that keep them from seeing the world the way the disabled do. "Talking is a portable communications system that enhances every other activity. We used to put some of our noncommunicators into the pool each day, and we could never figure out why they hated it. Then we realized that by removing electronic communications boards that couldn't tolerate water, their pool time was the equivalent of being gagged. We designed some simple, waterproof alphabet boards and the problem went away. Pool time became fun."

Michael B. Williams is an augmented communications technology user and a disability rights activist from Berkeley, California. He relies on three devices to communicate: two VOCAs (voice output communication aids, basically chip-controlled text-to-voice synthesizers) and a low-tech waterproof alphabet board. The board, he told me in an email, is there "for when California's power goes out," and for "private thoughts in the shower." Williams's smaller VOCA is a spell-and-speak device that is handy enough for dinner table conversations. His largest and most advanced VOCA is "heavy and hard on the knees," but has rapid word access that enables Williams to give public speeches in a kind of partial-playback mode, which he has been doing for years now.

Diagnosed with cerebral palsy as a young child, Williams struggled with the speech therapy recommended by medical and educational professionals to enable him to control his mouth and use his own voice. His eventual rejection of this mode of communication was a simple technology decision; the brain-machine interface called speech is, in his case, seriously flawed. He describes his voice as being "like used oatmeal," and he has instead acquired the tech to live on his own terms, according to his personal specifications. When Williams gives speeches, his advanced VOCA offers the choice of 10 different programmed voices (he prefers the one called Huge Harry for himself). When he quotes someone, he uses a different voice, and it sounds like two people are on stage.

"This bit of electronic tomfoolery seems to wow audiences," he says in an email, his sly showman's confidence coming through. So when you think about Williams, don't think courageous crippled guy giving a speech. Think puppetry, ventriloquism, Stephen Hawking.

Williams says it's impossible to evaluate any technology on function alone. For instance, he says the value of his ability to communicate is directly related to his mobility. "Someone recently asked me, 'If you were given a choice of having a voice or a power wheelchair, which would you choose?' This is a no-brainer for me. I would choose the power wheelchair. What would I do with only a voice—sit at home and talk to the TV? Another thing I wouldn't give up is my computer. With a computer and a modem I can get my thoughts, such as they are, out to the world."

Frank DeRuyter says designers need to think in the broadest possible terms when they approach human-interface technology. "We're just beginning to realize the importance of integrating movement technology with communications tech. We see that a GPS device can powerfully increase the functionality of a communications board. When people roll their wheelchairs into a grocery store, the GPS will automatically change the board's stored phrases and icons into ones relevant to shopping. Shifting context as you move—that's what the brain does. Now we can do it, too."

This idea of optimizing a personal brain-machine interface is as much an issue for engineers at Nokia, Motorola, and other manufacturers of wireless technology as it is for people designing for the disabled. Companies need people to actually buy and use their devices, not just gawk at them in glossy trade magazines. On a street in Manhattan last fall, it hit me: four people, one intersection. One man with a cell phone and headset was talking calmly and loudly, oblivious to the rest of the world. Another had a cell phone handset pressed to his head and was attempting to get a scrap of paper, one-handed, from his briefcase. A woman was at the pay phone looking for a quarter. The fourth person stood waiting for the light to change, looking at his wristwatch. If the four were frozen at that intersection, how would future paleontologists construe their fossilized differences? Four people, four different capabilities, four distinct species. Five, if you count me. Man with wheelchair . . . no cell phone.

"There is a calculus in this field that we have come to know from decades of experience," says Ron Triolo of the Cleveland FES Center. "People don't want to lose anything they already have, and that includes wasted time, as well as an arm or a leg. But if they can increase functionality without losing anything, they want to do that.

"How we thought people would benefit from FES is different from what actual users have told us," he continues. "For instance, we imagined that FES would be of no value unless it was nearly invisible and provided a level of function comparable to the pre-injured state. We discovered we were talking from an ivory tower. People enjoy the ability to make even the most rudimentary physical motions and don't particularly care if those motions don't lead to jobs or activities associated with their life pre-injury."

Triolo describes novel ways in which disabled people have taken off-the-shelf equipment and used it in sometimes alarming ways, well beyond the designer's imagination. A man who uses his FES system to stand has improvised a way to clumsily hop up and down stairs. A female FES user recently sent Triolo a picture of herself standing, à la *Titanic*, on the bow of a boat under full sail. "If she had gone into the water . . ." He pauses to find words to convey both his fear (of massive product liability, perhaps) and his admiration for the woman's guts. In the end he can only say, "Well, you know."

In my case, projecting my independence as a collaboration between machine, body, and brain is an important message, if difficult to convey. I can coast flat out and slalom effortlessly around pedestrians, and produce equal measures of awe and terror. No matter how skilled I am in my chair, people often wonder why I don't use a motorized one. I love using a machine I never have to read a manual to operate. Why can't they see the value of my ragged optimizing strategies? Think Xtreme sports, hot-dogging.

There are also deep cultural factors that sometimes surprise and frustrate designers of technology for the disabled. One of the first machine-to-brain devices, the cochlear implant, was heralded as a miracle cure for some forms of deafness when it was fully introduced in the 1990s. The electronic device, mounted inside the ear, works like FES on muscle tissue. In this case, the electrodes, responding to sound, stimulate different regions of the cochlea at a rate equivalent to a 91K modem. The cochlea, in turn, sends signals to the brain that can be processed as sound. The device requires training the brain to decipher the implant's stimulus and does not replace or completely restore hearing. Many deaf people view the implant as a form of ethnic cleansing and physical mutilation. The cochlear implant, according to opponents, is a direct confrontation to the shared experience of deafness, the language of signing, and all of the hot-dogging improvisations deaf people have developed over many generations to function without hearing.

Brenda Battat is the deputy executive director of Self-Help for Hard of Hearing People, a national organization in Bethesda, Maryland, that counsels people who are considering traditional hearings aids and cochlear implants. She believes opposition to the cochlear implant is moderating. Still, she says, technology requires an investment of time and emotion that engineers and users often aren't aware of. "Whatever technology you use, you're still a person with a hearing loss. When the battery breaks down, there is a moment of absolute panic. It's a very scary feeling." That feeling of dependence relates as much to the type A technoid having seizures over the dead batteries in his BlackBerry as it does to Johnny Ray adjusting to the imperfections of his brain implant. Anyone using an assistive technology system expects it will work every time, under a wide variety of conditions, without degrading any of their existing capabilities.

Perhaps the best example of a technology solution that interacts directly with the brain is the Ibot wheelchair, now in the final stage of prelaunch testing by Johnson & Johnson and the FDA. Designer Dean Kamen wanted to create a transportation device that would have the equivalent functionality of walking, climbing stairs, standing upright, and all-terrain motion. To operate in upright, two-wheel stand-up mode, the Ibot uses an onboard computer and a system of miniaturized aviation-grade gyros to assess the center of gravity and deliver a signal to high-speed motors. These turn the wheels accordingly to compensate and keep the user from falling over.

My first impression of the machine was not positive. The Ibot is a cumbersome, complicated thing that makes you dread being stuck somewhere without a tool kit. But watch the Ibot balancing, making little rocking motions to keep it upright, and you feel as though you're in the presence of some humanoid intelligence.

When Kamen began testing his chair with disabled users, he discovered an eerie and unanticipated brain-machine interface. "Each person we took up the stairs said, 'Great.' They said great when we took them through the sand and the gravel and up the curb and down the curb. But when we stood them up and made them eye level with another person, and they could feel what it was like to balance, every single one of them started crying."

Kamen believes that people who use the Ibot in its two-wheel balancing mode are literally feeling the experience of walking, even though the machine is doing the work. "If you could get an MRI picture of the balance center of the brain of some person in a wheelchair who goes up on the Ibot's two wheels, I bet you'd see some lights go on," he says. "I'm convinced the brain remembers balancing, and that's why people feel so much emotion."

I felt exactly that when I used the Ibot for the first time and stood upright. The chip was making the wheels move, but my brain's own sense of balance seemed to instantly merge with the machine. Its decisions seemed to be mine. No implants. No wires. It was truly extraordinary. Think FDR on a skateboard.

This raises a fairly revolutionary point about brains and the physical world. Bodies are perhaps a somewhat arbitrary evolutionary solution to issues of mobility and communication. By this argument, the brain has no particular preference for any physical configuration as long as functionality can be preserved.

Michael Williams believes that the disabled have helped humanity figure this out in terms of technology. He thinks people are rapidly losing their fear of gadgets. "The greatest thing people with disabilities have done for the general population is to make it safe to look weird. It's certainly true that the general population has glommed onto some principles of assistive tech. Just roll down the street and observe the folks with wires dangling from their ears. Look at the TV commercials featuring guys with computerized eyewear."

The history of assistive technology for the disabled shows that people will sacrifice traditional body image if they can have equivalent capabilities. It's a profound lesson for designers and people who irrationally fear brain implants. It perhaps has even more practical implications for people who are waiting for a cure to restore their functions. The brain-body-machine interface doesn't seem to need the body as much as we believe it does.

Think many different puppets . . . same show.

For those open to the possibility, the definition of human includes a whole range of biological-machine hybrids, of which I am
only one. The ultimate promise of brain-machine technology is to
add functionality—enhanced vision, hearing, strength—to people
without disabilities. There is nothing of a technological nature to
suggest that this can't happen, and in small but significant ways it
has already begun. The organic merging of machine and body is a
theme of human adaptation that predates the digital age.

As I think about the quarter century I've spent in a wheelchair,
there are almost no traditional concepts to describe the experience. As I weave around the obstructions of the world's low-
bandwidth architecture, with its narrow doors and badly placed
steps, I find my journey to be less and less some sentimental, stoic
"go on with your life, brave boy" kind of thing and more part of a
universal redrafting of the human design specification. I am drawn
back to Michael Williams and his disarming motto: "The disabled
have made it OK to look weird." There is such wisdom and promise
in that statement.

People with disabilities—who for much of human history died
or were left to die—are now, due to medical technology, living full
lives. As they do, the definition of humanness has begun to widen.
I remember encountering, on a street corner in Kinshasa in the former Zaire, a young man with the very same spinal cord injury as
my own, rolling around in a fabulous, canopied hand-pedaled
bike/wheelchair/street RV. He came up to me with a gleam of
admiration for my chair and invited me to appreciate his solution
to the brain-body interface problem. We shared no common language, but he immediately recognized how seamlessly my body
and chair merged. That machine-body integrity is largely invisible
to the people who notice only the medical/tragedy aspect of my experience. I could see how he had melded even more completely
with his chair—in fact, it was almost impossible to see where his
body left off and his welded-tube contraption began. It was clear
he was grateful for my admiration.

As time has passed, I am conscious of how little I miss specific
functions of my pre-accident body, how little I even remember them
in any concrete way. I used to think this was some psychological
salve to keep me from being depressed over what has been a so-far
irreversible injury. I have come to believe that what is really going on
is a much more interesting phenomenon. My brain has remapped
my physical functions onto the physical world by using my remaining nonparalyzed body, a variety of new muscle skills, tools, recon-
figured strategies for movement and other functions, and by making

the most of unforeseen advantages (good parking spaces, for instance). This is something that has taken me years to learn.

My daughters have never known any other way of looking at me. As they grow older, they will no doubt be introduced by people around them to the more conventional way of thinking about their poor, injured, incapacitated daddy. I suspect they will see the flaws in this old way of thinking far more quickly than their little friends who come though our house warily regarding the man in the purple chair with wheels.

In a straightforward way that needs no psychological jargon to explain, my former body simply doesn't exist anymore. Like Isaac Stern and his violin, I am now part chair, with some capabilities that exceed my original specifications.

There's a very old story about a puppet that worked so hard to live in the real world, it eventually stopped being a puppet. The experience of interacting in the world connected this wooden puppet to the humans around him to the point where he was indistinguishable from them. An unstated corollary of the fable is that the humans were equally indistinguishable from the wooden puppet. I'm not lying.

Think Pinocchio. Think real boy.

Topics for Thought and Discussion

1. Describe some of the metaphors that help Hockenberry organize this article. Identify as many as you can, and describe how they serve him as a writer.

2. Hockenberry begins by redefining *disability*, and ends by redefining *human*. What are these definitions and how do they serve to organize Hockenberry's larger argument?

3. Name some of the assistive technologies that you use. How are they like and unlike the technologies that Hockenberry describes?

4. Analyze Hockenberry's tone and his position as a narrator. Could a nondisabled person have written this essay? Explain.

5. What are some of the social, cultural, and scientific issues that Hockenberry's essay asks us to consider?

Suggestions for Writing

1. Write a paper in which you evaluate your own identity as a puppet. In what ways are you aware of the strategies of your brain to maximize performance and functionality?

2. Respond to Hockenberry's final claim that "the definition of human includes a whole range of biological-machine hybrids." Construct an argument in which you address the issue of what makes us human, particularly in the face of increasing use of assistive technologies.

3. Construct an argument in which you address the availability of assistive technologies. Should these biological-machine hybrids be available only to the disabled, or should all people be allowed, as Hockenberry says, "to add functionality—enhanced vision, hearing, strength"?

Will Drugs Make Us Smarter and Happier?
JAMES VLAHOS

James Vlahos is a writer whose work on science and the outdoors has appeared in a wide assortment of magazines and journals, including Esquire, Skiing, National Geographic Adventure, Popular Mechanics, *and* Popular Science. *Vlahos's work focuses on the relationship between humans and their world. Often he is interested in the physical challenge posed to humans by the outdoors. Other times, as in the following article, which first appeared in* Popular Science *in 2005, he investigates the impact on humanity of current trends in science. As you read the following essay, note the way that Vlahos moves around in time, and what that structure provides for him rhetorically.*

◆

J*une 6, 2025, 7:30 A.M. The alarm is going off, and I feel great. Thanks to Reposinex, I've had a full four hours of deep, restorative sleep. My head hit the pillow, and boom! I was right into slow-wave delta sleep. In the car, driving to work, I sip an Achieve latte. I love these things—they sensitize my dopamine receptors, shift my MAO levels, and send my noradrenaline levels soaring. I have no jitters, and my concentration is tack-sharp. Driving used to freak me out, actually. I was involved in a bad accident a few years back. Good thing the doctor prescribed that trauma blunter. I still remember the accident; it just doesn't bug me anymore. I'm no longer one of those Human 1.0s—I'm a human with complete control of his brain chemistry.*

June 6, 2005, 7:30 P.M. Ramez Naam has a queen and a six face-up on the green felt of the blackjack table. The dealer shows a six. The obviously correct strategy is for Naam to stay, but this is his first time gambling at a casino, and nothing is obvious to him. Naam is 32, with dark hair and a neatly trimmed goatee. He peers uncertainly at his hand through blue-rimmed glasses, then taps the table with his fingertips. The dealer flips a card: a jack. Naam is out. He's blown through his $40 stack of chips in less than 10 minutes.

Designing software for Microsoft is Naam's job; envisioning the future—one in which biotechnology would allow us to shatter natural evolutionary limits—is his calling. A senior member of futurist think tanks such as the Acceleration Studies Foundation and the Foresight Institute, he speaks regularly at technology trade shows and is the author of the provocative new book *More Than Human: Embracing the Promise of Biological Enhancement*. Like most over-achievers, Naam doesn't like to lose. In blackjack and in life, of course, many factors are beyond our control—we can't choose what we're dealt, from the card deck or the genetic one—and Naam argues that we should change the restrictive rules of the biological game. He asks: What if you could pop a pill to make you remember more, think faster, or become happier or higher-achieving? What if there were safe steroids for the brain? You could effectively stack the deck, and the payoff could be huge.

The prospect of drug-enabled superminds is not just a futurist's fantasy. In the past 20 years, scientists—aided by advances in computing, brain imaging and genetic engineering—have made significant progress toward understanding the biochemical systems that regulate cognition and emotion. This knowledge has raised the possibility of manipulating those systems more powerfully and precisely than ever before. One prominent neuroscientist, Anjan Chatterjee, calls what's coming the era of cosmetic neurology. "Prospecting for better brains may be the new gold rush," he says.

Roman Casino, where I've met Naam, is Caesar's Palace on a serious budget, located in a strip mall near Seattle rather than on the Strip in Vegas. Coming here was my idea. A casino—where quick thinking, a good memory and control of your emotions can pay—seemed like a fitting backdrop for getting an overview of the possibilities of enhancement drugs. After a fruitless go at the tables, Naam and I retreat to the bar and order rum-and-Cokes.

"We've been enhancing ourselves since the dawn of civilization," he says. The latest drugs are, to be sure, considerably more complex than the caffeine and alcohol we're sending toward our bloodstream at the moment. And the way new enhancement pills reach us is complex as well: A pharmaceutical company develops a medication to treat a recognized physical or mental illness; people gradually realize that the drug can help healthy users too; doctors prescribe the substance to patients "off label," meaning for purposes other than the ones recognized by the Food and Drug Administration; and other people obtain it illegally. Thus, college students end up popping Ritalin to help them ace exams. Concert pianists take propranolol, a hypertension and angina medication, to ease preperformance jitters. And coffee addicts switch to Provigil, a sleep-disorder medication, for powerful, enduring, jitter-free stimulation.

Naam argues that we shouldn't be limited to using bootlegs of therapeutic drugs (FDA rules prohibit the development of drugs just for enhancement). If companies could turn their attention directly to the task, he says, "in the next few decades, we could create new drugs to sculpt or alter any aspect of human behavior: infatuation, pair-bonding, empathy, appetite, spirituality, thrill-seeking, arousal, even sexual orientation."

These drugs wouldn't simply be nice to have, he and other enhancement advocates believe—they would enable a societal transformation every bit as significant as the one wrought by computers. To true believers like Naam, the issue with drugs of the future is about cognitive liberty, the right to do what we want with our minds. It is about a capitalistic fight for the neurocompetitive advantage: The country with the most drug-enhanced citizens wins. And it is an ideological war against bio-Luddites. Past technological revolutions have allowed us to master the world around us. The pharmaceutical one, he believes, will allow us to master the world within.

11:15 A.M. Five projects, 10 deadlines, an uncountable number of engineering calculations. And I'm on top of it all. Since I started taking a cognitive enhancer, I don't seem to forget a thing. And my mind runs so much faster. My boss doesn't appreciate all I do, of course, but that doesn't irritate me. Emoticeuticals—gotta love 'em. Zen-like calm, but I still feel the important stuff. If I did somehow get ticked and reached for a cigarette—my crutch from way back when— it wouldn't do any good. Nicotine vaccination. No point in ever taking a drag again.

The road to Naam's pharma-utopia may begin here: on a slide, under a microscope, where two slices of rat hippocampus are being stimulated by electrodes. The neurons in slice one have been treated with a type of drug known as an ampakine, while those in slice two have not. A computer records the levels of electrochemical signaling within each slice. The experiment looks low-tech, like something out of my seventh-grade science class, but it has far-reaching implications: Ampakines may prove to be the world's most powerful cognitive-enhancing, memory-boosting drugs.

I squint through the microscope for a few seconds, making out pale gray cell bodies surrounded by tangles of stringy dendrites, and then head down a hall to the office of Gary Lynch. A neuroscientist at the University of California at Irvine, Lynch made a series of discoveries in the late 1980s and early 1990s about memory and the ways in which it might be manipulated chemically. In 1987 he co-founded a biotech company called Cortex Pharmaceuticals, which has been working since 1993 to bring an ampakine drug to market.

Lynch is waiting for me behind his desk. Sixty-one years old, he looks like a curly-haired version of Martin Short, complete with broad upper lip, grin full of teeth, and eyes glinting with private mischief. After a few preliminaries, he launches into his favorite subject—memory—and quickly gains oratorical traction. "If these drugs do what I do expect them to do, which is to improve cognition, the social implications could be astounding," he says. "So much of our society is built around the idea of people thinking they're smart or dumb—maybe you'd have people taking the pills and saying, 'I should be a professor at Harvard instead of doing this daily grind.'"

Cortex isn't alone in the quest to boost cranial capacity. About 40 other companies, including behemoths such as Eli Lilly and GlaxoSmithKline, are pursuing what many consider the holy grail of pharmacology, a pill to boost sagging memory—Viagra for the brain. The profit potential is enormous. Some 4.5 million Americans suffer from Alzheimer's disease, which currently has only marginally helpful drug therapies; at least four million are afflicted with mild cognitive impairment, a precursor to Alzheimer's; and more than 10 million have age-associated memory impairment, which means their memories are far below average for their age. And, as is the case with drugs like Provigil, there's an off-label market as well. "Companies won't tell you this, but they are really gunning for the market of non-impaired people—the 44-year-old salesman trying to remember the names of his customers," James McGaugh, another U.C. Irvine neuroscientist, has said.

Cortex is attempting to improve cognition by tinkering with the brain's intricate system of electrochemical communication. To convey information, neurons release various types of neurotransmitter molecules, which bind to complementary receptor sites on adjoining neurons. Successful "docking" signals the neuron to open a channel that allows positive ions to flow inside, thus charging the cell. Ampakines crank up the volume of this neuronal conversation.

They bond to the ampa receptor, which receives the neurotransmitter glutamate, causing the channel to stay open longer, allowing a stronger electrical charge to build.

"You can take a rat's brain, stimulate one cortical region, and measure the electrical signal from another," Lynch says. "Wash in an ampakine, and the signal is bigger." Better signaling is thought to provide a cognitive boost, particularly in older brains with withering neurons. Aging baseball players have trouble hitting in part because they can't process visual information as quickly, Lynch says. "Nothing is going to change that fact. But with an ampakine, maybe you could hit a curveball."

Also intriguing to Lynch is the effect of ampakines on memory. When one neuron signals another, the connection between them becomes stronger. The frequency and strength of signaling helps determine how long the connection—known as potentiation—will endure. A link lasting for days or years is called long-term potentiation (LTP), and LTP is the fundamental biological mechanism of memory. Ampakines enhance LTP. Extending the amount of time that glutamate bonds to the ampa receptors triggers the opening of the neighboring NMDA receptors (another docking site for glutamate). They, in turn, admit calcium into the neuron, which signals the cell to establish LTP.

Ampakines have an additional, related benefit: They trigger the production of brain-derived neurotrophic factor (BDNF), which many researchers suspect will lead to the creation of more receptor sites. In other words, the drug doesn't just make the neurons listen longer, it also builds new ears. In rats, Lynch has been able to reverse memory decline using single injections of an ampakine, giving middle-aged animals memory abilities nearly equivalent to those of young ones. Maybe, Lynch speculates, ampakines will have the same regenerative effect in humans. "Can we make it go from the winter of the brain to the spring?" he asks.

Cortex has begun to gauge the efficacy of its drugs on people; earlier this year, the company tested CX717, its lead drug candidate, in a trial of 16 sleep-deprived British men. Fueled by ampakines, the impaired subjects showed improvements on a battery of cognitive tests. Three more trials, all in the U.S., are scheduled for this year: one for Alzheimer's patients, one for adult sufferers of attention-deficit hyperactivity disorder, and another for sleep-deprived men, this one funded by the Defense Advanced Research Projects Agency. Soldiers and pilots are often sleep-deprived during missions, and the military is keenly interested in finding cognitive boosters that work better than today's amphetamines.

Other companies, manipulating different neurochemical pathways, have also reported promising results in animals and are planning human trials. Both Memory Pharmaceuticals, co-founded by Nobel Prize–winning neuroscientist Eric Kandel, and Helicon Therapeutics, founded by neuroscientist Tim Tully, have developed drugs that improve the memories of rodents. "Memory enhancers could become 'lifestyle' drugs," Tully says, "to be used by anyone interested in learning a language, in playing a musical instrument, or in studying for an exam." But the drug researchers are cautious. The pharmaceutical industry is littered with would-be wonder drugs that didn't make the leap from animals to people. Cortex has learned that some of its most potent ampakine formulations, those that best influence LTP formation, can also cause seizures in rats. Even if ampakines are safe, their primary benefit—making memory stronger—may also be a liability. Remembering is important, but so is forgetting; otherwise the brain would become swamped with trivia. "I'm not at all clear what is going to happen when you take a drug that makes it harder to get rid of the things you've encoded," Lynch says.

Overall, though, he is an optimist. Gazing at a poster of the brain on his office wall, Lynch remarks that a thought is essentially an ad hoc network of communicating neurons. Ampakines, by improving that communication, would allow a larger network—and a larger thought?—to be formed. "I should say that the best implication of ampakines is that we make everybody go home happy when they're 50—fully powered sexually, memory back, age slipping off like a cloak," he says. "But actually, personally, I wonder: Will you be able to think things that you can't think right now? Ultimately we'd find out the limits of being human and go beyond them."

5:50 P.M. I'm driving home, and Senator Davidson is on the radio. I support this psychopharm-disclosure bill she's pushing. Shouldn't we have the right to know if our elected leaders are taking empathogens and avarice-reducers like they're supposed to? My wife is working late tonight; I'm with the kids. I love them, but sometimes my patience wears thin. With the advanced beta-blocker I take, though, a tantrum doesn't set me off. Before bed, we say prayers. Truthfully, I never used to believe. But one little white entheogen pill and I feel—I don't know, a presence. It's comforting.

Smarts, of course, don't guarantee happiness. In the pro-enhancement manifesto *The Hedonistic Imperative*, transhumanist philosopher David Pearce calls for liberation from our natural biochemistry—the "sick psycho-chemical ghetto bequeathed by our genetic past"—and the beginning of an era of "paradise engineering." With the help of drugs, he writes, we'll be able to chemically crank our dopaminergic systems so that "undiluted existential happiness will infuse every second of waking and dreaming existence."

Sounds great. Sounds familiar, too. Similar if slightly more modest claims circulated two decades ago about Prozac, Paxil and other selective serotonin reuptake inhibitor (SSRI) antidepressants. The drugs are indeed effective and popular. Still, most Americans don't use them. Their side effects—jitteriness, fuzzy thinking and diminished sex drive—are one reason they haven't been widely adopted as enhancers, says Samuel Barondes, a psychiatrist at the University of California at San Francisco and author of *Better Than Prozac: Creating the Next Generation of Psychiatric Drugs*. "The public's desire for a pure, selective-acting wonder drug remains."

For much of the 20th century, drug development relied on luck—usually in the form of a serendipitous discovery that a known substance had additional positive effects. Miltown, the first blockbuster psychiatric drug, launched in the 1950s, was originally an antibiotic; Prozac, created in 1972, was a descendant of a common over-the-counter antihistamine.

Going forward, drug development will become less dependent on chance. Studies of genetically modified lab animals are revealing valuable information about the genetic and biochemical mechanisms underlying mood. At the University of Colorado, behavioral geneticist John DeFries selectively bred dozens of generations of mice until he had a dark-haired strain that was 30 times as brave as an albino one, as measured by fearfulness tests. The gene variants governing mouse anxiety may turn out to be different than the human ones, but DeFries's discoveries will probably shed light on genetic contributions to human fear—and may lead to new drug targets.

The completion of the Human Genome Project in 2003 and the rapidly decreasing cost of tools to collect and analyze DNA samples are also aiding drug development. By examining the gene variants that distinguish a depressed man from his happy brother, for instance, researchers may be able to create a more effective mood-elevating drug. Maybe. This burgeoning field, known as psychiatric genetics, is controversial. Any given aspect of personality, behavior or mood is influenced by the interplay of multiple genes—often a dozen or more—as well as environmental factors.

Nevertheless, futurists hail these genetic advances; some drug developers do as well, though more cautiously. In 2001 Emory University neurobiologist Larry Young genetically engineered a line of male prairie voles to have extra receptors for the hormone vasopressin. The manipulated voles formed bonds with females more quickly than normal voles and didn't need to have sex before doing so. Futurists wonder: Will this knowledge pave the way for a drug to domesticate wayward men? Dean Hamer, chief of gene structure and regulation at the National Cancer Institute, has found that people with a variation of the VMAT2 gene, which affects the transport of the neurochemical monoamine, are more likely to report having transcendent spiritual experiences. Futurists wonder: A pill to make you believe in God?

And finally, happiness itself. Studies of twins have indicated that our fundamental dispositions may be 40 to 50 percent rooted in genetics. Futurist James Hughes writes in *Citizen Cyborg: Why Democratic Societies Must Respond to the Redesigned Human of the Future* that "the heritability of happiness . . . suggests that there could be future drugs and gene therapies that jack our happiness set-point to its maximum without negative side effects."

June 7, 2025, 8 P.M. I'm out at dinner with my wife, and things couldn't be better. Hard to believe we were so close to divorce. All that tiresome couples counseling. Then, simple oxytocin therapy. In a few sessions, it was as if we were dating again—such great chemistry. Right now, we're on our third bottle of Connect—serotonin levels up, corticosteroid levels down. Sure, you can have an intimate conversation without this stuff, but it's so much easier with it. We'll go dancing later. Not naturally my thing, but I can pop some Steppinex—it makes me feel ecstatic. Before driving home, I'll take an AntiStep and instantly be sober.

Let's say the optimists are right, and we're able to create powerful new enhancement drugs. Should we? To many people, the answer is clear: absolutely not. Social critic Francis Fukuyama, author of *Our Posthuman Future*, presents a disquieting vision of a pharma-enhanced population. "Stolid people can become vivacious; introspective ones extroverted; you can adopt one personality on Wednesday and another for the weekend," he writes. Fukuyama worries that the qualities that make us essentially human would be lost.

Biomedical philosopher Leon Kass, who recently chaired President Bush's Council on Bioethics, writes that "in those areas of human life in which excellence has until now been achieved only by discipline and effort, the attainment of those achievements by means of drugs . . . looks to be 'cheating.'" Enhancement, in his view, is wrong because it is unfair. And unnatural: "All of our encounters with the world . . . would be mediated, filtered, and altered." More than human, in his view, is no longer human at all.

Back at the casino, Naam and I decide to have another go at the tables. He watches closely, soaking up information from the dealer and other players. Soon he's hitting when he should hit, staying when he should stay, and doubling down. He goes up $120 before pushing back from the table, smiling and flipping the dealer a tip. Seldom is learning so rapid. Still, if Naam had been on a cognitive enhancer, maybe he would have learned even faster and lost less money up-front. Would that be unnatural? Unfair?

"I think it's unfair that Michael Jordan was born with better basketball genes than me," he says. "If somebody has a disposition toward being smarter or having a better memory than me, then maybe drugs could help even that out." Naam also disagrees that enhancement drugs are unnatural. "The urge to better ourselves has been a force in history as far back as we can see," he says as we head for the door. "Embracing the quest to improve ourselves doesn't call our humanity into question—it reaffirms it."

Topics for Thought and Discussion

1. Vlahos alternates between a day in 2025 and the same day today. How does the fictional part of this essay contribute to the clarification of the science fact?
2. If you could take performance-enhancing drugs without adverse effects, would you? Why or why not? What seem to be the most powerful arguments for taking such drugs? What are the arguments against? Which seem most convincing?
3. Is Naam right when he says: "I think it's unfair that Michael Jordan was born with better basketball genes than me." What is his point? Should we, or should we not, try to make the world a fairer place? Would these drugs do that?
4. What role does the casino play for Vlahos? Why does he open and close his essay there?

Suggestions for Writing

1. Collect some of the performance enhancers that Vlahos imagines in his description of a day in 2025 and write a short story that imagines more fully the impact of these drugs. Would it be a pharm-utopia?
2. Take a stand, and in a short essay, argue for or against the use of drugs to improve the individual. What issues are essential and must be dealt with in your essay?
3. Conduct research. What are some of the performance enhancers that people use legally today? Are they unfair? Fair? Develop an argument.

Launching the Right Stuff
NEIL DEGRASSE TYSON

Neil deGrasse Tyson is the Frederick P. Rose Director of the Hayden Planetarium in New York City. Throughout his career as an astrophysicist, Tyson has been committed to writing for and educating the public. Since 1995 he has written a monthly column for Natural History *magazine called "Universe;" he has also written a number of books, including* Merlin's Tour of the Universe *(1989),* Universe Down to Earth *(1994),* Just Visiting This Planet *(1998),* One Universe: At Home in the Cosmos *(written with Charles Liu and Robert Irion, 2000),* Origins: Fourteen Billion Years of Cosmic History *(with Donald Goldsmith, 2004),* Death by Black Hole, and Other Cosmic Quandries *(2006), and his memoir.* The Sky Is Not the Limit: Adventures of an Urban Astrophysicist *(2000). Dr. Tyson has won many academic and cultural awards, including having asteroid "12123 Tyson" named after him by the International Astronomical Union. The following essay first appeared in* Natural History *in 2004. As you read, consider how Tyson defines "the right stuff."*

———————— ✦ ————————

More than a year has passed since the space shuttle Columbia broke into pieces over central Texas. This past January President Bush announced a long-term program of space exploration that would return human beings to the Moon, and thereafter send them to Mars and beyond. As this magazine goes to press, the twin Mars Exploration Rovers, Spirit and Opportunity, are wowing the scientists and engineers at the rovers' birthplace—NASA's Jet Propulsion Laboratory (JPL)—with their skills as robotic field geologists. JPL's official rover Web site (marsrovers.jpl.nasa.gov) is being stampeded by visitors.

The confluence of these and other events resurrects a perennial debate: with two shuttle failures out of 112 missions, and the astronomical expense of the manned space program, can sending people into space be justified, or should robots do the job alone? Or, given society's sociopolitical ailments, is space exploration something we simply cannot afford to pursue? As an astrophysicist, as an educator, and as a citizen, I must speak my mind on these issues.

Modern societies have been sending robots into space since 1957, and people since 1961. Fact is, it's vastly cheaper to send robots: in most cases, a fiftieth the cost of sending people. Robots don't much care how hot or cold space gets; give them the right lubricants, and they'll operate in a vast range of temperatures. They don't need elaborate life-support systems, either. Robots can spend long periods of time moving around and among the planets, more or less unfazed by ionizing radiation. They do not lose bone mass from prolonged exposure to weightlessness, because, of course, they are boneless. Nor do they have hygiene needs. You don't even have to feed them. Best of all, once they've finished their jobs, they won't complain if you don't bring them home.

So if my only goal in space is to do science, and I'm thinking strictly in terms of the scientific return on my dollar, I can think of no justification for sending people into space. I'd rather send the fifty robots.

But there's a flip side to this argument. Unlike even the most talented modern robots, a person is endowed with the ability to make serendipitous discoveries that arise from a lifetime of experience. Until the day arrives when bioneurophysiological computer engineers can do a human-brain download on a robot, the most we can expect of the robot is to look for what it has already been programmed to find. A robot—which is, after all, a machine for embedding human expectations in hardware and software—cannot fully embrace revolutionary scientific discoveries. And those are the ones you don't want to miss.

In the old days, people generally pictured robots as a hunk of hardware with a head, neck, torso, arms, and legs—or maybe some wheels to roll around on. They could be talked to, and would talk back (sounding, of course, robotic). The standard robot looked more or less like a person. The fussbudget character C3PO, from the *Star Wars* movies, is a perfect example.

Even when a robot doesn't look humanoid, its handlers might present it to the public as a quasi-living thing. Each of NASA's Mars rovers, for instance, is described in JPL press packets as having "a body, brains, a 'neck and head,' eyes and other 'senses,' an arm, 'legs,' and antennas for 'speaking' and 'listening.'" On February 5, 2004, according to the status reports, "Spirit woke up earlier than normal today . . . in order to prepare for its memory 'surgery.'" On the 19th the rover remotely examined the rim and surrounding soil of a crater dubbed Bonneville, and "after all this work, Spirit took a break with a nap lasting slightly more than an hour."

In spite of all this anthropomorphism, it's pretty clear that a robot can have any shape: it's simply an automated piece of machinery that accomplishes a task—either by repeating an action faster or more reliably than the average person can, or by performing an action that a person, relying solely on the five senses, would be unable to accomplish. Robots that paint cars on assembly lines don't look much like people. The Mars rovers look a bit like toy flatbed trucks, but they can grind a pit in the surface of a rock, mobilize a combination microscope-camera to examine the freshly exposed surface, and determine the rock's chemical composition—just as a geologist might do in a laboratory on Earth.

It's worth noting, by the way, that even a human geologist doesn't go it alone. Unaided by some kind of equipment, a person cannot grind down the surface of a rock; that's why a field geologist carries a hammer. To analyze a rock further, the geologist deploys another kind of apparatus, one that can determine its chemical composition. Therein lies a conundrum. Almost all the science likely to be done in an alien environment would be done by some piece of equipment. Field geologists on Mars would schlep it on their daily strolls across a Martian crater or outcrop, where they might take measurements of the soil, the rocks, the terrain, and the atmosphere. But if you can get a robot to do the schlepping and deploy all the same instruments, why send a field geologist to Mars at all?

One good reason is the geologist's common sense. Each Mars rover is designed to move for about ten seconds, then stop and assess its immediate surroundings for twenty seconds, move for another ten seconds, and so on. If the rover moved any faster, or moved without stopping, it might stumble on a rock and tip over, becoming as helpless as a Galápagos tortoise on its back. In contrast, a human explorer would just stride ahead; people are quite good at watching out for rocks and cliffs.

Back in the late 1960s and early 1970s, in the days of NASA's manned Apollo flights to the Moon, no robot could decide which pebbles to pick up and bring home. But when the Apollo 17 astronaut Harrison Schmitt, the only geologist (in fact, the only scientist) to have walked on the Moon, noticed some odd, orange and black soil on the lunar surface, he immediately collected a sample. It turned out to be minute beads of volcanic glass. Today a robot can perform staggering chemical analyses and transmit amazingly detailed images, but it still can't react, as Schmitt did, to a surprise. By contrast, packed inside the 150-pound mechanism of a field geologist are the capacities to walk, run, dig, hammer, see, communicate, interpret, and invent.

And of course when something goes wrong, an on-the-spot human being becomes a robot's best friend. Give a person a wrench, a hammer, and some duct tape, and you'd be surprised what can get fixed. After landing on Mars this past January 3, did the Spirit rover just roll right off its lander platform and start checking out the neighborhood? No, its airbags were blocking the path. Not until January 15 did Spirit's remote controllers manage to get all six of its wheels rolling on Martian soil. Anyone on the scene on January 3 could have just lifted the airbags out of the way and given Spirit a little shove.

Let's assume, then, that we can agree on a few things: People notice the unexpected, react to unforeseen circumstances, and solve problems in ways that robots cannot. Robots are cheap to send into space, but can make only a preprogrammed analysis. Cost and scientific results, however, are not the only relevant issues. There's also the question of exploration.

The first troglodytes to cross the valley or climb the mountain ventured forth from the family cave not because they wanted to make a scientific discovery but because something unknown lay beyond the horizon. Perhaps they sought more food, better shelter, or a more promising way of life. In any case, they felt compelled to explore. The drive to explore may be hardwired, lying deep within the behavioral identity of the human species. To send a person to Mars who can look under the rocks or find out what's down in the valley is the natural extension of what ordinary people have always done on Earth.

Many of my colleagues assert that plenty of science can be done without putting people in space. But if they are between forty and sixty years old, and you ask what inspired them to become scientists, nearly every one (at least in my experience) will cite the high-profile Apollo program. It took place when they were young, and it's what got them excited. It's that simple. In contrast, even if they also mention the launch of Sputnik I, which gave birth to the space era, very few of those scientists credit their interest to the numerous other unmanned satellites and space probes launched by both the United States and the Soviet Union shortly thereafter.

So if you're a first-rate scientist drawn to the space program because you'd initially been inspired by astronauts rocketing into the great beyond, it's somewhat disingenuous of you to contend that people should no longer go into space. To take that position is, in effect, to deny the next generation of students the thrill of following the same path you did: enabling one of our own kind, not just a robotic emissary, to walk on the frontier of exploration.

Whenever we hold an event at the Hayden Planetarium that includes an astronaut, I've found there's a small but noticeable uptick in attendance. People invariably seek the astronaut's autograph. This celebrity status holds even for astronauts most people have never heard of. Any astronaut will do. The one-on-one encounter makes a difference in the hearts and minds of Earth's armchair space travelers—whether retired science teachers, hardworking bus drivers, thirteen-year-old kids, or ambitious parents.

Of course, people have been excited about robots lately, too. From January 3 through January 5, 2004, the NASA Web site that tracks the doings of the Mars rovers got more than half a billion hits—506,621,916 to be exact. That's a record for NASA.

The solution to the quandary seems obvious to me: send both robots and people into space. Space exploration needn't be an either/or transaction, because there's no avoiding the fact that robots are better suited for certain tasks, and people for others.

One thing is certain: in the coming decades, the U.S. will need to call upon multitudes of scientists and engineers from scores of disciplines, and astronauts will have to be extraordinarily well trained. The search for evidence of past life on Mars, for instance, will require top-notch biologists. But what does a biologist know about planetary terrains? Geologists and geophysicists will have to go, too. Chemists will be needed to check out the atmosphere and sample the soils. If life once thrived on Mars, the remains might now be fossilized, and so perhaps we'll need a few paleontologists to join the fray. People who know how to drill through kilometers of soil and rock will also be must-haves, because that's where Martian water reserves might be hiding.

Where will all those talented scientists and technologists come from? Who's going to recruit them? Personally, when I give talks to students old enough to decide what they want to be when they grow up, but young enough not to get derailed by raging hormones, I need to offer them a tasty carrot to get them excited enough to become scientists. That task is made easy if I can introduce them to astronauts looking for the next generation to share their grand vision of exploration and join them in space. Without such inspiring forces behind me, I'm just that day's entertainment. My reading of history tells me that people need heroes. Nobody ever gave a ticker-tape parade for a robot.

Twentieth-century America owed much of its security and economic strength to its support for science and technology. Some of the most revolutionary (and marketable) technology of the past several decades has been spun off the research done under the banner of U.S. space exploration: kidney dialysis machines, implantable pacemakers, corrosion-resistant coatings for bridges and monuments (including the Statue of Liberty), hydroponic systems for growing plants, collision-avoidance systems on aircraft, digital imaging, infrared hand-held cameras, cordless appliances, athletic shoes, scratch-resistant sunglasses, virtual reality. And that list doesn't even include Tang.

Although solutions to a problem are often the fruit of direct investments in targeted research, the most revolutionary solutions tend to emerge from cross-pollination with other disciplines. Medical investigators might never have known of X-rays, since they do not naturally occur in biological systems. It took a physicist, Wilhelm Conrad Röntgen, to discover them—light rays that could probe the body's interior with nary a cut from a surgeon.

Here's a more recent example of cross-pollination. Soon after the Hubble Space Telescope was launched in April 1990, NASA engineers realized that the telescope's primary mirror—which gathers and reflects the light from celestial objects into its cameras and spectrographs—had been ground to an incorrect shape. In other words, the billion-and-a-half-dollar telescope was producing fuzzy images.

That was bad.

As if to make lemonade out of lemons, though, computer algorithms came to the rescue. Investigators at the Space Telescope Science Institute in Baltimore, Maryland, developed a range of clever and innovative image-processing techniques to compensate for some of Hubble's shortcomings. Turns out, maximizing the amount of information that could be extracted from a blurry astronomical image is technically identical to maximizing the amount of information that can be extracted from a mammogram. Soon the new techniques came into common use for detecting early signs of breast cancer.

But that's only part of the story. In 1997, for Hubble's second servicing mission (the first, in 1993, corrected the faulty optics), shuttle astronauts swapped in a brand-new, high-resolution digital detector—designed to the demanding specs of astronomers whose careers are based on being able to see small, dim things in the cosmos. That technology is now incorporated in a minimally invasive, low-cost system for doing breast biopsies, the next stage after mammograms in the early diagnosis of cancer.

So why not ask investigators to take direct aim at the challenge of detecting breast cancer? Why should innovations in medicine have to wait for a Hubble-size blunder in space? My answer may not be politically correct, but it's the truth: when you organize extraordinary missions, you attract people of extraordinary talent who might not have been inspired by or attracted to the goal of saving the world from cancer or hunger or pestilence.

Today, cross-pollination between science and society comes about when you have ample funding for ambitious, long-term projects. America has profited immensely from a generation of scientists and engineers who, instead of becoming lawyers or investment bankers, responded to a challenging vision posed in 1961 by President John F. Kennedy. "We intend to land a man on the Moon," proclaimed Kennedy, welcoming the citizenry to aid in the effort. That generation, and the one that followed, was the same generation of technologists who invented the personal computer. Bill Gates, co-founder of Microsoft, was thirteen years old when the U.S. landed an astronaut on the Moon; Steve Jobs, co-founder of Apple Computer, was fourteen. The PC did not arise from the mind of a banker or artist or professional athlete. It was invented and developed by a technically trained workforce, who had responded to the dream unfurled before them, and were thrilled to become scientists and engineers.

Yes, the world needs bankers and artists and even professional athletes. They, among countless others, create the breadth of society and culture. But if you want tomorrow to come—if you want to spawn entire economic sectors that didn't exist yesterday—those are not the people you turn to. It's technologists who create that kind of future. And it's visionary steps into space that create that kind of technologist. I look forward to the day when human beings travel the solar system as if it's our own backyard—not only with robots, but with real live people, guided by our timeless and boundless need to explore.

Topics for Thought and Discussion

1. What is Tyson's argument in this essay? What are some of the argumentative strategies that Tyson uses? In what ways does Tyson engage with both sides of this issue?

2. Where does Tyson's title originate? What are its connotations? How is the title related to his argument?

3. Tyson's ostensible purpose is to resolve the issue of whether we should send humans, or robots, into space. But by the end of the essay, Tyson is clearly arguing for the importance of the space program in general. What is the importance of the space program? What techniques does Tyson turn to at the end to inspire and engage you?

4. What do you think? Should we continue with the space program? Should we send humans? (As you answer these questions, be sure you address one of Tyson's early points: "Given society's sociopolitical ailments, is space exploration something we simply cannot afford to pursue?".)

Suggestions for Writing

1. Tyson is an advocate of the space program, and he bases this advocacy on humanity's "boundless need to explore." Write a personal memoir in which you engage with this issue. How, in your own life, has the need to explore manifested itself? Has your exploration tended to lead to good or to bad?

2. Take a stand and write a letter to the editor (of your school paper, or a local paper, or your hometown paper) in which you address the central issue in question #4 above. Should we, or should we not, continue with the space program? Be convincing!
3. Conduct research. What are NASA's most recent projects? Research NASA's current long- and short-term projects. Does NASA seem to be taking Tyson's advice?

How to Build a Time Machine
PAUL DAVIES

Paul Davies, now at the Australian Centre for Astrobiology, is internationally acclaimed as both an astrophysicist and a writer, and is known for his ability to make complex ideas accessible to nonspecialist readers. He is the author of more than twenty books, including God and the New Physics *(1983),* The Mind of God: The Scientific Basis for a Rational World *(1992),* About Time: Einstein's Unfinished Revolution *(1995),* The 5th Miracle: The Search for the Origin and Meaning of Life *(1999), and* How to Build a Time Machine *(2002). The following essay first appeared in* Scientific American. com *in 2002, and is based on the work Davies did for his book of the same title. As you read this article, notice particularly how science enables—and confounds—our expectations of what is possible.*

———————— ✦ ————————

Time travel has been a popular science-fiction theme since H. G. Wells wrote his celebrated novel *The Time Machine* in 1895. But can it really be done? Is it possible to build a machine that would transport a human being into the past or future?

For decades, time travel lay beyond the fringe of respectable science. In recent years, however, the topic has become something of a cottage industry among theoretical physicists. The motivation has been partly recreational—time travel is fun to think about. But this research has a serious side, too. Understanding the relation between cause and effect is a key part of attempts to construct a unified theory of physics. If unrestricted time travel were possible, even in principle, the nature of such a unified theory could be drastically affected.

Our best understanding of time comes from Einstein's theories of relativity. Prior to these theories, time was widely regarded as absolute and universal, the same for everyone no matter what their physical circumstances were. In his special theory of relativity, Einstein proposed that the measured interval between two events depends on how the observer is moving. Crucially, two observers who move differently will experience different durations between the same two events.

The effect is often described using the "twin paradox." Suppose that Sally and Sam are twins. Sally boards a rocket ship and travels at high speed to a nearby star, turns around and flies back to Earth, while Sam stays at home. For Sally the duration of the journey might be, say, one year, but when she returns and steps out of the spaceship, she finds that 10 years have elapsed on Earth. Her brother is now nine years older than she is. Sally and Sam are no longer the same age, despite the fact that they were born on the same day. This example illustrates a limited type of time travel. In effect, Sally has leaped nine years into Earth's future.

JET LAG

The effect, known as time dilation, occurs whenever two observers move relative to each other. In daily life we don't notice weird time warps, because the effect becomes dramatic only when the motion occurs at close to the speed of light. Even at aircraft speeds, the time dilation in a typical journey amounts to just a few nanoseconds—hardly an adventure of Wellsian proportions. Nevertheless, atomic clocks are accurate enough to record the shift and confirm that time really is stretched by motion. So travel into the future is a proved fact, even if it has so far been in rather unexciting amounts.

To observe really dramatic time warps, one has to look beyond the realm of ordinary experience. Subatomic particles can be propelled at nearly the speed of light in large accelerator machines. Some of these particles, such as muons, have a built-in clock because they decay with a definite half-life; in accordance with Einstein's theory, fast-moving muons inside accelerators are observed to decay in slow motion. Some cosmic rays also experience spectacular time warps. These particles move so close to the speed of light that, from their point of view, they cross the galaxy in minutes, even though in Earth's frame of reference they seem to take tens of thousands of years. If time dilation did not occur, those particles would never make it here.

Speed is one way to jump ahead in time. Gravity is another. In his general theory of relativity, Einstein predicted that gravity slows time. Clocks run a bit faster in the attic than in the basement, which is closer to the center of Earth and therefore deeper down in a gravitational field. Similarly, clocks run faster in space than on the ground. Once again the effect is minuscule, but it has been directly measured using accurate clocks. Indeed, these time-warping effects have to be taken into account in the Global Positioning System. If they weren't, sailors, taxi drivers, and cruise missiles could find themselves many kilometers off course.

At the surface of a neutron star, gravity is so strong that time is slowed by about 30 percent relative to Earth time. Viewed from such a star, events here would resemble a fast-forwarded video. A black hole represents the ultimate time warp; at the surface of the hole, time stands still relative to Earth. This means that if you fell into a black hole from nearby, in the brief interval it took you to reach the surface, all of eternity would pass by in the wider universe. The region within the black hole is therefore beyond the end of time, as far as the outside universe is concerned. If an astronaut could zoom very close to a black hole and return unscathed—admittedly a fanciful, not to mention foolhardy, prospect—he could leap far into the future.

MY HEAD IS SPINNING

So far I have discussed travel forward in time. What about going backward? This is much more problematic. In 1948 Kurt Gödel of the Institute for Advanced Study in Princeton, N.J., produced a solution of Einstein's gravitational field equations that described a rotating universe. In this universe, an astronaut could travel through space so as to reach his own past. This comes about because of the way gravity affects light. The rotation of the universe would drag light (and thus the causal relations between objects) around with it, enabling a material object to travel in a closed loop in space that is also a closed loop in time, without at any stage exceeding the speed of light in the immediate neighborhood of the particle. Gödel's solution was shrugged aside as a mathematical curiosity—after all, observations show no sign that the universe as a whole is spinning. His result served nonetheless to demonstrate that going back in time was not forbidden by the theory of relativity. Indeed, Einstein confessed that he was troubled by the thought that his theory might permit travel into the past under some circumstances.

Other scenarios have been found to permit travel into the past. For example, in 1974 Frank J. Tipler of Tulane University calculated that a massive, infinitely long cylinder spinning on its axis at near the speed of light could let astronauts visit their own past, again by dragging light around the cylinder into a loop. In 1991 J. Richard Gott of Princeton University predicted that cosmic strings—structures that cosmologists think were created in the early stages of the big bang—could produce similar results. But in the mid-1980s the most realistic scenario for a time machine emerged, based on the concept of a wormhole.

In science fiction, wormholes are sometimes called stargates; they offer a shortcut between two widely separated points in space. Jump through a hypothetical wormhole, and you might come out moments later on the other side of the galaxy. Wormholes naturally fit into the general theory of relativity, whereby gravity warps not only time but also space. The theory allows the analogue of alternative road and tunnel routes connecting two points in space. Mathematicians refer to such a space as multiply connected. Just as a tunnel passing under a hill can be shorter than the surface street, a wormhole may be shorter than the usual route through ordinary space.

The wormhole was used as a fictional device by Carl Sagan in his 1985 novel *Contact*. Prompted by Sagan, Kip S. Thorne and his co-workers at the California Institute of Technology set out to find whether wormholes were consistent with known physics. Their starting point was that a wormhole would resemble a black hole in being an object with fearsome gravity. But unlike a black hole, which offers a one-way journey to nowhere, a wormhole would have an exit as well as an entrance.

IN THE LOOP

For the wormhole to be traversable, it must contain what Thorne termed *exotic matter*. In effect, this is something that will generate antigravity to combat the natural tendency of a massive system to implode into a black hole under its intense weight. Antigravity, or gravitational repulsion, can be generated by negative energy or pressure. Negative-energy states are known to exist in certain quantum systems, which suggests that Thorne's exotic matter is not ruled out by the laws of physics, although it is unclear whether enough antigravitating stuff can be assembled to stabilize a wormhole [see "Negative Energy, Wormholes and Warp Drive," by Lawrence H. Ford and Thomas A. Roman; *Scientific American*, January 2000].

Soon Thorne and his colleagues realized that if a stable wormhole could be created, then it could readily be turned into a time machine. An astronaut who passed through one might come out not only somewhere else in the universe but somewhen else, too—in either the future or the past.

To adapt the wormhole for time travel, one of its mouths could be towed to a neutron star and placed close to its surface. The gravity of the star would slow time near that wormhole mouth, so that a time difference between the ends of the wormhole would gradually accumulate. If both mouths were then parked at a convenient place in space, this time difference would remain frozen in.

Suppose the difference were 10 years. An astronaut passing through the wormhole in one direction would jump 10 years into the future, whereas an astronaut passing in the other direction would jump 10 years into the past. By returning to his starting point at high speed across ordinary space, the second astronaut might get back home before he left. In other words, a closed loop in space could become a loop in time as well. The one restriction is that the astronaut could not return to a time before the wormhole was first built.

A formidable problem that stands in the way of making a wormhole time machine is the creation of the wormhole in the first place. Possibly space is threaded with such structures naturally—relics of the big bang. If so, a supercivilization might commandeer one. Alternatively, wormholes might naturally come into existence on tiny scales, the so-called Planck length, about 20 factors of 10 as small as an atomic nucleus. In principle, such a minute wormhole could be stabilized by a pulse of energy and then somehow inflated to usable dimensions.

CENSORED!

Assuming that the engineering problems could be overcome, the production of a time machine could open up a Pandora's box of causal paradoxes. Consider, for example, the time traveler who visits the past and murders his mother when she was a young girl. How do we make sense of this? If the girl dies, she cannot become the time traveler's mother. But if the time traveler was never born, he could not go back and murder his mother.

Paradoxes of this kind arise when the time traveler tries to change the past, which is obviously impossible. But that does not prevent someone from being a part of the past. Suppose the time traveler goes back and rescues a young girl from murder, and this girl grows up to become his mother. The causal loop is now self-consistent and no longer paradoxical. Causal consistency might impose restrictions on what a time traveler is able to do, but it does not rule out time travel per se.

Even if time travel isn't strictly paradoxical, it is certainly weird. Consider the time traveler who leaps ahead a year and reads about a new mathematical theorem in a future edition of *Scientific American*. He notes the details, returns to his own time and teaches the theorem to a student, who then writes it up for *Scientific American*. The article is, of course, the very one that the time traveler read. The question then arises: Where did the information about the theorem come from? Not from the time traveler, because he read it, but not from the student either, who learned it from the time traveler. The information seemingly came into existence from nowhere, reasonlessly.

The bizarre consequences of time travel have led some scientists to reject the notion outright. Stephen W. Hawking of the University of Cambridge has proposed a "chronology protection conjecture," which would outlaw causal loops. Because the theory of relativity is known to permit causal loops, chronology protection would require some other factor to intercede to prevent travel into the past. What might this factor be? One suggestion is that quantum processes will come to the rescue. The existence of a time machine would allow particles to loop into their own past. Calculations hint that the ensuing disturbance would become self-reinforcing, creating a runaway surge of energy that would wreck the wormhole.

Chronology protection is still just a conjecture, so time travel remains a possibility. A final resolution of the matter may have to await the successful union of quantum mechanics and gravitation, perhaps through a theory such as string theory or its extension, so-called M-theory. It is even conceivable that the next generation of particle accelerators will be able to create subatomic wormholes that survive long enough for nearby particles to execute fleeting causal loops. This would be a far cry from Wells's vision of a time machine, but it would forever change our picture of physical reality.

Topics for Thought and Discussion

1. Science fiction writers make much of time travel paradoxes. How does Davies deal with these seeming impossibilities? Are you content with his explanation?
2. According to Davies, time travel is a theoretical possibility. Is it also a practical possibility? Comment on the ways that Davies suggests moving into the future and into the past.
3. What advantages does providing headings and dividing this essay into sections give Davies as a writer? Why divide up this essay as he does?
4. Given what Davies has told us, do you believe that humans will one day be able to travel through time? Explain your answer as well as you can.

Suggestions for Writing

1. Make a list of potential time-travel paradoxes. What sorts of things could not be done by a time-traveler and maintain the integrity of our understanding of cause and effect?
2. Write an essay or a short story in which you propose a use for a time machine. What are the social, cultural, and personal dangers involved in this type of travel for the purpose you have chosen?
3. Write an essay in which you argue either for or against pursuing research into time travel. Is this a kind of science that is too dangerous to be pursued?

Pondering the Future's Future
FRED GUTERL

Fred Guterl is a senior editor at Newsweek *magazine and a journalist specializing in science and technology issues. He currently directs* Newsweek's *science, technology, health, medicine, and environmental coverage, and has written about a wide variety of scientific topics for* Newsweek, Discover Magazine, *and others. In the following essay, first published in* Newsweek *in 2002, Guterl looks at the future of science. As you read, consider how Guterl uses Einstein as a model for, and against, how science is done.*

---- ✦ ----

He changed the future without ever winning an election or commanding an army. All Albert Einstein did was have an idea. It's not a particularly easy one to grasp in all its ramifications, but the basic insight he expressed in his 1905 paper on special relativity is almost childlike in its simplicity. And yet it ushered in a golden age of physics and did much to shape the course of the 20th century. It also transformed the way the future is made: not with wars and revolutions but with scientific insights.

But Einstein has also come to represent an obsolete stereotype. This disheveled, socially challenged scientist with the wild hair and the shabby cardigan epitomizes the popular notion that science proceeds in great leaps at the hands of the lone genius, who reinterprets everything and achieves, in one bold stroke, what science philosophers like to call a "paradigm shift." There's no doubt that Einstein did exactly that. Physics was never the same, and his insights cleared the way for the solid-state electronics that undergird the Internet and the atom bombs that loomed over the cold war. Einstein's brilliance set the 20th century in motion. But what about the next one? Will a towering figure emerge to shape its trajectory?

There's reason to think not. Times have changed since Einstein worked by day as a clerk in the Swiss Patent Office, and by night as a World-Historical Physicist. Early in the last century, science and technology were still largely the province of private patrons and individual inventors working in basement labs. These days vast networks of laboratories sponsored by governments, universities, corporations and venture capitalists are all pushing to find the next new thing. Discovery and invention—in developed countries, at least—have become regularized. The insights of individuals are still important, of course, but the overall effort relies less on any one genius. "In the late 19th century you had predominantly the private inventor," says Yale historian Daniel Kevles. "Now you have the organized inventor. Even the big conceptual scientific leaps are much less likely to occur nowadays. Scientific fields are crowded with geniuses. Everybody's working at the big problems all the time." The advances we take for granted in 2012 will have sprung not from one mind but from an army of them.

What that means is our society has become more steady in producing earth-shattering advances. The need for breakthroughs on-demand started during World War II, when the U.S. military wanted its antiaircraft shells to inflict damage even when they missed enemy planes. Nobody knew how to get the bombs to explode in midair at just the right moment, so the Pentagon funded the applied-physics lab at Johns Hopkins University in Baltimore and staffed it with experts in plastics, electromagnetics and other specialties. The proximity fuse they came up with was decisive in winning the war. And the effort to make it, along with the legendary Manhattan Project to build the atomic bomb, set the precedent for organizing an array of expertise based on the need for a particular invention.

This shift in the methodology of discovery has complicated matters. It gave inventors the wherewithal to build ever more complex machines, but made the act of inventing more complex as well. The Pentagon awards a contract for a new jet fighter to a prime contractor, which passes the various subsystems and components down through layers of subcontractors. "Henry Ford could understand every piece of his assembly line," says Don Kash, a technology expert at George Mason University in Fairfax, Va. "Nobody can do that at Toyota." Complexity has spread from big-ticket items like cars and planes to toasters, stuffed animals and Game Boys.

What's different now, though, is how comfortable we've become with complexity. Innovation is part of our lives in a way it wasn't for previous generations. In 1970 Alvin Toffler argued in *Future Shock* that technology was changing society so quickly that in the span of a single lifetime a person would find himself a stranger in his own culture. Toffler's best-selling book struck home because many people thought new technologies—in those days television, the birth-control pill and the transistor—were bringing about change at a pace that was disorienting and not a little disturbing. These days we've learned how to ride the rocket of innovation. "My father thought the world would be the same" says Kash. "My children wake up every day thinking the world will be different."

Just because we have grown accustomed to, even jaded by, our scientific and technological progress doesn't mean it hasn't been mind-boggling. Certainly it's easy to criticize the overheated rhetoric of the Internet boom. But we shouldn't forget that even if the Web didn't quite change everything, it certainly changed a lot of things. The past decade saw one of the most concentrated bursts of innovation ever—not just the Net but the decoding of the human genome and the cloning of a sheep named Dolly come to mind.

It's possible that the next 10 years will render even those radical changes forgettable. Science-fiction writer Arthur C. Clarke has said he seldom predicts the future; he merely extrapolates from the present. A decade ago, with the bloom just coming off Japan, few people predicted that the American economy would so thoroughly dominate the world's. An equal number of visionaries now argue that by 2012, Europe will have supplanted the United States as the prime mover in the global economy. The Internet opened new worlds by linking PCs to other computers. Now its reach is already beginning to spread to tiny chips embedded in everyday objects (and even the human body). "Grid" computing is making it possible to spread massive computing tasks over many machines. As the Internet's presence in our daily lives grows, we'll continue to grapple with the issues of security and privacy.

Based on what's happening in today's labs, the most potentially explosive field is genetics, which requires no lightning bolts of insight to shake things up. In vitro fertilization already gives scientists the ability to create an embryo in a petri dish. Should the technology get good enough to make many embryos at once, genetic-screening techniques, which already exist, will allow scientists to pick the one with the most highly prized traits. Outlawing unsavory practices, like eugenics, in the United States or Europe won't help much if biotechnology is being practiced elsewhere without ethical constraints.

On the positive side, diagnostic tests using gene chips and other technologies may tell us if we're susceptible to specific diseases or how we'll respond to certain drugs. Armed with this kind of information, doctors may be able to tailor our diets and treatments to our own genetic idiosyncrasies. Genetically modified plants may someday yield the raw materials for gasoline, turning petroleum into a renewable resource. Since the plants take carbon out of the air, burning them wouldn't add to global warming. "I've become a great believer in energy plants" says Freeman Dyson, a mathematician at the Institute for Advanced Study at Princeton.

All this change will have an even broader impact than what we've experienced so far: the steady churn of technological advances builds on itself, sometimes with unanticipated results. Birth control, which has made it commonplace to have fewer children later in life, means the world's population will get grayer, posing problems for governments as well as opportunities for business. As women continue to win in the global job market, men will have to adapt or accept a change in status. (Since they'll live longer, though, they'll have plenty of time to work it out.)

To figure out what the future will be like, look around: innovation has a way of emerging from the wheels and gears of daily life. Einstein, for instance, used the technology around him as a mental springboard for his thoughts about physics and the nature of time. To synchronize clocks in all the Continent's far-flung railway stations, European engineers sent out signals from Paris and Berlin through wires and radio links. Some of the many inventions needed for such a system—signal relays, electromechanical devices to reset the clocks and so forth—might even have passed across Einstein's desk at the patent office. "Every day Einstein took the short stroll from his house, left down the Kramgasse, to the patent office," writes science historian Peter Galison of Harvard. "Every day he must have seen the great clock towers that presided over Bern with their coordinated clocks, and the myriad of street clocks branched proudly to the central telegraph office." So maybe his great mental leap didn't come from left field at all, but had its genesis in the inventions of the day. Today's budding scientists have an even more remarkable panorama to explore. What seeds of change are they sowing?

Topics for Thought and Discussion

1. Look into the future. Based on what we now have and know, describe what the ten biggest scientific and technological innovations will be ten years from now.
2. Guterl contrasts the old model of doing science—"the paradigm shift"—to the current model of doing science. Describe the current model. If the lone

genius can be called "paradigm shift," what would you call the current model Guterl describes?

3. Guterl uses Einstein to anchor his essay. Describe the many ways Einstein works for Guterl, including whatever connotations Einstein may bring to the essay indirectly.

Suggestions for Writing

1. Choose a scientific discovery or technological innovation from the last five years and describe its social, cultural, and personal ramifications. How has this scientific discovery changed the world and the way we/you live?

2. Conduct research. Survey popular culture and write a review in which you describe how science is portrayed today in television, film, and other forms of media. One question you should certainly address is whether popular culture adheres to the "paradigm-shift" model, or to a more realistic, twenty-first century collaborative model of science.

Frontiers: Making Connections

1. Robots, cyborgs, and time machines have long been a part of the scientific and cultural imagination, and some (if not all) are quickly coming into reality. Using three of the essays in this chapter, address this question: What is the relationship between humanity and technology? Should we be afraid? Is technology dangerous? What safeguards must we put in place? What benefits can we expect?

2. Science is about pushing our knowledge into the unknown, learning how things work, and applying that knowledge to improve our lives (or, more cynically, to make a buck). Using three essays from this chapter, respond to this question: What can we expect to get out of science? How might the advances and ideas highlighted in your chosen essays affect our lives?

3. Given the essays from this chapter (and drawing upon at least three of them), define "the human." What are human beings like? Where would you draw our physical boundaries? Our psychological boundaries? Our emotional boundaries? What do we need? What are we driven to do? What can we tell about human beings from the science we are doing and the questions in which we are interested?

4. Choose any two of the essays from this chapter that you feel engage with similar issues and describe the social and cultural effect of the science being described. For example, what are the social and cultural issues raised by the work described by Dan Ferber and John Hockenberry? Or that discussed by Neil deGrasse Tyson and Paul Davies?

CREDITS

AIBS. "American Institute of Biological Sciences Ethics Statement," from The American Institute of Biological Sciences, revised 22 March, 2002. Reprinted with permission of The American Institute of Biological Sciences.

Angier, Natalie. "Of Altruism, Heroism, and Evolution," by Natalie Angier. Copyright © 2001 by The New York Times Co. Reprinted with permission.

Begley, Sharon. "Designer Babies," from *Newsweek*, November 9, 1998. © 1998 Newsweek, Inc. All rights reserved. Reprinted by permission.

Buss, David M. "The Strategies of Human Mating," from *American Scientist*, ©1994. Reprinted with the permission of *American Scientist*.

Davies, Paul. "How to Build a Time Machine," reprinted with permission. Copyright © 2002 by Scientific American, Inc. All rights reserved.

Diamond, Jared. "Easter Island's End," © 1995. Originally published in *Discover Magazine*. Reprinted with the permission of the author.

Duncan, David Ewing. "DNA as Destiny," © 2002 by David Ewing Duncan. Reprinted with permission of William Morris Agency, LLC on behalf of the Author, as first appeared in *Wired Magazine* (November 2002).

Ehrenreich, Barbara. "Science, Lies, and the Ulitmate Truth," © 1991 Time Inc. Reprinted by permission.

Everett, Jenny. "My Little Brother On Drugs," from *Popular Science*, April 2004. Copyright © 2004 Time 4 Media, Inc. Reprinted with permission of *Popular Science*.

Ferber, Dan. "The Man Who Mistook His Girlfriend for a Robot," from *Popular Science*, August, 2003. Reprinted with permission of *Popular Science*. Copyright © 2003 Time 4 Media, Inc.